Fodor's

Brooklyn

CONTENTS

ABOUT THIS GUIDE

Fodor's Brooklyn is unlike any guide-book we've ever published. Written entirely by Brooklynites and gorgeously illustrated by Clinton Hill–based artist Claudia Pearson, it includes features on Brooklyn's homegrown culinary and design scenes; and plenty of insider tips. The result is a curated compilation infused with authentic Brooklyn flavor, accompanied by easy-to-use maps and transit information. Whether you're vis-iting Brooklyn for the first time, moving in, or are a longtime borough resident looking to explore a new neighborhood, this is the guide for you.

While all Fodor's guidebooks have a local perspective, this one is especially close to us since we're based in New York City and Brooklyn is our backyard. We've handpicked the top things to do and rated the sights, shopping, dining, and nightlife in 29 dynamic neighbor-hoods. Truly exceptional experiences in all categories are marked with a ★.

Restaurants, bars, and cafés are a huge part of Brooklyn's appeal, of course, and you'll find plenty to savor in its diverse neighborhoods. We cover close

#INSIDEBKLYN

We've highlighted fun neighbor-hood facts throughout this guide. As you explore Brooklyn, we invite you to use #InsideBklyn to share your favorite discoveries with us.

to 50 cuisines in all price points, and everything from enduring institutions and groundbreaking chefs to the fixings for the perfect picnic. New hotels are opening all the time; we've reviewed our favorites, including pros and cons for each one. Use the $ to $$$$ price charts below to estimate meal and room costs. We list adult prices for sights; ask about discounts when purchasing tickets.

Brooklyn is constantly changing. All prices, opening times, and other details in this guide were accurate at press time. Always confirm information when it matters, especially when making a detour to a specific place.

Visit Fodors.com for expanded restuar-ant and hotel reviews, additional recom-mendations, news, and features.

WHAT IT COSTS: Restaurants			
$	$$	$$$	$$$$
Under $13	$13-$24	$25-$35	Over $35

Prices are the average cost of a main course at dinner or, if dinner is not served, at lunch.

WHAT IT COSTS: Hotels			
$	$$	$$$	$$$$
Under $300	$300-$449	$450-$600	Over $600

Prices are the lowest cost of a standard double room in high season.

1

Experience Brooklyn

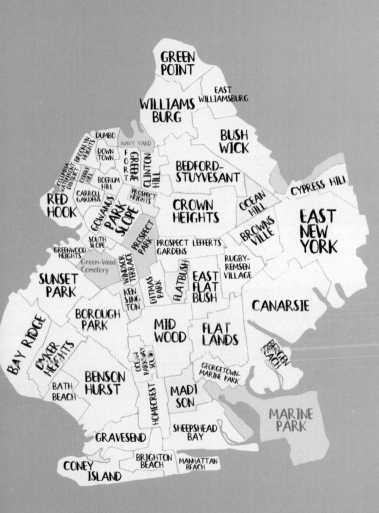

WELCOME TO BROOKLYN

In less than a generation, Brooklyn has transformed into a global capital of culture and creativity. It buzzes with energy, excitement, and the inherent tension of coupling reinvention with a dedication to authenticity.

BROOKLYN TODAY

Across the East River from Manhattan on Long Island's western edge, Brooklyn is one of New York City's five boroughs. At 71 square miles, it's more than three times the size of Manhattan. With more than 2½ million people, if Brooklyn were a city, it would be the fourth largest in the United States by population.

For decades Manhattan was New York City's most significant draw, but now visitors come specifically to Brooklyn: to eat, drink, see, absorb, and experience one of the most talked-about places in the world. What made Brooklyn the trendsetting destination it is today? It would be hard not to use the "H" word—referring to the L-train-riding hipsters who moved to Williamsburg in the 1990s when the rents were cheap, and put their creative DIY ideas into action. It was, at least in part, their energy that grew and spread to other neighborhoods in the borough, where old factories were turned into innovative maker spaces, rooftops into urban gardens, and parking lots into farm-to-table restaurants whose rustic chic "Brooklyn-style" decor can now be found in Paris, Bogotá, Tokyo, and beyond. Brooklyn today is, of course, more than a playground for tattooed and bearded skateboarders; it's a place where old and new mingle, and continue to change—in some places slowly and at breakneck speed in others.

HISTORY

The Lenape, a Native American people, originally inhabited much of the land Brooklyn now occupies. The Dutch settled here in 1636, but the British displaced them in 1664. Over the next two-plus centuries Brooklyn—an Anglicization of Breuckelen, the area's Dutch name—developed into the independent city incorporated in 1854. Four decades later residents narrowly voted to join Manhattan, Queens, the Bronx, and Staten Island to form New York City. Before and after the 1898 merger, many key events in U.S. history took place in Brooklyn. Gowanus hosted the largest battle of the American Revolution in 1776; Walt Whitman pioneered a uniquely American style of free-verse poetry in the mid-19th century; the Brooklyn Bridge, completed in 1883, was among the era's premier engineering feats; and Brooklyn Dodger Jackie Robinson became professional baseball's first African American player in 1947. And that's just for starters. The Brooklyn Historical Society is a great place to delve deeper into the borough's past and present.

IMMIGRATION

From the 19th century to the present, successive waves of immigrants reshaped Brooklyn every generation or two. Irish, Germans, Italians, Poles, and Russians were among the Europeans who emigrated in large numbers early on, with many of the new arrivals finding work in factories and shipyards. Jewish people came in several waves, as did Puerto Ricans, whose earliest significant migration occurred in the 1940s. A 21st-century study credits immigrants from Asia, Latin America, and the Caribbean, many of whom settled in Brooklyn during the 1970s and 1980s, with sparing New York City from the depopulation Detroit and other rust belt cities experienced during the late 20th century. With nearly half of current residents speaking a language other than English at home, it's possible to hear conversations in Urdu, Arabic, Spanish, Yiddish, and Mandarin in a single afternoon—or on a single subway car.

GENTRIFICATION

Many Brooklyn neighborhoods have become upscale in recent decades, a development that native son and film director Spike Lee disparaged in 2014 during an impromptu exchange at Brooklyn's Pratt Institute. Lee mocked what he dubbed the Christopher Columbus syndrome, one group "discovering" a neighborhood that other people already live in. Lee also reproved newcomers who "come in when people have a culture that's been laid down for generations" and ignore or disrespect it. What Lee described isn't a new phenomenon: the completion of the Brooklyn Bridge prompted similar disruption when many Manhattan residents, seeking lower rent, larger living spaces, and an easy commute, relocated here. Flash forward a century later to Park Slope, Williamsburg, and elsewhere, and the same dynamic unfolded.

Contemporary gentrification is admired by some, and cause for concern among others. Proponents applaud higher property values and improved infrastructure. Critics decry the evictions of long-term residents and the loss of neighborhood character. Wherever you stand, know that gentrification is a touchy subject for many Brooklynites. Keep in mind, too, that all of Brooklyn isn't gentrified, affluent, and fashionable. There are also many residents, among them Williamsburg's Hasidic Jews, who strive to maintain their traditional ways, while in other highly visitable areas housing project residents struggle with poverty.

WHAT'S WHERE IN BROOKLYN

Each of Brooklyn's neighborhoods has its own allure. To help you choose where to visit, here's a rundown of the areas we cover in detail. The numbers refer to chapter numbers.

2. WILLIAMSBURG
An industrial neighborhood turned creative mecca, this popular choice for visitors generates worldwide buzz with its vibrant nightlife, chic boutiques, innovative restaurants, and happening arts scene.

3. GREENPOINT
Predominantly Polish Greenpoint has been absorbing the spillover of Williamsburg, its trendsetting neighbor. Family-run corner stores and Eastern European restaurants abound, but you'll also find fantastic boutiques, restaurants, and bars.

4. BUSHWICK AND EAST WILLIAMSBURG
Older homes and mom-and-pop shops in these neighborhoods coexist with DIY music venues and happening bars and eateries. Street art and avant-garde galleries are daytime draws; at night, huge warehouses open for edgy dance parties.

5. BEDFORD-STUYVESANT AND CROWN HEIGHTS
Though undergoing rapid change, Bed-Stuy and Crown Heights retain their mostly residential ambience. Up-and-coming bars and ethnic eateries that reflect the flourishing diversity are reasons to visit.

6. FORT GREENE AND CLINTON HILL
Tree-lined residential streets and historic architecture provide the backdrop for sophisticated dining and mellow nightlife in these side-by-side neighborhoods. The Brooklyn Academy of Music anchors the borough's performing arts scene.

7. PROSPECT HEIGHTS
Adjacent to Park Slope, with easy access to Brooklyn Botanic Garden, the Brooklyn Museum, and the Barclays Center, Prospect Heights is a must for culture lovers. Cool cocktail bars and locavore restaurants thrive here.

8. PARK SLOPE AND PROSPECT PARK
Family-friendly Park Slope entices with historic streets, brownstone stoops, specialty shops, and well-regarded restaurants. Adjoining Prospect Park hosts copious festivals and summer concerts.

9. GOWANUS
Creative types enliven this neighborhood that once bustled with factory workers. Quirky performance spaces

and innovative food and drink destinations keep things hopping.

10. DUMBO

The chic area known as Down Under the Manhattan Bridge Overpass seduces with cobblestone streets, boutiques, arts spaces, and killer Manhattan views.

11. BROOKLYN HEIGHTS AND DOWNTOWN BROOKLYN

The borough's oldest neighborhood, Brooklyn Heights, pleases with its varied architecture and enchanting promenade. The Brooklyn Historical Society mounts outstanding shows; Downtown Brooklyn is a convenient transportation hub.

12. BOERUM HILL AND COBBLE HILL

These delightful neighborhoods are perfect for strolling. Brownstones, redbrick row houses, and cozy cafés lend the area an upscale, family-friendly suburban feel. Antiques stores and bright boutiques are plentiful.

13. CARROLL GARDENS

This neighborhood owes its down-to-earth vibe to its Italian-American base. Innovative restaurants and boutiques share the streets with old-style bakeries and butcher shops.

14. RED HOOK AND COLUMBIA WATERFRONT DISTRICT

These waterfront locales win points for their artsy vibe, knockout views, and destination bars and restaurants. The remoteness only adds to their attraction.

15. WINDSOR TERRACE, GREENWOOD HEIGHTS, AND SOUTH SLOPE

A deep sense of community characterizes these areas near Prospect Park. Their bars, restaurants, and shops exude local energy, and Green-Wood Cemetery is an oasis of greenery with historic cachet.

16. DITMAS PARK AND MIDWOOD

Victorian homes and landscaped front yards impart a suburban air to these areas south of Prospect Park, but their historic districts, and range of bars and restaurants radiate big city appeal.

17. SUNSET PARK

Home to Brooklyn's Chinatown, this multiethnic enclave also has a rapidly developing waterfront. The neighborhood is a prime contender for the borough's next exciting frontier.

18. BAY RIDGE

Waterfront parks and stunning views of the Verrazano-Narrows Bridge set the scene for the architectural charms of Bay Ridge's residential streets and diverse dining options.

19. BRIGHTON BEACH AND CONEY ISLAND

Golden sands, a fabulous boardwalk, amusement park rides, restaurants, and retro nightclubs make for a giddy good time at these beachside playgrounds.

TOP EXPERIENCES IN BROOKLYN

Everyone has favorite things to do or see in Brooklyn, the ones to go back to again and again, and to recommend to friends and family. These top 10 experiences will guide you to the best of the borough.

GRAND ENTRANCES

A stroll across the **Brooklyn Bridge** from Manhattan is an exhilarating way to enter the borough. Along the way, you can take in the bridge's Gothic Revival towers, read the plaques detailing the challenging construction process, and marvel at the views of the Manhattan and Brooklyn skylines. You'll want to snap a few photos, too. You can also enjoy sweeping vistas of the bridges and the city via the NYC Ferry or the New York Water Taxi to various points in Brooklyn.

WATERFRONT VIEWS

Brooklyn's waterfront provides unparalleled city and harbor views. For perspectives on Manhattan, head to **Brooklyn Bridge Park, WNYC Transmitter Park,** and **East River State Park.** To enjoy the scenery with a cocktail in hand, slip inland three blocks to **The Ides,** on the Wythe Hotel's roof, or head to **The River Café** to appreciate the views accompanied by a special meal. The Statue of Liberty is in clear view from **Louis Valentino Jr. Park & Pier,** whose panorama includes a generous portion of New York Harbor. From its perch overlooking its namesake neighborhood, **Sunset Park,** though not on the water, delivers bird's-eye views of New York Harbor and Lower Manhattan.

EATING AND DRINKING

Farm-to-table restaurants, traditional ethnic eateries, loungey cocktail dens, artisanal coffee roasters, and craft-beer bars make for dynamite eating and drinking options around the clock. For fine dining and glamorously casual cafés, head to **Williamsburg, Boerum Hill,** and **Carroll Gardens. Fort Greene, Prospect Heights,** and **Cobble Hill** shelter influential restaurants that source everything from the tenderloin to the tableware thoughtfully and sustainably. Bartenders and mixologists across the borough prove equally adept at fashioning classic and innovative cocktails. **Bay Ridge** and **Sunset Park** showcase Mexican, Middle Eastern, Italian, Chinese, and other cuisines. In good

weather, the patios and rooftop spaces of Brooklyn's restaurants and bars are the best places to be.

HAPPENING NIGHTLIFE

Brooklyn's cool kids convene in **Williamsburg, East Williamsburg, Greenpoint, Gowanus,** and elsewhere for nighttime revelry. To tap into Williamsburg's limitless vitality, check out a concert at the **Music Hall of Williamsburg,** catch the buzzy vibe at **Maison Premiere,** and go dancing at **Output.** For hanging out in chill backyards, stop in at **Hot Bird** or **Lavender Lake.** For something unique, head to the **Nitehawk Cinema,** which screens indie films and serves dinner. For games, there's bowling at the **Gutter** or **Brooklyn Bowl,** shuffleboard at **Royal Palms Shuffleboard,** bocce at **Floyd** and **Union Hall,** and arcade games at **Barcade.**

URBAN HISTORY

Brooklyn reveals its long history indoors and out. Thanks to the iconic bridge and fabulous architecture, you need only step outside to sense the borough's rich past, and a visit to the museums and institutions can heighten the impression. The curators at the **Brooklyn Museum** and the **Brooklyn Historical Society** assemble dynamic, sometimes interactive exhibits from their institutions' collections of prints, photographs, and artifacts. The diverting **New York Transit Museum** celebrates subways, trolleys, trams, and other public conveyances, and the **Old Stone House** re-creates life at a 17th-century Dutch farmhouse

that played a key role in the Battle of Brooklyn. The **Weeksville Heritage Center** pays homage to one of New York's first communities of free blacks.

THE ART SCENE

The **Brooklyn Museum** stands as a testament to its borough's enduring commitment to art. A stop here is essential, but numerous other venues merit investigation. The spaces at the multidisciplinary **BRIC Arts Media House** include a large gallery specializing in works by Brooklyn-based artists. The **Museum of Contemporary African Diaspora Arts** focuses on works with a social or political message about the African diaspora. Meanwhile, the **Pratt Institute Sculpture Park** includes more than 50 sculptures and the **Bushwick Collective** presents several dazzling blocks of street art. A fun way to survey the current art scene is to attend various neighborhoods' block parties, festivals, and open-studios events.

PARKS AND GARDENS

Green spaces small and large, waterside and inland, grace Brooklyn's landscape. At **Brooklyn Bridge Park** you can stroll the waterfront, picnic in the bridge's shadow, ride **Jane's Carousel,** and admire the Manhattan views. **Louis Valentino Jr. Park & Pier** and **Sunset Park** also have distinctive city and harbor vistas, and the **Shore Park and Parkway** affords stunning takes on the **Verrazano–Narrows Bridge,** which links Brooklyn with Staten Island. Inland, **Fort Greene Park** is a local favorite steeped in history, and 500-acre **Prospect Park** entices with lush greenery, winding paths, and walking and horseback-riding trails. With its large grounds and conservatory, the extraordinary **Brooklyn Botanic Garden** provides a colorful sanctuary year-round.

FESTIVALS AND EVENTS

Fun festivals and events happen year-round, and many are free. For the quintessential Brooklyn summer experience, tote a blanket and picnic fixings to Prospect Park for **Celebrate Brooklyn!** concerts and performances, or head to one of the parks in Williamsburg, Greenpoint, DUMBO, and Red Hook for outdoor movie screenings. The Bushwick Collective throws a massive summer block party, with street artists at work, food stands, and live music. Art galleries in Williamsburg, Greenpoint, and DUMBO often stay open late (and sometimes serve drinks) on Thursday and Friday for exhibit openings. Sunset Park's **Industry City** complex hosts fun, family-friendly dance parties ⇨ *See our Best Brooklyn Events listings in this chapter for more ideas.*

BROOKLYN SHOPPING

The borough attracts designers, craftspeople, and artists, so you'll find shops and galleries here touting all sorts of made-in-Brooklyn merchandise and artworks. **Williamsburg, Carroll Gardens, Boerum Hill, Cobble Hill, Greenpoint,** and **DUMBO** are pivotal stops for clothing, objects, and art, while the seasonally open DUMBO outpost of the Flea is a great place to browse for just about anything. There are also plenty of Brooklyn bookstores, most of which sell wonderful Brooklyn-made gifts and handmade stationery and cards in addition to books, many by Brooklyn's literati.

PERFORMING ARTS

As major performing-arts consumers, Brooklynites support diverse venues and cultural organizations. The stalwart and innovative **Brooklyn Academy of Music** (BAM) presents concerts, plays, dance, and other performances; so, too, do quirky loft and storefront spaces. The renowned **St. Ann's Warehouse** has commissioned cutting-edge theater, music, and high-art puppeteering for three-plus decades, while the **Kings Theatre,** a renovated movie palace, emerged in 2015 as an exciting new venue. Children's-literature-based performances and puppet shows at the **Brooklyn Center for the Performing Arts** and **Puppetworks** delight budding arts devotees, while classical-music lovers take in concerts in the **BAM** halls, the floating **Bargemusic** barge, and other spaces.

BROOKLYN WITH KIDS

Interactive museums, roller coasters, carousels, and state-of-the-art playgrounds make it a snap to entertain kids in Brooklyn. The only problem you'll have is figuring out what to do first.

AQUARIUM, ZOO, MUSEUM

There are museums that kids enjoy and there are museums made with kids in mind. The **Brooklyn Children's Museum** is the latter, and it's paradise for the under-eight set, who can dig in at the greenhouse, play in the sand and the water feature, and pretend to be pizza makers, bakers and travel agents. The **New York Aquarium** has plenty of watery wonders to delight children and adults, including playful penguins, otters, and seals, while the **Prospect Park Zoo** has a petting zoo with farm animals, a giant outdoor sea lion tank, and lots of other animals, large and small. Exhibits at the **New York Transit Museum** gets raves from all ages; the entrance resembles that of a subway station, and the subterranean space is full of vintage train cars and fun transportation-related activities.

SHOPPING

Who doesn't love a new toy? Take the kids to **Norman and Jules** for the most desirable handmade blocks and games, fun room accessories, and arts-and-crafts projects that will absorb attention for hours, if not days and weeks.

Area Kids is another one-stop shop for whimsical playthings as well as a small selection of adorable children's clothes. The borough's many bookstores have wonderful children's books and lots of fun storytelling events. In particular, check out **Books are Magic, Community Bookstore, Word, Greenlight Books,** and **Barnes and Noble.**

PLAY TIME

Great parks and playgrounds are plentiful in this borough. **Brooklyn Bridge Park** is a must, with several playgrounds, including the Water Lab's water jets, Swing Valley's swings and Tarzan-style ropes, Sandbox Village, and Slide Mountain. Brooklyn has several carousels, including the lovingly restored **Jane's Carousel** in Brooklyn Bridge Park and the **Carousel in Prospect Park.** Out at **Coney Island**, take the kids for a spin on the iconic **Wonder Wheel** and, for those tall enough to ride, the **Cyclone** roller coaster. The **LeFrak Center** in Prospect Park is a hit year-round, with ice-skating in the colder months and roller skating and water jets in summer.

FOOD AND DRINK IN BROOKLYN

Locally minded, innovative chefs, bartenders, baristas, and bakers can be found all over the borough. A hop on the subway is all you need to experience outstanding restaurants, bars, and cafés.

PIZZA

From old-school coal-oven-baked slices to nouveau pies dressed with innovative toppings, this is the pizza capital of the country. Legendary pizza makers have been slinging pies in Brooklyn for decades, while in recent years the borough has been the incubator for the new-wave Neapolitan craze. What makes the pizza so good here? Some say it's the special qualities of New York City water.

WORLD CUISINE

Think of a cuisine, and there's a good chance you can find it deliciously represented in Brooklyn. In a single day, you can have a superb Mexican breakfast, an authentic Chinese or Vietnamese lunch, a toothsome Czech Republic or Central American afternoon snack, and an outstanding Middle Eastern or Italian dinner. You'd still only be scratching the surface of the variety of eats you can enjoy here.

BEER AND COCKTAILS

Brooklynites take their drinks seriously. Want to sip artfully mixed cocktails made with house-brand bitters, guzzle Brooklyn brews in a happening beer hall, or taste Brooklyn-distilled liquor at its source? You can do all this and much more here.

COFFEE

Coffee has a serious presence in Brooklyn and pour-overs and local roasts are a source of pride. The profusion of local coffee bars and minichains, as well as top names from around the country, mean there's an abundance of cool or cozy spots for coffee connoisseurs looking to get a cup (to go or to stay).

SWEETS

No sweet tooth goes unsatisfied in Brooklyn, where cookies, cakes, pies, and pastries get local and creative. Small-batch chocolate factories, ice-cream shops with cult followings, bakeries that specialize in pie, and doughnut shops with lines out the door are among the local institutions churning out irresistible confections. Try not to leave the borough without tasting a hibiscus-glazed doughnut, a slice of chocolate julep pie, or a scoop of Ooey Gooey Buttercake ice cream.

MADE IN BROOKLYN

Brooklyn is a melting pot of makers, so what could be a better souvenir than something Brooklyn made? Here's a short list of local brands to look for when you're browsing.

....

CLOTHING

Madison Avenue may be famed for luxury shopping, but Brooklyn is where you go to discover up-and-coming talents. Be tempted by breezy silk blouses and dresses by Rachel Rose, wonderful Indian-inspired prints by Ace & Jig, and sleekly silhouetted frocks by Ilana Kohn. For a one-stop shop, hit one of the four **Bird** boutiques in the borough: they're in Carroll Gardens, Fort Greene, Park Slope, and Williamsburg.

ACCESSORIES

Accessories purchased on location are the perfect way to remember a trip. Digby & Iona, Scosha, and AILI are all known for their unique yet casual jewelry. Look for them and others at **Catbird**, in Williamsburg. The shop is also known for its own line of delicate pieces. For purses and totes, keep your eye out for Brooklyn brands like Hayden-Harnett's clever zip pouches and cross-body styles, as well as sumptuous leathers by KikaNY.

BEAUTY PRODUCTS

Homemade beauty brands abound in Brooklyn. Lip and body-care lines like Stewart & Claire, Apotheke, and MeowMeow Tweet have literally been cooked up in the borough. The **Shen Beauty** emporium carries these and many, many others.

HOME DECOR

Buy yourself, or a friend, something for the home: everyone adores the totes and tea towels with whimsical motifs hand-drawn by *Fodor's Brooklyn*'s own illustrator Claudia Pearson. Design lovers rave about the stunning wood cutting boards from Gowanus Furniture, coasters by Brooklyn Slate, offbeat dishware by Recreation Center, and everything from custom cabinets to small goods like coasters and trays from Noble Goods. The **Brooklyn Flea** in DUMBO and **Artists & Fleas** are good places to shop.

EDIBLES

Dozens of Brooklyn-based purveyors produce delicious snacks, nibbles, and spreads—pickles by Brooklyn Brine, Mike's Hot Honey, jams and jellies by Anarchy in a Jar, Mama O's kimchi, and so much more. **Whole Foods** is the perfect place to stock your kitchen or find a gift.

WHAT TO WATCH AND READ

To learn more about Brooklyn, before or after you visit, consider these movies, TV shows, books, magazines, and blogs as a primer to the borough's past, present, and ever-changing future.

MOVIES

Movies can capture time and place so perfectly, sometimes so much so that they quickly become dull and dated: not so these Brooklyn-based films, which both entertain and capture slices of Brooklyn life over time. Hal Ashby's 1970 film *The Landlord* takes a comedic look at Park Slope real estate and the diverse neighborhood. Hometown hero Spike Lee's revolutionary debut, *She's Gotta Have It* (1986), depicts the now-legendary independent arts scene brewing in Fort Greene in the 1980s. Called Brooklyn Boheme, the movement established the neighborhood—and Brooklyn itself—as a creative destination with global impact. Lee's *Do The Right Thing* (1989) also harks back to the 1980s, with a riveting portrayal of the racial tensions in Bedford-Stuyvesant at that time. As neighborhood demographics continue to shift through contemporary Brooklyn, the film remains powerfully relevant. *Requiem for a Dream,* Darren Aronofsky's 2000 screen adaptation of Hubert Selby's 1978 novel, is a searing look at addiction, set largely in Coney Island. Revisit 1977's *Saturday Night Fever,* in which John Travolta got his start as Italian-American Bay Ridgeite Anthony "Tony" Manero, and the Verrazano-Narrows Bridge plays a significant role. *Moonstruck,* Norman Jewison's 1987 film, is one of the era's quintessential romantic comedies, set against the backdrop of Brooklyn Heights. Another favorite, *The Squid and the Whale,* Noah Baumbach's award-winning 2005 indie flick, captures the fiercely intellectual, vaguely neurotic character of Park Slope. Baumbach's 2015 film, *While We Were Young,* is a wryly comedic look at very contemporary life in Brooklyn.

TV SHOWS

With Brooklyn's outsize personality, it's no wonder the borough is more than just a backdrop for many a screenwriter. Several recent series showcase Brooklyn front and center. *Girls* (2012–17), Lena Dunham's much-lauded HBO series about four twentysomething women in Greenpoint, is populated by the sort of lovable yet flawed characters that some feel are representative of Brooklyn's young, creative class. *Bored to Death* (2009–11), a neo-noir HBO series created by Jonathan Ames, depicts a Brooklyn-based writer and sometime private detective exploring Brooklyn themes like gentrification in Park Slope, pollution in the Gowanus Canal, and the changing ideas of contemporary parenting and publishing. Look farther back, to shows like *Welcome Back, Kotter* (1975–79) and even *The Honeymooners* (1955–56) for different perspectives of the borough.

BOOKS

The number of literary lions who have lived in Brooklyn over the centuries, from Walt Whitman to Norman Mailer to Pulitzer Prize–winning contemporary novelist Jennifer Egan, are far too many to enumerate. A reading list for understanding Brooklyn as a place, though, could start with poetry, including Whitman's "Crossing Brooklyn Ferry" (1856) and Hart Crane's "The Bridge" (1930). Moving to books, dig into classic American works like Betty Smith's 1943 novel *A Tree Grows in Brooklyn* and Alfred Kazin's memoir *A Walker in the City* (1978), both of which were inspired by Brooklyn's immigrant communities. Paule Marshall's critically acclaimed *Brown Girl, Brownstones* (1959) focuses on Bajan émigrés and Chaim Potok's *The Chosen* (1967) delves into Jewish society in Williamsburg. For rich history, David McCullough's *The Great Bridge: The Epic Story of the Building of the Brooklyn Bridge* (1972) is unforgettable. Brooklyn Heights is the setting for "Ghosts," the second story in Paul Auster's now-iconic *New York Trilogy,* from 1987. *Motherless Brooklyn,* Jonathan Lethem's 1999 novel about a detective with Tourette's syndrome, takes place in Gowanus, Boerum Hill, Cobble Hill, and Carroll Gardens. Adelle Waldman's *Love Affairs of Nathanial P.,* published in 2013, covers romance and narcissism within literary circles in contemporary Prospect Heights. Jennifer Egan's latest, *Manhattan Beach* (2017), is a fascinating tale set largely in the Brooklyn Navy Yards of the 1940s.

MAGAZINES AND BLOGS

To immerse yourself further in all things Brooklyn, check out the online Brooklyn Magazine, for excellent feature stories, news, and cultural updates. *Edible Brooklyn* is the borough's food-focused magazine and website, full of tantalizing stories about food, restaurants, and where to eat. Blogs like Brooklyn-Based, Brownstoner, and Brokelyn have information about events, news, community listings, and local gossip. Neighborhood-based blogs like Brooklyn Heights Blog, Bushwick Daily, Ditmas Park Corner, Free Williamsburg, Greenpointers, and Here's Park Slope get even more granular.

BROOKLYN TIMELINE

So much has happened on this plot of land that is today called Brooklyn. These are just some of the game-changing events that have made the borough what it is since its founding in 1636.

....

1636–46: A settlement known as Breuckelen is created by the Dutch, around Brooklyn Heights, and named after a town near Utrecht, in the Netherlands.

1776: The Battle of Long Island (aka the Battle of Brooklyn) begins George Washington's New York campaign during the Revolutionary War.

1801: The Brooklyn Navy Yard is established as an active naval base.

1816: Incorporation of the Village of Brooklyn under the Constitution of the State of New York.

1830s: Brooklyn is incorporated as a city (1834). Green-Wood Cemetery is founded (1838).

1840s: Walt Whitman is editor of the *Brooklyn Eagle* (1846–48). Brooklyn Borough Hall is built as City Hall in the Greek Revival style (1848). Weeksville, one of the first free black communities in the United States, is established in parts of what are now Bedford-Stuyvesant and Crown Heights (1840–80s).

1855: Additional areas including Williamsburg, Greenpoint, and Bushwick become part of Brooklyn.

1860s: Brooklyn Academy of Music opens and presents its inaugural performance (1861). Brooklyn plays an important role in the Civil War, providing a seaport, a manufacturing center, and troops. Prospect Park is designed by Fredrick Law Olmsted and Calvert Vaux, after they finish Manhattan's Central Park; the park is opened to the public while still under construction (1867).

1870s: Williamsburgh Savings Bank is built.

1880s: Industry booms throughout the decade, exemplified by the Domino Sugar Refinery in Williamsburg (1882), the largest sugar refinery in the world at the time. The Brooklyn Bridge is built, connecting Brooklyn to Manhattan by bridge for the first time and ushering in an era of economic prosperity (1883). The Brooklyn Elevated Railroad (known as the El) begins operating (1885). The Pratt Institute is established (1887). Peter Luger's opens (1887).

1890s: Soldiers & Sailors Arch, in Grand Army Plaza, is dedicated to the casualties of the Civil War (1892). The Brooklyn Public Library is established (1896). The Brooklyn

Museum is designed by McKim, Mead & White (1893). The City of Brooklyn becomes one of the five boroughs of New York City (1898). Al Capone is born in Brooklyn (1899) and grows up near the Navy Yard and then in Park Slope.

1900s: The Williamsburg Bridge is completed (1903). Coney Island's Luna Park debuts (1903). The Manhattan Bridge opens (1909).

1910s: Brooklyn Botanic Gardens is founded (1910). The Brooklyn Army Terminal is built (1919).

1920s: The Cyclone opens at Coney Island (1927). The 37-story Williamsburgh Savings Bank Tower is built, becoming the tallest office building in Brooklyn (1929).

1930s: European Jews escaping Nazism establish a Hasidic enclave in Williamsburg.

1940s: The Central Library at Grand Army Plaza is completed (1941). *A Tree Grows in Brooklyn* is published (1943). Jackie Robinson debuts for the Brooklyn Dodgers, becoming the first African American to play for a Major League Baseball team (1947).

1950s: The population of Brooklyn hits a high of 2.7 million people in the 1950s before it declines through the '60s, '70s, and '80s. Toward the end of the '50s, many middle-class families begin leaving Brooklyn for the suburbs of Westchester and Long Island. The Brooklyn Dodgers decamp to Los Angeles (1958).

1960s: The Brooklyn-Queens Expressway (also known as the BQE) is completed after 25 years in the works (1960). The Verrazano-Narrows Bridge is constructed, connecting Brooklyn to Staten Island (1964). Following a period of economic decline, the Brooklyn Navy Yard shuts down (1966). Brooklyn's first West Indian-American Carnival parades down Eastern Parkway (1969).

1970s: The National Register of Historic Places adds the Park Slope Historic District and several others (1973–79). The Red Hook Food Vendors set up shop (1974); Brooklyn's last breweries shut down (1976). White flight gains momentum; crime and poverty are major issues throughout Williamsburg, Bushwick, Park Slope, and other neighborhoods. The blackout of 1977 results in looting and arson in Bushwick.

1980s: More additions to the National Register of Historic Places: Ditmas Park Historic District (1981), Clinton Hill Historic District (1981), and Greenpoint Historic District (1982). The Brooklyn

Chinese-American Association is founded (1987) to support the influx of Chinese immigrants settling in Sunset Park, Brooklyn's first Chinatown. Many neighborhoods are still plagued with high crime rates. Spike Lee's *Do the Right Thing* depicts racial tension and violence in Bedford-Stuyvesant (1989).

1990s: Brooklyn's population increases for the first time since the 1950s. Artists who can't afford rising rents in Manhattan begin moving into lofts and vacant warehouses in Williamsburg and DUMBO. The mayor's office targets Brooklyn's waterfront for revitalization (1992). The MetroTech Center business and educational area in Downtown Brooklyn is founded, revitalizing the area (1992). Brooklyn Brewery sets up a permanent home in Williamsburg (1996), sparking a renaissance in Brooklyn brewing. Diner opens in the same neighborhood, paving the way for the farm-to-table movement to arrive in Brooklyn (1999).

2000s: Steiner Studios opens in the Brooklyn Navy Yard, bringing the film industry to Brooklyn (2004). The Brooklyn Book Festival debuts (2005). Café Grumpy starts roasting coffee in Greenpoint, when there was little happening north of McCarren Park (2005). Etsy gets its start in a Fort Greene apartment (2005). The DUMBO Historic District is added to the National Register of Historic Places (2007). Roberta's pizza opens in industrial East Williamsburg (2008). The Brooklyn Flea is founded (2008).

2010s: King's County Distillery opens, becoming New York City's first whiskey distillery since Prohibition (2010). Chef's Table at Brooklyn Fare is the borough's first restaurant awarded two Michelin Stars (2010). The first phase of Brooklyn Bridge Park renovations are unveiled (2010). Jane's Carousel is installed in the park (2011); Smorgasburg is created as an extension of the Brooklyn Flea, drawing foodies across the East River (2011). The Barclays Center opens (2012). The Wythe Hotel opens (2012). HBO's *Girls* puts Greenpoint on the map (2012). The Domino Sugar Refinery, abandoned since 2004, is demolished to make room for a mixed-use residential and commercial development (2015). Hillary Clinton sets up her 2016 presidential campaign headquarters in Brooklyn Heights (2015). Though some protested, Brooklyn Bridge Park's ecoluxury hotel, 1 Hotel Brooklyn Bridge, opened in 2017.

BEST BROOKLYN EVENTS

You can always find something special to do in Brooklyn, but these are the standouts that Brooklynites plan their calendars around. These are organized by month, with ongoing events at the end.

MARCH

Greenpoint Gallery Night

Locals and visitors alike have the chance to go gallery-hopping two Friday nights a year thanks to Greenpoint Gallery Night, which is fortunate because many of the neighborhood's art spaces fly under the radar. (Some are open to the public throughout the year, usually on weekends.) One place to start is 67 West Street, which houses many small galleries, including the Greenpoint Terminal Gallery and Calico, then follow the map of participating galleries posted online. ⊠ *Greenpoint* ⊕ *www.greenpointgalleries.org* Ⓜ *G to Greenpoint Ave. or Nassau Ave.*

MAY

Greenpoint Film Festival

To see what's behind North Brooklyn's reputation as a haven for avant-garde artists and filmmakers, check out the four-day-long Greenpoint Film Festival, held every May. It features films in four categories (Documentary, Narrative, Experimental, and Animation), plus Q&As with filmmakers. The festival also includes an "Environmental" themed section with a special emphasis on Greenpoint. ⊠ *Wythe Hotel, 80 Wythe Ave., Greenpoint* ⊕ *www.greenpointfilmfestival.org* Ⓜ *L to Bedford Ave.; G to Greenpoint Ave.*

Park Slope House Tour

For nearly 60 years, the annual Park Slope house tour has offered a glimpse inside beautiful private family homes. The self-guided, ticketed event takes place on a Sunday afternoon in May, rain or shine, and shuttle buses connect key sites. Ticket-holders receive an illustrated brochure with the history and details of the participating homes. ⊠ *Poly Prep Lower School, 50 Prospect Park W, Park Slope* ☎ *347/871–0477* ⊕ *www.parkslopeciviccouncil.org* ⊠ *From $25* Ⓜ *2, 3 to Grand Army Plaza; F, G to 7th Ave.*

JUNE THROUGH AUGUST

Afropunk Fest

This annual multicultural fete brings artists like Macy Gray, D'Angelo, Big Freedia, and Chuck D to an urban park near the Brooklyn Navy Yard, at the far north end of Fort Greene. The fashion scene is as fabulous as the music. Local food trucks provide sustenance and a thrift market keep fans occupied between sets. ⊠ *Commodore Barry Park, Flushing*

Ave., Fort Greene ⊕ afropunkfest. com/brooklyn/ Ⓜ A, C, F, R to Jay St.– MetroTech; B, Q, R to DeKalb Ave.

Bastille Day

The French equivalent of the Fourth of July, Bastille Day is celebrated annually on Smith Street on a Sunday in July that falls closest to July 14, the actual date of the holiday. The street is closed off and transformed into a massive party, with area restaurants setting up booths and a temporary pétanque court near Bar Tabac. ⊠ Smith St., Carroll Gardens ⊕ www.bartabacny. com/bastille-day/ Ⓜ F, G to Bergen St., Carroll St., or Smith–9th Sts.

Celebrate Brooklyn!

New York City's longest-running summer outdoor performance festival began in 1979 and remains a top-notch crowd-pleaser with its diverse roster of mostly free (and some benefit) star acts. There's ample band shell seating, but locals tend to favor arriving early with a blanket to get a good seat on the grassy slope. Acts range from artists such as Janelle Monáe, the National, Neutral Milk Hotel, and St. Vincent to the Shen Wei Dance Arts company and Dance Theatre of Harlem. Look for silent film nights accompanied by innovative live music as well as spoken word performances. Pack a picnic or buy food from local, on-site vendors. ⊠ Prospect Park Bandshell, Entrance on Prospect Park W, Prospect Park ☎ 718/683–5600 ⊕ www.bricartsme-dia.org/performing-arts/celebrate-brooklyn Ⓜ F, G to 7th Ave.

Mermaid Parade

Plan a trip to Coney Island in mid to late June for the neighborhood's biggest event of the year, and you'll without a doubt have something to talk about for months to come. The costumes (or lack thereof) and floats are memorable, with some pretty outlandish presentations. It can get hot and crowded and hedonistic—more akin to Mardi Gras, with some nudity, than the Thanksgiving Parade, so you may wish to leave the kids at home. ⊠ Coney Island ⊕ www.coneyisland. com/programs/mermaid-parade.

Northside Festival

North Brooklyn's largest festival for music, film, and innovation comes alive for one week every June. Organized by Northside Media (the people behind Brooklyn Magazine and The L Magazine), the festival brings thousands together for an epic series of live performances by up-and-coming bands and indie rock stars, art, film screenings, and talks by Brooklyn's influencers—in venues across Williamsburg and Greenpoint. McCarren Park is Northside's heart, and several free events take place there. Check the website for the full schedule and to purchase tickets. ⊠ Williamsburg ⊕ www.northsidefestival.com.

Red Hook Flicks

This weekly summer movie series runs through July and August at the Louis Valentino Jr. Park & Pier. Films are projected against a ware-house as the sun fades behind the Statue of Liberty. Bring a blanket and make a picnic out of it. There's usually food for sale, too. ⊠ *Louis Valentino Jr. Park & Pier, Red Hook* ⊕ *www.redhookflicks.com* Ⓜ *F, G to Smith–9th Sts.*

SummerScreen

Every summer, New York City's parks become enormous outdoor movie theaters, and McCarren Park in Williamsburg is no exception. Presented by Northside Media, SummerScreen shows a different film every Wednesday. Past films include crowd-pleasers like *Dirty Dancing*, *Ferris Bueller's Day Off*, and *The Princess Bride*. Though the film doesn't start until the sun sets, the lawn opens at 6 pm; it's best to bring a blanket and arrive early to score a spot. There are food and drink vendors on-site. ⊠ *Brooklyn* ⊕ *www.summerscreen.org* Ⓜ *G to Nassau Ave.*

Victorian Flatbush House Tour

This biannual self-guided tour happens on even-numbered years and gives design and architecture buffs a look inside turn-of-the-century masterpieces. The event takes place, rain or shine, from 1 to 6 pm on the Sunday before Father's Day. You can go at your own pace and walk the entire route or use the shuttle bus. The tour starts at Temple Beth Emeth of Flatbush, where you can purchase or pick up tickets and collect the detailed guidebook and map. ⊠ *Temple Beth Emeth of Flatbush, 83 Marlborough Rd., Brooklyn* ☎ *718/859–3800* ⊕ *www.fdconline. org/house-tour* Ⓜ *B, Q to Church Ave.; Q to Beverley Rd.*

Atlantic Antic

Food, music, and a lot of fun are the features of this gigantic yearly party that closes down Atlantic Avenue from 4th Avenue to the waterfront on a Sunday in late September. There are several stages for performances and all kinds of antics at this family-friendly event, which celebrated its 43rd anniversary in 2017. ⊠ *New York* ⊕ *www. atlanticave.org/index.php.*

Brooklyn Book Festival

National and international stars of the book world headline talks and readings at the largest free literary event in New York City, started back in 2006. A week's worth of book talks, parties, and screenings in various venues around Brooklyn—as well as Queens and Manhattan—lead up to the Sunday main event, based at Brooklyn Borough Hall. ⊠ *New York* ⊕ *www. brooklynbookfestival.org.*

Bushwick Open Studios

The volunteer-run organization Arts in Bushwick puts together festivals and activities throughout the year. The main event, Bushwick Open Studios, is a huge art fair that takes place over a weekend in summer or early fall. Hundreds of artists throughout the neighborhood open their studios to the public, and there are events, performances, and panel discussions. ⊠ *Bushwick* ⊕ *www. artsinbushwick.org.*

Greenpoint Gallery Night.
See March.

Taste Talks
With so many exciting develop-
ments in the United States within
the fields of food and drink, the
annual Taste Talks festival program
has grown to include events in
Chicago, Los Angeles, and Miami,
but the main event still takes place
over a fall weekend in Brooklyn.
Panel discussions by influential
chefs and representatives from
various food publications, as well
as parties and supper clubs are
just some of the tasty experiences
to look forward to. ⊠ *Brooklyn*
⊕ *www.tastetalks.com/festivals.*

West Indian Day Parade
Each year on Labor Day, millions of
spectators and participants attend
the West Indian Day Parade, which
celebrates Carnival and West Indian Caribbean culture with dozens
of floats, city dignitaries, march-
ing bands, live music, and food
vendors. The parade route typically
heads from Crown Heights to Prospect Heights, along Eastern Parkway, from Utica Avenue to Grand
Army Plaza. Celebrations actually
begin early the morning before the
parade with *j'ouvert* (French for
"daybreak") but this isn't officially
part of the parade. ⊠ *Eastern Pkwy.,
Crown Heights* ☎ *718/467–1797*
⊕ *www.wiadcacarnival.org.*

OCTOBER
Bushwick Film Festival
Founded in 2007, the Bushwick
Film Festival draws a diverse audience of industry professionals and
film fans to its annual multiday
October event. Features, shorts,
and documentaries are submitted
by domestic and international filmmakers. Film education programs,
with workshops throughout the
year, help bridge the gap between
craft and community. ⊠ *Bushwick*
☎ *347/450–3464* ⊕ *www.bushwick-
filmfestival.com.*

Gowanus Open Studios
The factories, warehouses, and
studios of Gowanus foster many an
artisan, and for one weekend in October, literally hundreds of makers
open their work spaces to the public. There are events all weekend,
with studios open noon to 6 pm on
weekends. ⊕ *www.artsgowanus.org.*

NOVEMBER TO DECEMBER
Christmas Markets
From November through Christmas, holiday markets pop up
all over Brooklyn, many with a
creative, DIY bent. Some are one
day or weekend only, others recur
for several weeks. Artists & Flea is
a year-round market with a holiday
spin leading up to December,
while annual events like the BUST
Holiday Craftacular (⊕ *www.bust.
com*), the Brooklyn Holiday Bazaar
(⊕ *www.brooklynholidaybazaar.
com*), and the Etsy NY Handmade
Cavalcade (⊕ *www.handmadecav-
alcade.com*) each take place
over one weekend in November
or December. One-day events
include the Greenpointers Holiday
Market (⊕ *www.greenpointers.com*).
⊠ *Brooklyn.*

Dyker Heights Christmas Lights

Every holiday season, Dyker Heights becomes aglow with utterly extravagant light displays. Driving is convenient, but walking can be more fun, if the weather is agreeable—between 11th and 13th avenues, and from 83rd to 86th streets are a good bet. Here are a couple of tips: take a thermos of hot chocolate to keep you warm, and if you're driving, don't wait until the days right before Christmas because the traffic can get horrendous. ⊠ *Brooklyn.*

ONGOING EVENTS

DUMBO First Thursday Gallery Walk

This monthly happening provides after-hours access to more than 20 of DUMBO's galleries, retailers, and exhibition halls, plus happy hour specials at neighborhood bars and restaurants. Maps are available throughout the neighborhood. ⊠ *DUMBO* ⊕ *www.artindumbo. com/#first-thursday* Ⓜ *2, 3 to Clark St.; A, C to High St.; F to York St.*

Franklin Park Reading Series

This Crown Heights reading series at the Franklin Park bar and beer garden occurs on the second Monday of each month. Previous readers have included headliners like best-selling author Hannah Tinti and comedian Michael Showalter. ⊠ *Franklin Park, 618 St. John's Pl., Crown Heights* ☎ *718/975-0196* ⊕ *www.franklinparkbrooklyn.com/ reading-series* Ⓜ *2, 3, 4, 5 to Franklin Ave.*

Pete's Candy Store Reading Series

Williamsburg's premier reading series takes place year-round at a narrow bar in a converted train car; it's free to the public, has been patronized by Jonathan Ames and Dani Shapiro, and is held every other Thursday evening. There's also a poetry series, the second Friday of every month. ⊠ *Pete's Candy Store, 709 Lorimer St., Brooklyn* ☎ *718/302-3770* ⊕ *www. petescandystore.com/all-events* Ⓜ *L to Lorimer St., G to Metropolitan Ave.*

BEST BETS

With so many places to go and things to do in Brooklyn, how will you decide? Fodor's writers and editors have chosen our favorites to help you plan. Search the neighborhood chapters for more recommendations.

ACTIVITIES AND SIGHTS

ARCHITECTURE

Clinton Hill Architecture Walk, Clinton Hill

"Fruit Streets," Brooklyn Heights

Park Slope Historic District, Park Slope

Prospect Heights Historic Distict, Ditmas Park

Stuyvesant Heights, Bed-Stuy

MUSEUMS AND GALLERIES

Brooklyn Museum, Prospect Heights

Bushwick Collective, Bushwick

New York Transit Museum, Brooklyn Heights

PARKS AND GREEN SPACES

Brooklyn Botanic Garden, Park Slope

Fort Greene Park, Fort Greene

Green-Wood Cemetery, Greenwood Heights

Narrows Botanical Gardens, Bay Ridge

Prospect Park

VIEWS

Brooklyn Bridge, Brooklyn Heights

Brooklyn Bridge Park, Brooklyn Heights

Brooklyn Heights Promenade, Brooklyn Heights

Bush Terminal Park, Sunset Park

East River State Park, Williamsburg

Louis Valentino Jr. Park & Pier, Red Hook

Shore Park and Parkway, Bay Ridge

Sunset Park, Sunset Park

WNYC Transmitter Park, Greenpoint

SHOPPING

BROOKLYN-MADE

Annie's Blue Ribbon General Store, Park Slope

Artists & Fleas, Williamsburg

Better Than Jam, East Williamsburg

Brooklyn ARTery, Ditmas Park

Gowanus Souvenir Shop, Gowanus

Green in BKLYN, Clinton Hill

CLOTHING BOUTIQUES

Alter, Greenpoint

Bird, Carroll Gardens, Fort Greene, Park Slope, and Williamsburg

Friends NYC, Bushwick

In God We Trust, Greenpoint and Williamsburg

Marche Rue Dix, Bed-Stuy

JEWELRY

Catbird, Williamsburg

Clay Pot, Park Slope

Erie Basin, Red Hook

VINTAGE STORES

Beacon's Closet, Greenpoint and Park Slope

Chess and the Sphinx, Bushwick

Front General Store, DUMBO

10 Ft. Stella Dallas, Williamsburg

FOOD

BAKED GOODS

Baked, Red Hook

Bakeri, Greenpoint and Williamsburg

Dough, Bed-Stuy

Four & Twenty Blackbirds, Gowanus

One Girl Cookies, Carroll Gardens and DUMBO

BARBECUE

Fette Sau, Williamsburg

Hometown Bar-B-Que, Red Hook

Pig Beach, Gowanus

BRUNCH

Aurora, Williamsburg

Chavela's, Crown Heights

Five Leaves, Greenpoint

Iris Cafe, Brooklyn Heights

Le Barricou, Williamsburg

Maria's Bistro Mexicano, Sunset Park

Rabbithole, Williamsburg

BURGER

Cherry Point, Greenpoint

Emily, Fort Greene

Five Leaves, Greenpoint

Henry Public, Cobble Hill

Hope and Anchor, Red Hook

Korzo, South Slope

Ox Cart Tavern, Ditmas Park

Peter Luger, Williamsburg

Reynard, Williamsburg

Threes Brewing, Gowanus

FARM-TO-TABLE FARE

The Farm on Adderley, Ditmas Park

Glasserie, Greenpoint

Marlow & Sons, Williamsburg

Olmsted, Prospect Heights

Reynard, Williamsburg

Rose Water, Park Slope

Rucola, Boerum Hill

Vinegar Hill, DUMBO

ICE CREAM

Ample Hills Creamery, Gowanus and Prospect Heights

Milkmade Tasting Room, Carroll Gardens

Van Leeuwen, Boerum Hill and Greenpoint

ITALIAN

al di là Trattoria, Park Slope

Aurora, Williamsburg

Brucie, Cobble Hill

Convivium Osteria, Park Slope

Frankie's 457, Carroll Gardens

OUTDOOR DINING

Brooklyn Crab, Red Hook

El Almacen, Williamsburg

Frankie's 457, Carroll Gardens

Watty & Meg, Cobble Hill

Habana Outpost, Fort Greene

PIZZA

Barboncino, Crown Heights

Di Fara Pizza, Midwood

L&B Spumoni Gardens, Gravesend

Lucali, Carroll Gardens

Paulie Gee's, Greenpoint

Roberta's, East Williamsburg

Totonno's Pizza, Coney Island

ROMANTIC DINING

Aita, Fort Greene

Aurora, Williamsburg

Colonie, Brooklyn Heights

Convivium Osteria, Park Slope

El Almacen, Williamsburg

Rucola, Boerum Hill

Zenkichi, Williamsburg

TACOS
Fonda, Park Slope

Tacos Matamoros, Sunset Park

Taqueria de los Muertos, Prospect Heights

Tortilleria Mexicana Los Hermanos, Bushwick

Zona Rosa, Williamsburg

DRINK

COFFEE
Blue Bottle Coffee, Boerum Hill and Williamsburg

Brooklyn Roasting Company, DUMBO

Devoción, Williamsburg

Little Skips, Bushwick

Steeplechase, Windsor Terrace

Toby's Estate, Williamsburg

COCKTAILS
Alameda, Greenpoint

Blueprint, Park Slope

Clover Club, Carroll Gardens

Donna, Williamsburg

Featherweight, East Williamsburg

Hotel Delmano, Williamsburg

Maison Premiere, Williamsburg

The Richardson, Williamsburg

Tooker Alley, Prospect Heights

Weather Up, Prospect Heights

CRAFT BEER
Circa Brewing Company, Downtown Brooklyn

Great Bar Harry, Carroll Gardens

Left Hand Path, Bushwick

Spuyten Duyvil, Williamsburg

Tørst, Greenpoint

OUTDOOR DRINKING
Brooklyn Barge, Greenpoint

Brooklyn Bavarian Biergarten, South Slope

Greenwood Park, Greenwood Heights

Hot Bird, Clinton Hill

The Ides, Williamsburg

Lavender Lake, Gowanus

Paul's Daughter, Coney Island

Threes Brewing, Gowanus

NIGHTLIFE AND PERFORMING ARTS

DANCING
Baby's All Right, Williamsburg

Bembe, Williamsburg

Diamond Lil, Greenpoint

Frank's Cocktail Lounge, Fort Greene

The Good Room, Greenpoint

Lot 45, Bushwick

Output, Williamsburg

LIVE MUSIC
Barbès, Park Slope

The Bell House, Gowanus

Brooklyn Bowl, Williamsburg

Kings Theatre, Ditmas Park

Music Hall of Williamsburg, Williamsburg

Pete's Candy Store, Williamsburg

Rock Shop, Gowanus

St. Mazie, Williamsburg

Sunny's, Red Hook

Union Pool, Williamsburg

READING SERIES
Books are Magic, Cobble Hill

Greenlight, Fort Greene

Franklin Park, Crown Heights

Pete's Candy Store, Williamsburg

THEATER AND PERFORMANCE
Brooklyn Academy of Music, Fort Greene

Littlefield, Gowanus

St. Ann's Warehouse, DUMBO

2

Williamsburg

Greenpoint

NORTH WILLIAMSBURG

East Williamsburg

SOUTH WILLIAMSBURG

Bedford-Stuyvesant

Clinton Hill

tseeing ★ ★ ★ ★ ☆ | Shopping ★ ★ ★ ★ ★ | Dining ★ ★ ★ ★ ★ | Nightlife ★ ★ ★ ★

The kinetic energy of this trendsetting Brooklyn neighborhood hits you the moment you exit the L train at Bedford Avenue, Williamsburg's main drag. Chic boutiques abound, the arts are in evidence everywhere, happening restaurants and dimly lit cocktail bars beckon, local denizens sport the latest street style, and it's immediately apparent that this is the neighborhood that defines Brooklyn's international image. It wasn't always this way, though. As the 20th century dawned, immigrants transformed Williamsburg into a dense area of tenements and factories—everything from chemicals and glassware to beer and sugar was made here. Hasidic Jews began settling in the southern section before World War II, with increasing numbers, including many Holocaust survivors, arriving in the late 1940s. By the 1960s, industrial production declined—and with it the neighborhood—but a few decades later an enterprising creative class began to reenergize the enclave, and the rest, as they say, is history. It's worth noting that although Williamsburg is one large neighborhood, residents often make the distinction between the more redeveloped northern part and the southern section, where the majority of the Hasidic Jews reside and maintain their traditional lifestyle, with Grand Street as the informal border between them. We divided our coverage into North Williamsburg and South Williamsburg to reflect that.—*Updated by Laura Itzkowitz*

North Williamsburg

Sights

Brooklyn Art Library
The library's chief draw is the fascinating Sketchbook Project, thousands of crowd-sourced sketchbooks created by artists and amateurs from around the globe. You could easily while away an afternoon perusing these 32-page meditations, whose topics range from comics, travelogues, and memoirs to catalogs of extinct genetic muta-tions. Should the addictive musings activate your own imagination, there are art supplies for sale on-site. ⊠ *28 Frost St., Brooklyn* ☎ *718/388–7941* ⊕ *www.brooklynartlibrary. com* ⊘ *Closed Mon. and Tues.* Ⓜ *L to Bedford Ave.*

Bushwick Inlet Park
A $30 million investment turned a former parking lot into this lush green space adjacent to East River State Park. Part of a major revitalization project aimed at the Williamsburg and Greenpoint

waterfront, the renovation added a sloped pavilion leading up to a public promenade, a playground, an athletic field, and an environmentally sophisticated building (with restrooms) for community activities. The views are expansive, taking in everything from the Williamsburg Bridge to the Empire State Building. ⊠ *Kent Ave. between N. 9th and N. 10th Sts., Brooklyn* ⊕ *www.bushwickinletpark.org* Ⓜ *L to Bedford Ave.*

City Reliquary

Subway tokens, Statue of Liberty figurines, antique seltzer bottles, and other artifacts you might find in a time capsule crowd the cases of this museum that celebrates New York City's past and present. Temporary exhibits here have included one about doughnut shops and another about Jewish gangsters of the Lower East Side. ⊠ *370 Metropolitan Ave., Brooklyn* ☎ *718/782-4842* ⊕ *www.cityreliquary. org* ⊴ *$7* ⊗ *Closed Mon.–Wed.* Ⓜ *L to Lorimer St.; G to Metropolitan Ave.*

East River State Park

Cherished by residents for its grassy knolls and superb Manhattan views, this park contains vestiges of the 19th-century dock that once occupied these 7 acres. On Saturday, more than a hundred vendors sell artisanal goods at the Smorgasburg open-air market (see Chapter 8, Park Slope and Prospect Park, for full listing). The park can get crowded on summer weekends, so don't be surprised if you find yourself scavenging for an open patch of grass. ⊠ *Kent Ave.,*

Brooklyn ☎ *718/782-2731* ⊕ *www. parks.ny.gov/parks/155/details.aspx* Ⓜ *L to Bedford Ave.*

McCarren Park

On warm weekends, locals flock to this park that forms the border between Williamsburg and Greenpoint. The 35 acres include baseball diamonds, benches, tree-lined paths, and plenty of dogs out enjoying the sunshine with their owners. Across Driggs Avenue are a running track, soccer field, and tennis courts. The outdoor McCarren Park Pool, open in summer, tends to hit capacity pretty quickly. There's a skating rink in winter. ⊠ *Bordered by N. 12th St., Berry St., Nassau Ave., Lorimer St., Manhattan Ave., and Bayard St., Brooklyn* ⊕ *www.nycgovparks.org/ parks/mccarren-park* Ⓜ *G to Nassau Ave.; L to Bedford Ave.*

New York Distilling Company

This young distillery makes two kinds of rye and three types of gin. The knowledgeable staff is delighted to explain their nuances; visit on a weekend afternoon for a free tour and tasting (check the website for additional tour times). The bartenders at the attached Shanty bar, open nightly (weekends from 2 pm), make a serious gin gimlet. Be warned: the Dorothy Parker and Perry's Tot gins are potent. ⊠ *79 Richardson St., Brooklyn* ☎ *718/412-0874* ⊕ *www. nydistilling.com* Ⓜ *L to Lorimer St.; G to Metropolitan Ave.*

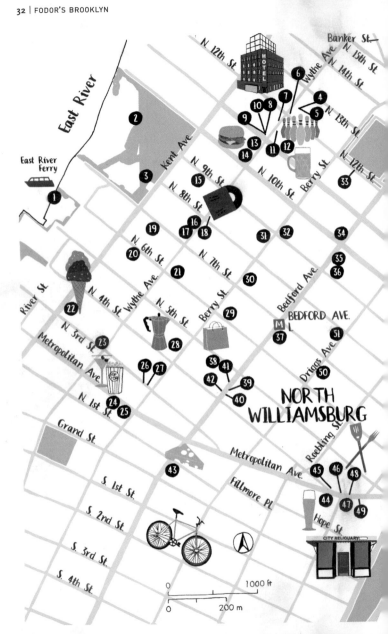

East River

East River
Ferry

Banker St.

N. 12th St.

Wythe Ave.

N. 15th St.

N. 14th St.

N. 13th St.

N. 12th St.

Kent Ave.

N. 10th St.

Berry St.

N. 9th St.

N. 8th St.

N. 7th St.

N. 6th St.

Wythe Ave.

N. 5th St.

Berry St.

Bedford Ave.

BEDFORD AVE.

River St.

N. 4th St.

N. 3rd St.

Metropolitan Ave.

N. 1st St.

Driggs Ave.

NORTH
WILLIAMSBURG

Grand St.

Metropolitan Ave.

Roebling St.

S. 1st St.

Fillmore Pl.

S. 2nd St.

Hope St.

CITY RELIQUARY

S. 3rd St.

S. 4th St.

0   1000 ft

0   200 m

North 6th St. Pier
NYC Ferry's East River route stops in North Williamsburg at this clean, modern pier, but even if you're not taking the ferry, it's a nice place for a walk, with benches and excellent views of the Manhattan skyline. On summer days, you're likely to see teens skateboarding and people eating ice cream from OddFellows, just two blocks away. ⊠ *N. 6th St., Brooklyn* ⊕ *www.ferry.nyc* Ⓜ *L to Bedford Ave.*

 Shopping

★ Artists & Fleas
Hands down the best place to lay eyes on the latest cool creations from Brooklyn-based artists and designers, this huge warehouse lures canny connoisseurs seeking one-of-a-kind items. Every weekend, nearly 100 vendors sell everything from handmade jewelry and objets d'art to custom clocks made from old hardcover books and T-shirts with vintage cartoons. ⊠ *70 N. 7th St., Brooklyn* ☎ *917/488–4203* ⊕ *www.artistsandfleas.com* Ⓜ *L to Bedford Ave.*

Awoke Vintage
In a neighborhood known for indie shops and often overpriced second-hand stores, this vintage shop stands out for its great selection and sales on clothing and accessories. Whether or not you're hunting for something particular, you can enjoy browsing curated racks of women's and men's fashions here or at its Greenpoint location. ⊠ *132 N. 5th St., Williamsburg* ☎ *718/387–*

GETTING HERE

The L train to Bedford Avenue is a direct route to the epicenter of Williamsburg. Much of North Williamsburg and parts of South Williamsburg are an easy walk from here. For the southern parts of South Williamsburg, go to Marcy Avenue. For the scenic route, the NYC Ferry's East River route stops at N. 6th Street in North Williamsburg and at Schaefer Landing in South Williamsburg.

3130 ⊕ *www.awokevintage.com* Ⓜ *L to Bedford Ave.*

★ Bedford Cheese Shop
A cheese lover's dream, this small fromagerie sells everything needed for a gourmet antipasto. The more than 200 artisanal cheeses are arranged by style—hard, soft, Bries, blues, etcetera. Dry goods include crackers, biscuits, premium olive oils, small-batch jams, and chocolates. Prosciutto di Parma and Serrano ham are among the cured meats; you'll also find foie gras, quail eggs, and other comestibles. Expert cheesemongers will help you navigate the offerings. ⊠ *265 Bedford Ave., Brooklyn* ☎ *718/599–7588* ⊕ *www.bedfordcheeseshop.com* Ⓜ *L to Bedford Ave.*

Brooklyn Charm
An amateur jewelry designer's paradise, this shop stocks more than a thousand charms and stones and sells everything needed to make necklaces, earrings, bracelets, and rings—wire, chain

by the yard, beads, and tools. The New York state charms and vintage adornments make great gifts. ⊠ 145 Bedford Ave., Brooklyn ☎ 347/689–2492 ⊕ www.brooklyncharm.com Ⓜ L to Bedford Ave.

The Brooklyn Kitchen

Recreational home cooks and advanced chefs adore this shop that stocks a dazzling array of kitchen tools and supplies, from cookbooks to hard-to-find ingredients. Informative and well-organized classes on everything from knife skills to home brewing to pasta making are held in the kitchen labs. ⊠ 100 Frost St., Brooklyn ☎ 718/389–2982 ⊕ www.thebrooklynkitchen.com Ⓜ L to Lorimer St.; G to Metropolitan Ave.

★ Catbird

Known for its trademark stackable rings and other dainty jewelry, the tiny store also sells soft cashmere hats, candles, and gift items, all curated with an emphasis on area designers. Any gift you buy here—for a friend or for yourself—will be cherished. ⊠ 219 Bedford Ave., Brooklyn ☎ 718/599–3457 ⊕ www.catbirdnyc.com Ⓜ L to Bedford Ave.

★ Dépanneur

Foodies have many reasons to stop at Dépanneur: artisanal products, cookbooks, food magazines, gourmet sandwiches, pastries, and coffee by Toby's Estate. The specialty store's shelves are lined with small-batch jams, pickles by Brooklyn Brine, flavored hot sauces, syrups, cordials, and bitters, not to mention a well-chosen selection of cheeses and

salumi. ⊠ 242 Wythe Ave., Brooklyn ☎ 347/227–8424 ⊕ www.depanneur.com Ⓜ L to Bedford Ave.

Desert Island Comics

The sign above the storefront says Sparacino's bakery, but the shop is actually home to a comic book utopia. Desert Island packs all kinds of illustrated media into the small shop, from kids' books to graphic novels and zines. You might find a rare vintage comic book or discover new work by a neighborhood graphic artist. ⊠ 540 Metropolitan Ave., Brooklyn ☎ 718/388–5087 ⊕ www.desertislandbrooklyn.com Ⓜ G to Metropolitan Ave.; L to Lorimer Ave.

Heatonist

Where will you find a specialty store dedicated entirely to hot sauce? In Williamsburg, of course! Owner/hot sauce aficionado Noah Chaimberg curated a selection of more than 100 varieties from all over the world—all without additives, preservatives, or extracts. Stop by the shop to taste them before you buy. ⊠ 121 Wythe Ave., Brooklyn ☎ 718/599–0838 ⊕ heatonist.com Ⓜ L to Bedford Ave

ID New York

Williamsburg's dapper gents head to this small boutique for high-quality apparel and accessories. Scotch & Soda, Life After Denim, WeSC, and similar brands fill the shelves. Don't miss the colorful, patterned bow ties. There's also a shop at 107 North 5th Street (at Berry). ⊠ *232 Bedford Ave., Brooklyn* 🕾 *718/599–0790* ⊕ *www.idnewyork. com* Ⓜ *L to Bedford Ave.*

In God We Trust. Branch location at 129 Bedford Ave. *See Chapter 3, Greenpoint, for full listing.*

★ Mast Brothers

The elegantly wrapped bars of Brooklyn's artisanal bean-to-bar chocolatiers are ubiquitous in New York City, but to experience the magic as it transpires, head to the Mast flagship on North 3rd Street, where you can tour the factory and sample goodies ($10, register online). The all-natural, single-origin chocolate bars are earthy and barely sweet. Two doors down at Brew Bar, cocoa beans are brewed like coffee—the taste is like nothing you've tried before. ⊠ *111 N. 3rd St., Brooklyn* 🕾 *718/388–2644* ⊕ *www. mastbrothers.com* Ⓜ *L to Bedford Ave.*

★ Pema New York

Stylish shoppers stop into this boutique for affordable dresses, tops, and skirts by the likes of Olivaceous, Everleigh, Lucy Paris, and Gracia, shoes by New York–based Chelsea Crew, as well as eclectic jewelry. The shop also carries yak-wool scarves and hats knitted in the Himalayas by the owner's family. ⊠ *225 Bedford Ave., Brooklyn* 🕾 *718/388–8814* ⊕ *www. pemany.com* Ⓜ *L to Bedford Ave.*

Rough Trade Records

This cavernous, London-based store sells LPs, CDs, and books, and doubles as a 250-seat concert venue and art gallery. The shop's cool, of-the-moment design incorporates recycled shipping containers. ⊠ *64 N. 9th St., Brooklyn* 🕾 *718/388–4111* ⊕ *www.roughtrad-enyc.com* Ⓜ *L to Bedford Ave.*

Spoonbill & Sugartown Booksellers

Top-notch art and design monographs as well as harder-to-find magazines like *Edible Brooklyn*, *Bomb*, and *Monocle* share shelf space with used and new best sellers, essay collections, and philosophy titles at this indie bookshop. The back of the shop has Brooklyn-made cards and notebooks. ⊠ *218 Bedford Ave., Brooklyn* 🕾 *718/387–7322* ⊕ *www.spoonbill-books.com* Ⓜ *L to Bedford Ave.*

10 Ft. Single by Stella Dallas

For vintage clothes, look no further. The store is enormous, with rack upon rack of secondhand clothes ranging from '40s cocktail dresses to '80s printed blouses. The back room has well-kept pieces from the 1940s to the 1960s, including an impressive array of fur coats. There's plenty for guys, too: T-shirts, varsity jackets, cowboy boots, and more. Head next door for antique textiles and rugs. ⊠ *285 N. 6th St., Brooklyn* 🕾 *718/486–9482* Ⓜ *L to Lorimer St.; G to Metropolitan Ave.*

☕ Coffee and Quick Bites

Bakeri. Branch location at 150 Wythe Ave. *See Chapter 3, Greenpoint, for full listing.*

★ Blue Bottle Coffee

$ | Café. Self-described coffee aficionados line up for the espresso and pour-overs at Blue Bottle, which originated in Oakland but feels very much at home in Williamsburg. The former factory building has light streaming in through large windows so the La Marzocco espresso machine seems to shine, and a Kyoto-style iced-coffee dripper, which looks like it belongs in a science lab, is displayed opposite the coffee counter. **Known for:** third-wave coffee; great pastries; cool design. *Average main: $4 ⊠ 160 Berry St., Brooklyn ☎ 718/387–4160 ⊕ www.bluebottlecoffee.com Ⓜ L to Bedford Ave.*

★ Du's Donuts & Coffee

$ | Bakery. After closing his famed restaurant WD~50, experimental chef Wylie Dufresne is back on New York's dining scene with—of all things—a doughnut shop. With flavors like pink lemonade pistachio, espresso cardamom, and brown butter key lime, these doughnuts are delicious little works of art. **Known for:** famous chef; creative flavors; superlative donuts. *Average main: $4 ⊠ 107 N. 12th St., Brooklyn ☎ 718/215–8870 ⊕ www.dusdonuts.com Ⓜ L to Bedford Ave.*

Fortunato Brothers Café & Pasticceria

$ | Bakery. Of the few old-school Italian pastry shops remaining in Williamsburg, this family-run café and bakery is by far the best. The three Fortunato brothers emigrated from Naples in 1971 and opened this Italian bakery in 1976; the fact that they may not have updated the decor since then only makes the place feel more authentic. **Known for:** old-school Italian-American pastries; delicious gelato; vintage decor. *Average main: $5 ⊠ 289 Manhattan Ave., Brooklyn ☎ 718/387–2281 ⊕ www.fortunatobrothers.com Ⓜ L to Graham Ave.*

Kinfolk 90

$ | Café. Multitasking is taken to a high level at this fabulous space that includes a coffee shop, a men's boutique, and a nightclub, all of which ascribe to the same überhip lifestyle. At Kinfolk 90, creative types meet for locally roasted coffee in a former garage decorated with custom artwork. **Known for:** coffee; cocktails; street-style men's clothing store. *Average main: $6 ⊠ 90–94 Wythe Ave., Brooklyn ☎ 347/799–2946 ⊕ www.kinfolklife.com Ⓜ L to Bedford Ave.*

OddFellows Ice Cream

$ | Café. In summer, lines stream out the door for unique and delicious ice cream flavors like extra virgin olive oil and Thai iced tea. Everything is homemade in small batches, even the cones, which are pressed in a waffle iron and hand rolled. **Known for:** oddball ice cream flavors; all-natural ingredients;

carnival-themed shop. *Average main: $5* ⊠ *175 Kent Ave., Brooklyn* ☎ *347/599-0556* ⊕ *www.oddfellowsnyc.com* Ⓜ *L to Bedford Ave.*

★ Patisserie Tomoko

$ | Bakery. Tokyo-born chef Tomoko Kato came up through New York's famed Le Bernardin and the East Village teahouse Cha-An before opening this pastry shop. Her inspired desserts marry Japanese flavors and French techniques, resulting in original creations like black-sesame crème brûlée, sake ice cream, and green tea mousse cake. **Known for:** Japanese-French pastries; matcha lattes; great design. *Average main: $7* ⊠ *568 Union Ave., Brooklyn* ☎ *718/388-7121* ⊕ *www.patisserietomoko.com* ⊙ *Closed Mon.* Ⓜ *L to Bedford Ave.*

Toby's Estate

$ | Café. With five cafés in New York City, Toby's Estate is expanding quickly, a mini coffee empire that started in Brooklyn. The coffee drinks are outstanding, as are the made-to-order sandwiches (think egg on a roll with espresso-lacquered bacon) and salads. **Known for:** excellent coffee; yummy sandwiches; cool design. *Average main: $7* ⊠ *125 N. 6th St., Brooklyn* ☎ *347/586-0063* ⊕ *www.tobysestate.com* Ⓜ *L to Bedford Ave.*

Dining

Allswell

$$ | Modern American. An alum of Manhattan's much-lauded Spotted Pig gastropub opened this popular spot, where closely packed tables, medieval-looking chandeliers, and a patchwork of patterned wallpaper are a rustic backdrop for elevated pub fare. At dinner the roast chicken is a standout; at brunch it's hard to choose between fluffy pancakes and eggs Benedict. **Known for:** gastropub fare; old-time decor; no reservations. *Average main: $24* ⊠ *124 Bedford Ave., Brooklyn* ☎ *347/799-2743* ⊕ *www.allswellnyc.com* Ⓜ *L to Bedford Ave.*

Antica Pesa

$$$ | Italian. The Williamsburg outpost of the historic Roman restaurant serves handmade pastas in an upscale setting. Though the decor is modern, the recipes uphold tradition: try the *spaghetti cacio e pepe* (al dente pasta with pecorino Romano and crushed black pepper) or the carbonara. **Known for:** Roman cuisine; sleek modern design; A-list clientele. *Average main: $25* ⊠ *115 Berry St., Brooklyn* ☎ *347/763-2635* ⊕ *www.anticapesa.com* ⊙ *No lunch* Ⓜ *L to Bedford Ave.*

Cafe Colette

$$ | Modern American. An owner of the Hotel Delmano bar across the street operates this charming corner bistro with an enclosed garden that's open year-round. Inside, the weathered wood, a zinc bar, leather banquettes, and candlelit tables lend the place a romantic, old-world feel and provide a backdrop to fresh, simple New American food influenced by the cuisines of Italy, France, Spain, and Central America. **Known for:** old-world atmosphere; bistro fare; charming garden. *Average main: $18* ⊠ *79 Berry St., Brooklyn* ☎ *347/599–1381* ⊕ *www.cafe-colette. com* Ⓜ *L to Bedford Ave.*

D.O.C. Wine Bar

$$ | **Italian.** There's simply nowhere else in Williamsburg like this rustic enoteca: You'd have to sail to Sardinia to savor a comparable meal. Pastas highlight the island's specialties, among them *fregola* (similar to couscous) with pistachio pesto and mascarpone, and the all-Italian wine list has plenty of accessible choices to pair with the artisanal cheeses. **Known for:** excellent wine list; Sardinian cuisine; rustic design. *Average main: $18* ⊠ *83 N. 7th St., Brooklyn* ☎ *718/963–1925* ⊕ *www.docwinebar.com* ☉ *No lunch* Ⓜ *L to Bedford Ave.*

El Almacen

$$$ | **Argentine.** The focus at this Argentine steak house is on grass-fed beef, served on wooden platters and paired with an Argentine Malbec from the extensive wine list. The restaurant has a warm bistro feel, with lace curtains and a pressed-tin ceiling. **Known for:** Argentine steaks; great wine list; romantic atmosphere. *Average main: $30* ⊠ *557 Driggs Ave., Brooklyn* ☎ *718/218–7284* ⊕ *www.elalmacennyc.com* ☉ *No lunch weekdays* Ⓜ *L to Bedford Ave.*

Fada

$$ | **French.** A typical French bistro in the heart of Williamsburg, Fada serves Provençal specialties, including classic *moules marinière,*steak au poivre, and ratatouille. The owner hails from Marseille, so both the menu and decor are in keeping with the traditions of the French Riviera. **Known for:** French bistro fare; charming garden; live gypsy jazz. *Average main: $15* ⊠ *530 Driggs Ave., Brooklyn* ☎ *718/388–6105* ⊕ *www. fadabistro.com* ☉ *Closed Mon. No lunch Tues.–Sat.* Ⓜ *L to Bedford Ave.*

Fette Sau

$$ | **Barbecue.** It might seem odd to go to a former auto-body repair shop to feast on meat, but the funky building and courtyard are just the right setting for the serious barbecue served here. A huge wood-and-gas smoker delivers brisket, sausages, ribs, and even duck—all ordered by the pound. **Known for:** Southern-style barbecue; excellent whiskey list; no reservations. *Average main: $13* ⊠ *354 Metropolitan Ave., Brooklyn* ☎ *718/963–3404* ⊕ *www.fettesaubbq. com* ☉ *No lunch Mon.* Ⓜ *L to Lorimer St.; G to Metropolitan Ave.*

★ Fornino

$$ | **Pizza.** The chefs here consider pizza-making both art and science, and their wood-fired creations prove just how deftly they balance the equation. The *funghi misti*—a white pie with mozzarella, wild mushrooms, and truffle oil—is downright irresistible. **Known for:** wood-fired pizza; casual vibe;

great for families. *Average main: $15 ✉ 291 Kent Ave., Brooklyn ☎ 718/384–6004 ⊕ www.fornino.com* Ⓜ *L to Bedford Ave.*

Lilia

$$$ | Italian. Having cut her teeth at Spiaggia in Chicago (a favorite of Obama's) and A Voce in New York, award-winning chef Missy Robbins is now earning accolades for her own chic restaurant in a former auto-body shop. Her handmade pastas are to die for and complement wood-fired fish, bruschetta, and other dishes that hew to the lighter side of Italian cuisine. **Known for:** award-winning chef; handmade pastas; healthy Italian cuisine. *Average main: $25 ✉ 567 Union Ave., Brooklyn ☎ 718/576–3095 ⊕ www.lilianewyork. com* ⊘ *No lunch* Ⓜ *L to Bedford Ave.*

★ Reynard

$$$ | Modern American. The largest of Andrew Tarlow's Williamsburg restaurants (which include Diner and Marlow & Sons), Reynard has all the hallmarks of a Tarlow venture. Farm-to-table fare highlights the season's freshest ingredients, and everything is made in-house, even the granola. **Known for:** pioneering restaurateur; farm-to-table fare; urban-rustic digs in the Wythe Hotel. *Average main: $26 ✉ Wythe Hotel, 80 Wythe Ave., Brooklyn ☎ 718/460–8004 ⊕ www. reynardnyc.com* Ⓜ *L to Bedford Ave.*

St. Anselm

$$ | Steakhouse. This modest spot grills high-quality meat and fish, all sustainably and ethically sourced, and at very reasonable prices. The

sides, ordered à la carte, deserve special attention: The spinach gratin is dependably hearty, and the seasonal special of delicata squash with manchego (cheese from sheep's milk) is divine. **Known for:** grilled meat and fish; casual vibe; no reservations. *Average main: $19 ✉ 355 Metropolitan Ave., Brooklyn ☎ 718/384–5054 ⊕ www.stanselm.net* ⊘ *No lunch weekdays* Ⓜ *L to Lorimer St.; G to Metropolitan Ave.*

★ Zenkichi

$$$ | Japanese. Modeled on Tokyo's intimate brasseries, this hidden Japanese restaurant serves no sushi: they specialize in exqui-sitely composed small plates, best enjoyed as part of the eight-course *omakase* (chef's tasting menu), though you can also order à la carte. Instead of a dining room, guests are seated in private booths separated by bamboo curtains, so other diners are audible but not visible. **Known for:** Japanese omakase; private booths; romantic date spot. *Average main: $26 ✉ 77 N. 6th St., Brooklyn ☎ 718/388–8985 ⊕ www.zenkichi.com* ⊘ *No lunch* Ⓜ *L to Bedford Ave.*

Zona Rosa

$$ | Mexican. You can't miss this fun taquería inspired by Mexico City's Zona Rosa neighborhood, thanks to the 1946 Airstream trailer embedded in the facade—the eatery started as a food truck and the restaurant was built around it. Tacos, like the flavorful mahimahi with grilled pineapple, onion, and cilantro, arrive on the bottom of a two-tiered wooden platter, with three salsas on top. **Known for:**

Airstream trailer; fun atmosphere; great tacos. *Average main: $16 ⊠ 571 Lorimer St., Brooklyn ☎ 917/324–7423 ⊕ www.zonarosabrooklyn.com ⊗ No lunch weekdays Ⓜ L to Lorimer St.; G to Metropolitan Ave.*

Bars and Nightlife

Barcade
Stop reminiscing about your arcade-loving youth and start playing the more than 30 vintage video games (most cost a mere quarter) lining the walls of this high-spirited bar-arcade. Challenge yourself with favorites like Ms. Pac-Man or rarities like Rampage. Barcade isn't just about the games, though: there's a good selection of micro-brews, as well as snacks. ⊠ *388 Union Ave., Brooklyn ☎ 718/302–6464 ⊕ www.barcadebrooklyn.com Ⓜ G to Metropolitan Ave.; L to Lorimer St.*

Brooklyn Bowl
A former ironworks foundry now houses a setup the original workers might have appreciated: 16 bowling lanes, a cocktail bar, a music stage, and a restaurant. The team behind the Blue Ribbon restaurant-bar empire handles the menu, which features Louisiana-style southern specialties like their signature fried chicken. There's a fine selection of brews on tap. Weekends bring out the crowds—and there are no lane reservations—so it can take a while to get a lane. ⊠ *61 Wythe Ave., Brooklyn ☎ 718/963–3369 ⊕ www.brooklynbowl.com ⊴ $20 per lane for 30 mins. Ⓜ L to Bedford Ave.; G to Nassau Ave.*

★ Brooklyn Brewery
This brewery put the borough's once-active craft beer scene back on the map when it opened in this former matzo factory in Williamsburg in 1996. Free 15-minute guided tours are offered on weekend afternoons, and there are always at least 8 or 10 offerings in the convivial taproom: the signature lager is popular, as is the Belgian-inspired Local 1, or try one of the seasonal options. Note that no open-toed shoes are allowed on the tours. ⊠ *79 N. 11th St., Brooklyn ☎ 718/486–7422 ⊕ www.brooklynbrewery.com Ⓜ L to Bedford Ave.; G to Nassau Ave.*

The Commodore
The door may be unmarked, but this bar is far from unknown: on weekends, it gets packed so tight it can be hard to navigate the sea of hip kids who come for reasonably priced drinks, renowned fried chicken, and nachos piled high with veggies, beans, and cheese. A retro vibe, fueled by the jukebox, enhances the cool factor. There are a few spacious booths, but get here early to snag one. ⊠ *366 Metropolitan Ave., Brooklyn ☎ 718/218–7632 Ⓜ L to Lorimer St.; G to Metropolitan Ave.*

★ Hotel Delmano
It's easy to miss the unmarked entrance to this cocktail bar on Berry Street, but head to the entrance on North 9th Street and you'll feel whisked away to an old-world parlor. Despite the name, this isn't a hotel, though the owners were inspired by lobby bars. Patrons imbibe cocktails around

marble-top tables or at the curved bar, where bartenders blend fresh fruit and homemade syrups into classic and original libations. Jazz and dim lighting make the place feel intimate. ⊠ *82 Berry St., Brooklyn* ☎ *718/387–1945* ⊕ *www.hoteldel-mano.com* Ⓜ *L to Bedford Ave.*

★ Ides Bar

One of the buzziest bars in Williamsburg, the Ides benefits from its privileged position on the Wythe Hotel's rooftop. Well-heeled patrons from all over the world line up for entry ($10 on Fridays and Saturdays after 6 pm) and the jaw-dropping views of the Manhattan skyline. It's a hot spot on weekends, and crowded—it's more than worth it to go early and have that memorable view all to yourself. ⊠ *Wythe Hotel, 80 Wythe Ave., 6th fl., Brooklyn* ☎ *718/460–8000* ⊕ *www.wythehotel.com/the-ides* Ⓜ *L to Bedford Ave.*

Knitting Factory

Rock, indie, and underground hip-hop performances draw crowds at this well-established concert venue that does double duty as a neighborhood watering hole, with a dimly lit front bar offering happy hour specials before and after shows. Sunday is comedy night in the front bar. ⊠ *361 Metropolitan Ave., Brooklyn* ☎ *347/529–6696* ⊕ *www.knittingfactory.com* Ⓜ *L to Bedford Ave. or Lorimer St.; G to Metropolitan Ave.*

Music Hall of Williamsburg

This intimate, tri-level music venue in a former mayonnaise factory has excellent acoustics, so it's no surprise that it draws die-hard fans of rock and indie music. There's balcony seating and an additional bar upstairs. If you love Manhattan's Bowery Ballroom, you'll feel the same way about this venue; it's run by the bookers at Bowery Presents, so you can expect the same quality lineups. ⊠ *66 N. 6th St., Brooklyn* ☎ *718/486–5400* ⊕ *www.musichallof-williamsburg.com* Ⓜ *L to Bedford Ave.*

Night of Joy

A night out at Night of Joy feels like drinking in a bohemian, slightly run-down fortune teller's den—the kind of place in a novel by Oscar Wilde or Gabriel García Márquez. The spacious lounge is outfitted with plush, mismatched sofas, oriental rugs, antique wall sconces, and a Victorian birdcage; peeling plaster gives it the air of dilapidated luxury. The libations are worth savoring—try the basil-lime gimlet or the rosemary and ginger bourbon. The rooftop patio is the place to be in summer: it has its own bar and patio furniture for lounging. ⊠ *667 Lorimer St., Brooklyn* ☎ *718/388–8693* ⊕ *www.nightofjoybar.com* Ⓜ *L to Lorimer St.; G to Metropolitan Ave.*

Output

This is Brooklyn's hottest nightclub and the cavernous converted ware-house draws top DJs spinning for crowds dancing under disco balls until the sun comes up. Stay in the main bilevel space, or head to the smaller Panther Room. The rooftop has great views. ⊠ *74 Wythe Ave., Brooklyn* ⊕ *www.outputclub.com* Ⓜ *L to Bedford Ave.*

Pete's Candy Store

Nope, it's not a candy store; it's an intimate bar that hosts nightly music performances as well as spelling bees, bingo, and a "quizz-off" contest every Wednesday night. The reading series held here on alternate Thursday evenings attracts high-caliber partici-pants. ⊠ *709 Lorimer St., Brooklyn* ☏ *718/302-3770* ⊕ *www.petescandys-tore.com* Ⓜ *G to Metropolitan Ave.; L to Lorimer St.*

Radegast Hall & Biergarten

The vibe is boisterous at this sprawling beer garden, with plenty of communal tables that foster a convivial atmosphere. The Central European beers on tap and in bottles pair well with hearty foods like schnitzel, goulash, and deli-cious hot pretzels. There's live music most nights. ⊠ *113 N. 3rd St., Brooklyn* ☏ *718/963-3973* ⊕ *www. radegasthall.com* Ⓜ *L to Bedford Ave.*

The Richardson

This corner bar serves classic cock-tails, beer, and wine. The decor takes its cues from a century-old saloon, with dark wood, damask wallpaper, and dim lighting. Whiskey-barrel tables and vintage cash registers further set the scene. Though the drinks and the gregarious bartenders who craft them are the stars here, there are some good nibbles, too. An excellent cheese plate—perfect for sharing—comes with your choice of locally sourced specimens. ⊠ *451 Graham Ave., Brooklyn* ☏ *718/389-0839* ⊕ *www.therichardsonnyc.com* Ⓜ *L to Graham Ave.*

Skinny Dennis

This honky-tonk has everything you'd want in a dive bar: peanut shells littering the floor, a vintage jukebox, a long bar with vinyl stools, and cheap drinks. This is Williamsburg, so the quality of beer is better than average—in addition to Coors and Guinness, there are craft beers by Brooklyn Brewery, Allagash, and Sixpoint. Live country music starts around 9 pm most nights. ⊠ *152 Metropolitan Ave., Brooklyn* ⊕ *www.skinnydennisbar.com* Ⓜ *L to Bedford Ave.*

Spuyten Duyvil

You might need to be a beer geek to recognize the obscure names of the more than 100 imported microbrews available here, but the connoisseurs behind the bar are more than happy to offer detailed descriptions and make recommen-dations. They'll also help you choose cheese and charcuterie platters to match your beverages. The space is narrow, with limited seating: all the more reason to take advantage of the huge backyard in summer. ⊠ *359 Metropolitan Ave., Brooklyn* ☏ *718/963-4140* ⊕ *www.spuyten-duyvilnyc.com* Ⓜ *L to Lorimer St.; G to Metropolitan Ave.*

Union Pool

A former pool-supply store now serves as a funky multipurpose venue, complete with a corrugated tin-backed bar, a photo booth, a small stage for live music, and cheap PBR. It's a popular spot on the Friday-night circuit, especially for late-night dancing. The back patio has a taco truck and a fire pit. ⊠ *484 Union Ave., Brooklyn* ☎ *718/609–0484* ⊕ *www.union-pool. com* Ⓜ *G to Metropolitan Ave.; L to Lorimer St.*

★ Westlight

Perched high on the 22nd floor of the William Vale Hotel, this is Brooklyn's hottest new spot for drinks with mind-blowing views, and it appeared on Aziz Ansari's Netflix show *Master of None.* Acclaimed chef Andrew Carmellini designed the menu of internationally inspired small plates like tuna tartare puffs and shrimp cocktail dumplings with Thai chili sauce to pair with the creative cocktails. Reservations are highly recommended. ⊠ *William Vale Hotel, 111 N. 12th St., 22nd fl., Brooklyn* ☎ *718/307–7100* ⊕ *westlightnyc.com* Ⓜ *L to Bedford Ave.*

Performing Arts

★ Nitehawk Cinema

The only movie theater of its kind in the New York City area, Nitehawk shows first-run and repertory films in three theater spaces and serves a full menu in-theater, as well as popcorn and snacks. Themed dining specials are paired with each indie film. Movies often sell out on weekends, so buy tickets in advance. After the film, bring your ticket stub down to the ground-level bar for $4 beers and well drinks. ⊠ *136 Metropolitan Ave., Brooklyn* ☎ *718/782–8370* ⊕ *www.nitehawk-cinema.com* 🎟 *Tickets $12* Ⓜ *L to Bedford Ave.*

🛏 Hotels

Hotel Le Jolie

$ | Hotel. This no-frills favorite has excellent service and is convenient not only to Williamsburg's arts, culture, and dining scenes but also to the subway and the Brooklyn-Queens Expressway, the latter handy should you want to get into Manhattan via car. **Pros:** good value; free parking on a first-come, first-served basis; convenient part of Brooklyn. **Cons:** proximity to highway can mean noise; can feel remote even though near to subways; not hip or trendy. *Rooms from: $199* ⊠ *235 Meeker Ave., Williamsburg* ☎ *718/625–2100* ⊕ *www.hotellejolie.com* 🛏 *52 rooms* ⦿ *Breakfast* Ⓜ *L to Lorimer St.; G to Metropolitan Ave.*

McCarren Hotel and Pool

$$ | Hotel. With funky design details like an underfoot, glass-encased river in the lobby (plus a fireplace), and a plum location overlooking McCarren Park, this hotel sizzles with scenester savvy. **Pros:** high hip factor; quality rooftop restaurant-bar; close to main thoroughfare Bedford Avenue. **Cons:** potential for noise from concerts in McCarren Park; some room details like lighting controls could be more user-friendly; the pool gets crowded in summer. *Rooms from: $315* ⊠ *160 N. 12th St., Brooklyn* ☎ *718/218–7500* ⊕ *www. mccarrenhotel.com* 🛏 *64 rooms* ⦿ *No meals* Ⓜ *L to Bedford Ave.*

★ Urban Cowboy B&B

$ | B&B/Inn. Williamsburg's only B&B, which occupies a renovated 100-year-old town house, combines the neighborhood's renegade spirit with an eye for design. **Pros:** beautiful design with personal touches; backyard Jacuzzi; personable staff. **Cons:** most rooms share a bathroom; a bit far from Williamsburg's main attractions; it can get a bit noisy. *Rooms from: $250 ⊠ 111 Powers St., Brooklyn ☎ 347/840–0525 ⊕ www.urbancowboybnb.com ⌿ 4 rooms, 1 cabin* ⊙ *Breakfast* Ⓜ *L to Lorimer St.; G to Metropolitan Ave.*

The Williamsburg Hotel

$$ | Hotel. This new boutique entry aims to embody the hip local spirit with a polished design, coveted skyline views, and great restaurant and bar offerings. **Pros:** nice design; great views from Manhattan-facing rooms; fun bar scene. **Cons:** a bit pricey; a bit far from the subway; only half of the rooms have a balcony. *Rooms from: $300 ⊠ 96 Wythe Ave., Brooklyn ☎ 718/362–8100 ⊕ www.thewilliamsburghotel.com ⌿ 147 rooms* ⊙ *No meals* Ⓜ *L to Bedford Ave.*

The William Vale

$$ | Hotel. The splashiest new opening to hit Brooklyn since the Wythe Hotel debuted in 2012, the 23-story William Vale towers above the neighborhood's low-slung buildings like a high-rise spaceship with a buzzy rooftop bar. **Pros:** every room has a balcony; destination-worthy restaurant and bar by an acclaimed chef; swimming pool only open to guests. **Cons:** service could use some improvement; doesn't feel very authentic to Williamsburg; pricey for what you get. *Rooms from: $350 ⊠ 111 N. 12th St., Brooklyn ☎ 718/631–8400 ⊕ thewilliamvale.com ⌿ 183 rooms* ⊙ *No meals* Ⓜ *L to Bedford Ave.*

★ Wythe Hotel

$ | Hotel. A former cooperage on the Brooklyn waterfront has found new life as the Wythe Hotel, a stunner for its Manhattan-skyline views, locally sourced design touches and amenities, and super-cool restaurant (Reynard) and bar (Ides). **Pros:** unique building history; Brooklyn-based design and environmentally friendly products; fabulous views from rooms or rooftop bar; destination-worthy restaurant. **Cons:** somewhat removed from the subway; no room service. *Rooms from: $295 ⊠ 80 Wythe Ave., Brooklyn ☎ 718/460–8001 ⊕ www.wythehotel.com ⌿ 70 rooms* ⊙ *No meals* Ⓜ *L to Bedford Ave.*

South Williamsburg

Sights

★ Grand Ferry Park

Hipsters, Hasidic Jews, and others hang out at this small waterfront park named for the ferry that for a century connected Williamsburg to Manhattan. The views of Manhattan and the Williamsburg Bridge are sublime anytime. Sand covers the ground in summer, and if you sit on a bench near the waves that crash against the rocks, you can almost

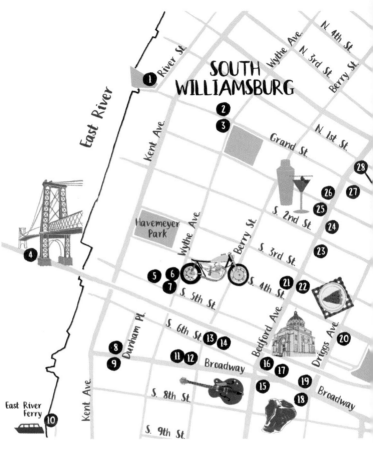

pretend you're at the beach. Check out the inscription on the redbrick smokestack, which figured in the development of penicillin. ⊠ *Grand St., Brooklyn* ⊕ *www.nycgovparks. org/parks/grand-ferry-park* Ⓜ *L to Bedford Ave.*

Schaefer Landing
The East River Ferry provides a fast and easy connection to nearby North Williamsburg, Greenpoint, DUMBO, and Manhattan. The landing on the South Williamsburg waterfront was named for the 19th-century Schaefer Brewery— the last operating brewery in Williamsburg before Brooklyn Brewery brought beer-making back to the neighborhood. The pier is clean, with great views of the Brooklyn Bridge, but there's not much nearby except new high-rise condos. ⊠ *440 Kent Ave., at S. 9th St., Brooklyn* ⊕ *www.eastriverferry. com* Ⓜ *J, M, Z to Marcy Ave.*

Sideshow Gallery
The quality varies from show to show at this pioneering gallery that specializes in works by emerging and established Brooklyn-based artists, but it remains a good place to take the creative pulse of Williamsburg and the borough. In its current space since 2000, Sideshow hosts edgy (sometimes peculiar) local and traveling exhibits, along with occasional readings, concerts, and other events. ⊠ *319 Bedford Ave., Brooklyn* ☎ *718/486–8180* ⊕ *www.sideshow-gallery.com* ⊘ *Closed Mon.–Wed.* Ⓜ *L to Bedford Ave.; J, M, Z to Marcy Ave.*

Weylin
An icon of the Williamsburg cityscape, the original headquarters of the Williamsburgh Savings Bank has been lavishly restored and renamed Weylin. Completed in 1875, the beaux arts building with its granite exterior and gold-tipped dome is a landmarked site. It's also a private event space, so don't be surprised to see a bride and groom posing on the steps. If you're lucky, you can peek inside. Be sure to look up: the ornately painted great dome is incredible. ⊠ *175 Broadway, Brooklyn* ☎ *718/963–3639* ⊕ *www. weylin.com* ⊘ *Only open for events* Ⓜ *J, M, Z to Marcy Ave.*

Williamsburg Art & Historical Center
WAH, as it's known locally, occupies one of New York City's earliest land-marked structures—a mansionlike 1867 former bank building designed in the French Second Empire style— but you have to enter through a side door to reach the high-ceiling, light-filled gallery. The exhibits showcase the works of contemporary artists in many media. ⊠ *135 Broadway, Brooklyn* ☎ *718/486–7372* ⊕ *www. wahcenter.net* ⊴ *$7 suggested donation* ⊘ *Closed Mon.–Thurs.* Ⓜ *J, M, Z to Marcy Ave.*

Williamsburg Bridge
The distinctive and quite beautiful steel bridge that links Williamsburg to Manhattan's Lower East Side was the world's longest suspension bridge when it was completed in 1903. More than 200,000 people cross it every day by car, train, bike, and on foot. A small plaza at

the corner of Bedford Avenue and Broadway, on the Brooklyn side, provides a great vantage point from which to admire the bridge. ⊠ *Pedestrian entrance at Bedford Ave. and S. 6th St., Brooklyn* ⊕ *www. nyc.gov/html/dot/html/infrastructure/ williamsburg-bridge.shtml* Ⓜ *J, M, Z to Marcy Ave.*

Shopping

Bird. Branch location at 203 Grand St. *See Chapter 13, Carroll Gardens, for full listing.*

GGrippo art+design
Argentinean GGrippo moved to Williamsburg 20 years ago and set up this very design-conscious shop focused on sustainable goods. At his studio in the back, he sews upcycled cashmere, creating beautiful patchwork sweaters, dresses, and coats. The shop is a sight in itself—the main floor has a balcony looking down on the showroom and workshop. Rotating installations might take the form of colorful flowers made of recycled bottles. It's closed Monday and Tuesday. ⊠ *174 Grand St., Brooklyn* ⊕ *www.ggripposhop. bigcartel.com* Ⓜ *L to Bedford Ave.; J, M, Z to Marcy Ave.*

Jane Motorcycles
Taking the boutique–coffee shop combo to the next level, Jane Motorcycles sells—you guessed it—motorcycles and coffee. Owners Adam and Alex wanted to open a place where anyone could stop by to admire the bikes (which they work on at nearby garages) without feeling pressured to buy. Bikers shop for helmets, apparel, and accessories, while the café set sips Parlor coffee (roasted in Brooklyn), munches on baked goods, and accesses the free Wi-Fi. ⊠ *396 Wythe Ave., Brooklyn* ☎ *347/884–9075* ⊕ *www.janemotorcycles.com* Ⓜ *J, M, Z to Marcy Ave.*

Coffee and Quick Bites

Abracadabra
$ | Café. This Turkish-owned bakery is a cozy stop for a quick breakfast, lunch, or afternoon snack. Grab a table in front of the street art–style mural and settle in with sandwiches and wraps, or vegan and gluten-free pastries like the coffee cake (served with berries in summer, pumpkin in fall). **Known for:** bakery with vegan and gluten-free options; street art mural; small but cozy space. *Average main: $6* ⊠ *347 Bedford Ave., Brooklyn* ☎ *347/884–9157* ⊕ *www. abracadabrabk.com* ⊟ *No credit cards* Ⓜ *J, M, Z to Marcy Ave.*

▲ Devoción
$ | Café. At this coffee shop with roots in Bogotá, the beauty of the space is matched by the quality of the coffee, which comes exclusively from small farms in Colombia. Fresh beans are brought directly to Brooklyn, where they're roasted on-site within a few days of arrival. **Known for:** third-wave Colombian coffee; bright, welcoming space; living plant wall. *Average main: $7* ⊠ *69 Grand St., Brooklyn* ☎ *718/285–6180* ⊕ *www.devocion.com* Ⓜ *L to Bedford Ave.*

Oneg Heimishe Bakery

$ | **Bakery.** Deep in the Hasidic section of South Williamsburg, with nary a fashionista in sight, this bakery produces superlative chocolate babka. The anachronistic storefronts around here haven't been recreated to look "old timey," they simply haven't been updated in decades, and Oneg is no exception. **Known for:** chocolate desserts; friendly service. *Average main: $8* ⊠ *188 Lee Ave., at Rutledge St., Brooklyn* ☎ *718/797-0971* ⊘ *Closed Sat.* ⊟ *No credit cards* Ⓜ *G to Flushing Ave.; J, M to Hewes St.*

🍴 Dining

★ Aska

$$$$ | **Scandinavian.** An unassuming door on a quiet street near the Williamsburg Bridge serves as the gateway to a two-Michelin-starred restaurant serving transportive Scandinavian cuisine in a restored 1860s warehouse. Swedish chef Fredrik Berselius uses local ingredients to create inspired tasting menus (there is no à la carte option) that would feel at home in Copenhagen. **Known for:** modern Scandinavian cuisine; acclaimed chef; sublime (and pricey) tasting menu. *Average main: $175* ⊠ *47 S. 5th St., Brooklyn* ☎ *929/337-6792* ⊕ *askanyc.com* ⊘ *Closed Sun. and Mon.* Ⓜ *J, M, Z to Marcy Ave.*

★ Aurora

$$ | **Italian.** Handmade pastas, exceptional antipasti, and wonderful brunch have earned homey Aurora a loyal following. Most ingredients are locally sourced, though the mozzarella and burrata hail from Italy. **Known for:** rustic space with an enclosed garden; authentic Italian food; superlative brunch. *Average main: $22* ⊠ *70 Grand St., Brooklyn* ☎ *718/388-5100* ⊕ *www.aurorabk. com* Ⓜ *L to Bedford Ave.*

Barano

$$ | **Italian.** At this large yet intimate restaurant near the Williamsburg Bridge, chef Albert Di Meglio conjures up specialties from the region around Barano d'Ischia, where his grandmother was born. That means hand-pulled mozzarella, wood-fired pizzas, pastas, and seafood get their due. **Known for:** wood-fired pizzas; intimate atmosphere; talented chef. *Average main: $16* ⊠ *26 Broadway, Brooklyn* ☎ *347/987-4500* ⊕ *www.baranobk. com* ⊘ *No lunch Mon.–Sat.* Ⓜ *J, M, Z to Marcy Ave.*

★ Diner

$$ | **American.** The word "diner" might evoke a greasy spoon, but this trendsetting restaurant under the Williamsburg Bridge is nothing of the sort. Andrew Tarlow—the godfather of Brooklyn's farm-to-table culinary renaissance—opened it in 1999 and launched an entire movement. **Known for:** trailblazing restaurateur; farm-to-table fare; intimate space in a vintage dining car. *Average main: $21* ⊠ *85 Broadway, Brooklyn* ☎ *718/486-3077* ⊕ *www.dinernyc.com* Ⓜ *J, M, Z to Marcy Ave.*

Le Barricou

$$ | French. The team behind nearby Maison Premiere operates this Parisian-style brasserie serving escargots, coq au vin, and other French bistro classics. Diners sit at rustic wooden tables, and the walls are collaged with vintage French newspapers. **Known for:** French bistro classics; popular brunch spot; old-world atmosphere. *Average main: $18* ✉ 533 Grand St., Brooklyn ☎ 718/782-7372 ⊕ www.lebarricouny.com Ⓜ *L to Lorimer St.; G to Metropolitan Ave.*

Loosie Rouge

$$ | Southern. Hip locals and French expats flock to this all-day and all-night trifecta composed of Loosie Rouge (the über-cool bar with cocktails on tap), Loosie's Kitchen (the restaurant with white-washed brick walls and Eames chairs), and Loosie's Café (the bright, airy daytime café with iced matcha and a greenhouse feel). You can't go wrong at any time of day, but the place really comes alive after 6 pm, when the bar fills up and hungry hipsters tuck into fried chicken and New Orleans–inspired Cajun fries and nutella beignets. **Known for:** superhip bar scene; New Orleans–inspired food and drinks; great design. *Average main: $20* ✉ 91 S. 6th St., Brooklyn ☎ 718/384-2904 ⊕ www.loosierouge.com Ⓜ *J, M, Z to Marcy Ave.*

★ Marlow & Sons

$$ | American. With its green-and-white-striped awning, you might easily mistake this buzzy bistro for an old-timey grocery store, but this is a wood-paneled dining room packed nightly with foodies for remarkable locavore cuisine. Part of the Andrew Tarlow empire, Marlow & Sons serves food that sounds simple until you take that first bite. **Known for:** pioneering restaurateur; inspired locavore fare; vintage grocery store–inspired design. *Average main: $23* ✉ 81 Broadway, Brooklyn ☎ 718/384-1441 ⊕ www.marlowandsons.com Ⓜ *J, M, Z to Marcy Ave.*

★ Meadowsweet

$$$ | Modern American. Amid Williamsburg's culinary landscape of casual, comfort food–centric bistros with rock-and-roll sound tracks, this Michelin-starred restaurant and bar feels thoroughly grown-up. Chef-owner Polo Dobkins serves New American cuisine in an airy space with blond-wood accents. **Known for:** sophisticated design; Michelin-starred New American cuisine; excellent tasting menu. *Average main: $28* ✉ 149 Broadway, Brooklyn ☎ 718/384-0673 ⊕ www.meadowsweetnyc.com ☾ *Closed Tues. No lunch Mon. and Wed.* Ⓜ *J, M, Z to Marcy Ave.*

★ Peter Luger Steak House

$$$$ | Steakhouse. Steak lovers come to Peter Luger for the exquisite dry-aged meat and the casual atmosphere. You can order individual steaks, but the porterhouse is highly recommended and served only for two, three, or four people. **Known for:** excellent steak; historic Brooklyn ambience; no credit cards.

Average main: $50 ✉ *178 Broadway, Brooklyn* ☎ *718/387-7400* ⊕ *www. peterluger.com* 🚫 *No credit cards* Ⓜ *J, M, Z to Marcy Ave.*

Pies 'N' Thighs

$$ | Southern. Opened by three Diner alums, this little restaurant takes its moniker seriously, serving famously delicious fried chicken and pies made with organic and local ingredients. Perched on chairs from an elementary school, diners enjoy Southern-style meals that come with a protein (catfish and pulled pork for those who don't want chicken) and two sides (grits, mac 'n' cheese, and biscuits are favorites). **Known for:** fried chicken and pies; fun, casual vibe; good value. *Average main: $15* ✉ *166 S. 4th St., Brooklyn* ☎ *347/529-6090* ⊕ *www.piesnthighs.com* Ⓜ *J, M, Z to Marcy Ave.*

Rabbithole

$$ | American. A wooden sign with an illustrated carrot marks the entrance to a charming bistro that serves up well-executed standards from hanger steak to pan-seared salmon to house-made gnocchi and taglietelle. Inside, exposed brick, old wood flooring, and time-worn antiques make for an endearingly low-key atmosphere in the main dining space. **Known for:** urban-rustic atmosphere; unfussy food; charming garden. *Average main: $17* ✉ *352 Bedford Ave., Brooklyn* ☎ *718/782-0910* ⊕ *www.rabbithole-restaurant.com* Ⓜ *J, M, Z to Marcy Ave.; L to Bedford Ave.*

Rye

$$ | American. An atmospheric hideaway on a little-trod block, Rye serves French bistro classics and creative American fare. Dark wood, leather cushions, a mosaic-tile floor, and a century-old oak bar hark back to the days of speakeasies and illicit booze. **Known for:** Prohibition-era vibe; American comfort food; great cocktails. *Average main: $20* ✉ *247 S. 1st St., Brooklyn* ☎ *718/218-8047* ⊕ *www.ryerestaurant.com* ⊗ *No lunch weekdays* Ⓜ *L to Bedford Ave.; G to Metropolitan Ave.; J, M, Z to Marcy Ave.*

Shalom Japan

$$ | Japanese Fusion. Williamsburg's melting-pot aspirations past and present express themselves with intelligence and flair at this Japanese-Jewish fusion restaurant. Chefs Sawako Okochi and Aaron Israel, veterans of top New York City restaurants, wanted to explore their respective roots, and in merging these two cuisines, they advanced something unique, as shown in a menu of shared plates including sake kasu challah, traditional Jewish bread infused with sake lees and served with raisin butter; matzo-ball ramen with foie gras dumplings; and the popular lox bowl, a sort of deconstructed salmon avocado roll. **Known for:** Jewish-Japanese fusion cuisine; talented chefs; casual vibe. *Average main: $23* ✉ *310 S. 4th St., Brooklyn* ☎ *718/388-4012* ⊕ *www. shalomjapannyc.com* ⊗ *Closed Mon. No lunch weekdays* Ⓜ *J, M, Z to Marcy Ave.*

Zizi Limona

$$ | Middle Eastern. This casual neighborhood bistro serves mouth-wateringly good Middle Eastern and Mediterranean dishes, drawing inspiration from the cuisines of Israel, Morocco, Greece, Turkey, and Southern Italy. You could easily make a meal of the tapas-style "Small Zi's," like the baba ghanoush with basil and feta, the silky hummus, and falafel with tomato salsa and yogurt sauce—but then you'd miss out on the delicious *tagines* (stews) and kebabs. **Known for:** Mediterranean mezze; cozy atmosphere; local favorite. *Average main: $16* ✉ *129 Havemeyer St., Brooklyn* ☎ *347/763-1463* ⊕ *www.zizilimona.com* ☽ *No lunch Mon.–Thurs.* Ⓜ *J, M, Z to Marcy Ave., L to Lorimer St.; G to Metropolitan Ave.*

 Bars and Nightlife

Baby's All Right

You'd be hard-pressed to categorize this eclectic place. With a diner up front, a '70s German disco–inspired music venue in the back, and a full bar in between, Baby's All Right is an amalgam of cool and a magnet for creative types. There's live music most nights, a DJ until 4 am, and "bottomless brunch" on the weekends. ✉ *146 Broadway, Brooklyn* ☎ *718/599-5800* ⊕ *www.babysallright.com* Ⓜ *J, M, Z to Marcy Ave.*

Bembe

This steamy, bi-level lounge is Williamsburg's answer to Miami clubbing, though decorated with salvaged items including an old redwood front door from a New York State winery. The crowd is as eclectic as the DJ-spun beats that range from reggae to Brazilian—often accompanied by live drumming. The tropical bar menu adds to the place's Latin cred. ✉ *81 S. 6th St., Brooklyn* ☎ *718/387-5389* ⊕ *www.bembe.us* Ⓜ *J, M, Z to Marcy Ave.*

★ Donna

This cocktail bar bills itself as "an elegant space for dirty kids"—that is, just because you like nice things doesn't necessarily mean you want to dress fancy. And Donna certainly is elegant, with a white vaulted ceiling, a long curved bar, reclaimed-wood benches and tables, and beautiful people drinking fabulous cocktails like the signature frozen Brancolada (a piña colada riff with Branca Menta). Tacos and other Latin fare provide the terrific, appropriately downscale nibbles. DJs spin most weekend nights. ✉ *27 Broadway, Brooklyn* ☎ *646/568-6622* ⊕ *www.donnabklyn.com* Ⓜ *J, M, Z to Marcy Ave.*

Larry Lawrence

It might be hard to find this hidden bar, but traverse the long, bare hallway and you're in for a treat. The high-ceiling space is generally filled with cool locals drinking beers on the chunky wooden furniture, the voice of Johnny Cash on the sound system, and chill vibes all around. Check out the custom-built roof terrace; it has a window that allows you to peer down into the bar below. ✉ *295 Grand St., Brooklyn* ☎ *718/218-7866* ⊕ *www.larrylawrencebar.com* Ⓜ *L to Lorimer St.; G to Metropolitan Ave.*

Lucky Dog

The moniker fits this laid-back, canine-friendly dive bar. With a jukebox, shuffleboard, and a large selection of craft beers (and pitchers) available, it's a great spot for day drinking, happy hour, or pretty much any hour. It's small and narrow inside, but there's a great back patio. ⊠ *303 Bedford Ave., Brooklyn* Ⓜ *L to Bedford Ave.; J, M, Z to Marcy Ave.*

★ Maison Premiere

Step inside this buzzy bar and restaurant, marked only by a small "Bar, Oysters" sign, and you'll instantly feel whisked away to New Orleans. Sip expertly made cocktails at the horseshoe-shape bar, or dine on platters of oysters at one of the café tables (there are full dinner and brunch menus as well). In spring and summer, the back garden is a lush oasis with cast-iron tables amid wisteria and palms. ⊠ *298 Bedford Ave., Brooklyn* ☎ *347/335–0446* ⊕ *www.maisonpremiere.com* Ⓜ *L to Bedford Ave.*

Miss Favela Brazilian Botequim

The flag outside announces Miss Favela's allegiance to Brazil—a favela is a Brazilian slum—and the theme continues inside, where the brick walls are painted green and yellow, and rickety metal tables are covered in brightly colored oilcloth. There are Brazilian specialties for lunch and dinner, but after 10 pm the tables are cleared and the place becomes an all-out dance party, fueled by pitchers of caipirinhas, Brazil's cachaça-laced favorite drink. On Saturday, people dance samba to a live band until the DJ takes over and the vibe becomes more clubby. ⊠ *57 S. 5th St., Brooklyn* ☎ *718/230–4040* ⊕ *www.missfavela.com* Ⓜ *J, M, Z to Marcy Ave.*

★ St. Mazie Bar & Supper Club

On Grand Street nearly abutting the highway is the 1920s-style St. Mazie, which presents excellent gypsy jazz and flamenco music to a crowd that favors listening over dancing. The cocktails are simple but done right. The intimate cellar, a speak-easy during Prohibition, serves European-inspired cuisine for dinner and weekend brunch. ⊠ *345 Grand St., Brooklyn* ☎ *718/384–4807* ⊕ *www.stmazie.com* Ⓜ *L to Lorimer St.; G to Metropolitan Ave.*

Videology

Depending on whom you ask, Videology is a bar with a screening room or a screening room with a bar. The laid-back space is divided in two: locals drink craft beer and cocktails—like the Don Draper (a twist on the old-fashioned)—up front, and film screenings, trivia contests, and comedy events unfold in back. The place started as a video rental store and still loans out DVDs, including out-of-print films and new releases. ⊠ *308 Bedford Ave., Brooklyn* ☎ *718/782–3468* ⊕ *www.videologybarandcinema.com* Ⓜ *J, M, Z to Marcy Ave.; L to Bedford Ave.*

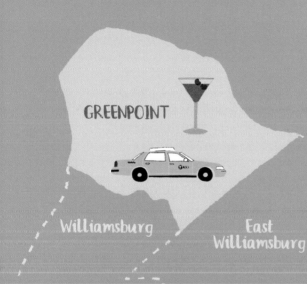

GREENPOINT

Williamsburg

East
Williamsburg

tseeing ★☆☆☆☆ | Shopping ★★★☆☆ | Dining ★★★★☆ | Nightlife ★★★★☆

Greenpoint, Brooklyn's northernmost neighborhood, above Williamsburg and below Queens, is often described as "up and coming," but Greenpointers know it's already arrived—again. A major 19th-century hub, first for shipbuilding and later for glassmaking, printing, and other manufacturing pursuits, Greenpoint prospered by welcoming successive waves of German, Irish, Italian, and Polish immigrants. Still predominantly Polish today, the area retains a village feel even as upscale businesses open and new residents move in. It has evolved more slowly than nearby Williamsburg, in part because the subway line that services Greenpoint is the borough's only one that doesn't travel to Manhattan. With more than 7,500 new housing units planned by around 2025—some in repurposed factories, others, among them the waterfront Greenpoint Landing development, new construction—the mood could shift. For now, though, Greenpoint plays amiable host to outstanding restaurants, creative bakeries, independent boutiques, and cozy bars. All of these, along with the now-ended HBO hit *Girls*, whose main character, Hannah, lived here, have raised Greenpoint's contemporary profile, but it's still easy to get a sense of the area's layered history. Town houses from the 1800s add architectural gravitas to the side streets off Manhattan Avenue, the neighborhood's main artery, and a half mile west, the waterfront is a striking juxtaposition of spruced-up parks and the remnants of the area's industrial past.—*Updated by Laura Itzkowitz*

Sights

Greenpoint Historic District

Landmarked in 1982, this historic district is lined with beautiful town houses. The area extends roughly from Calyer Street north to Kent Street, between Manhattan Avenue and Franklin Street. The brick homes date to the 1850s, when Greenpoint was a major hub for shipbuilding and the manufacturing.

Walking along Franklin Street, north of Greenpoint Avenue, it's easy to feel like you've stepped into an Edward Hopper painting. ✉ *Calyer St. to Kent St., Greenpoint* Ⓜ *G to Greenpoint Ave.*

India Street Pier

This spruced-up, modern pier serves the NYC Ferry's East River route. Take in the stunning views of Midtown while you wait for

the ferry to arrive. ⊠ *India St.,
Greenpoint* ⊕ *www.ferry.nyc* Ⓜ *G to
Greenpoint Ave.*

Monsignor McGolrick Park

The tree-lined allées and historic
colonnaded pavilion (1910) of this
park in southeastern Greenpoint
evoke 18th-century France.
Neighborhood kids skateboard and
play on the paths after school and
on weekends. On Sunday between
10 and 4, local purveyors like
Brooklyn Grange (rooftop farmers)
and Ovenly (bakers) sell their wares
at the farmers' market. ⊠ *Russell
to Monitor St., Greenpoint* ⊕ *www.
nycgovparks.org/parks/msgr-mcgol-
rick-park* Ⓜ *G to Nassau Ave.*

★ WNYC Transmitter Park

Greenpoint residents of all ages
head to this waterfront park to
soak up the sun and stunning views
of the Midtown skyline. From the
manicured lawn and the benches on
the esplanade, the Chrysler Building
and the Empire State Building seem
just a stone's throw away. Formerly
the site of WNYC radio's transmis-
sion towers, this pristine public
space opened in 2012, part of the
city's ongoing project to redevelop
waterfront property throughout the
five boroughs. ⊠ *West St., Greenpoint
* ⊕ *www.nycgovparks.org/parks/trans-
mitter-park* Ⓜ *G to Greenpoint Ave.*

🛍 Shopping

Adaptations

This pint-size shop is a treasure
trove of vintage home decor. The
pieces tend to have a feminine
appeal, with items like vintage
champagne coupes, Millennial pink
sofas, Lucite desks, and chrome-
and-glass end tables. Owner Kyla
Burney is constantly on the hunt
for cool new finds, so the inventory
changes frequently. ⊠ *109 Franklin
St., Greenpoint* ☏ *347/529–5889*
⊕ *www.adaptationsny.com* Ⓜ *G to
Greenpoint Ave.*

★ Alter

Sartorialists come to this fashionable boutique to snag unique ward-
robe pieces like drapey sweaters,
Cheap Monday jeans, and minimalist
jewelry, as well as retro-inspired
sunglasses, canvas bags, and shoes
for men and women. Area designers
are well represented. ⊠ *140 Franklin
St., Greenpoint* ☏ *718/349–0203*
⊕ *www.alterbrooklyn.com* Ⓜ *G to
Greenpoint Ave.*

Archestratus

This bookstore specializes in
cookbooks and other food-centric
volumes that showcase recipes,
art, and theory, and hosts readings, classes, tastings, and other
events. Once stoked by the books,
let your appetite lead you to the
café area that serves Sicilian baked
goods, tea, coffee, and other café
treats. ⊠ *160 Huron St., Greenpoint*
☏ *718/349–7711* ⊕ *www.archestrat.us*
Ⓜ *G to Greenpoint Ave.*

★ Beacon's Closet

The racks are organized by category
and color at this trove of secondhand and vintage clothes, so you
can find an entire section of black
dresses and another just for jeans.
Be patient sorting through the huge

selection—you might find gems like a vintage Yves Saint Laurent jacket or purple-sequined, peep-toe heels by Marc Jacobs. There are enough brocade gowns and fur (real and fake) to outfit the entire cast of a 1960s period drama. ✉ *74 Guernsey St., Greenpoint* ☎ *718/486–0816* ⊕ *www.beaconscloset.com* Ⓜ *G to Nassau Ave.*

★ Bellocq Tea Atelier

This jewel box of a tea shop is a bit out of the way, but it's a must for tea aficionados. Bellocq sources organic and exotic teas from China, India, and Japan, and sells them as single-origin varieties or custom blends. Though the shop isn't a full-service tea salon, you can always find a pot or two brewed for tasting. With their elegant yellow canisters, Bellocq teas make great gifts. ✉ *104 West St., Greenpoint* ☎ *347/463–9231* ⊕ *www.bellocq.com* Ⓜ *G to Greenpoint Ave.*

Homecoming

There aren't many places where you can purchase handcrafted floral arrangements and home decor accents alongside coffee and pastries; Homecoming does both with panache. The airy, white-painted boutique sells one-of-a-kind ceramics and potted plants, art prints, notebooks, and flowers by the stem, as well as Verve coffee and artisanal doughnuts by Dough. ✉ *107 Franklin St., Greenpoint* ☎ *347/457–5385* ⊕ *www.home-coming.com* Ⓜ *G to Greenpoint Ave.*

GETTING HERE

NYC Ferry's East River route is the most scenic way to travel to Greenpoint. Alternatively, take the subway to either Greenpoint Avenue or Nassau Avenue station.

★ In God We Trust

Stylish shoppers love this boutique for the homespun clothes and cheeky accessories, like gold penne pasta on a delicate chain or business-card cases emblazoned "Talented Mother Fucker." Of the two Brooklyn locations, the Bedford Avenue shop in Williamsburg gets the most foot traffic, but the clothes and jewelry are made in the studio behind this Greenpoint Avenue outpost. ✉ *70 Greenpoint Ave., Greenpoint* ☎ *718/389–3545* ⊕ *www.ingodwetrustnyc.com* Ⓜ *G to Greenpoint Ave.*

★ Porter James

Mid-century design fans should make a beeline to this store, which sells a curated selection of vintage home furnishings and decor. You might find a set of 1950s Bertoia chairs, a Hans Wegner headboard from the '60s, or a Herman Miller sofa. Owner Kyla Burney (who also runs Adaptations up the street) takes orders for custom velvet upholstering in a range of colors. ✉ *116 Franklin St., Greenpoint* ☎ *929/337–9387* ⊕ *porterjamesny. com* Ⓜ *G to Greenpoint Ave.*

WORD

What this pint-size bookshop lacks in space, it more than makes up for in community spirit and book enthusiasm. It's known for popular readings, meet-the-author events, and book-club discussions. The stock focuses on classic paperback fiction and cookbooks, as well as greeting cards and gift items, including Brooklyn-centric souvenirs. ✉ 126 Franklin St., Greenpoint ☎ 718/383–0096 ⊕ www.wordbookstores.com Ⓜ G to Greenpoint Ave.

☕ Coffee and Quick Bites

★ Bakeri

$ | Bakery. When Williamsburg's best European-style bakery wanted more space, it opened a Greenpoint outpost and included a rustic communal table, antique finishes, and hand-painted wallpaper. From house-made focaccia to financiers, there are plenty of mouthwatering choices (including vegan and gluten-free options) for breakfast and lunch. At breakfast you can watch the bakers in the open kitchen as you sip your morning coffee and snack on a raspberry pistachio muffin or Norwegian kolebrød. Soups and sandwiches on freshly baked bread are served at lunch. **Known for:** croissants and other European pastries; rustic chic vibe; vegan and gluten-free options. *Average main: $6* ✉ *105 Freeman St., Greenpoint* ☎ *718/349–1542* ⊕ *www.bakeribrooklyn.com* Ⓜ *G to Greenpoint Ave.*

> **SMOKED SNACKS**
>
> Heads up to smoked-fish lovers: the Acme Smoked Fish Corporation opens its factory at 30 Gem Street every Friday morning from 8 to 1 and sells its goods to the public at wholesale prices (⊕ www.acmesmokedfish.com).

★ Búdin

$ | Café. Coffee aficionados head to Greenpoint for Búdin's $10 latte—it's pricey because it's made with Danish licorice syrup, topped with licorice powder, and served on a silver tray. Come during the day for coffee by the Oslo-based roaster Tim Wendelboe, whose beans are favored by top European chefs, or after hours for wine and Nordic craft beer. The back of the shop is stocked with a rotating selection of Scandinavian-design goods. **Known for:** a $10 licorice-inflected latte; Scandinavian design; Nordic craft beer. *Average main: $8* ✉ *114B Greenpoint Ave., Greenpoint* ☎ *347/844–9639* ⊕ *www.budin-nyc. com* Ⓜ *G to Greenpoint Ave.*

Café Grumpy

$ | Café. Made famous by the HBO television show *Girls*—the character Ray works here—this indie coffee shop roasts its beans in the roastery next door and sends them to its other cafés around the city. Café Grumpy serves all the usual drip coffee and espresso drinks plus pastries, with gluten-free options. This location, opened in 2005, was the first. **Known for:** artisanal coffee; appearing on HBO's *Girls*;

freelancer-friendly. *Average main: $10* ✉ *193 Meserole Ave., Greenpoint* ☎ *718/349-7623* ⊕ *www.cafegrumpy. com* Ⓜ *G to Greenpoint Ave. or Nassau Ave.*

★ Frankel's Delicatessen & Appetizing

$$ | **Deli.** Inspired by old-school Jewish delis like Russ & Daughters, this family-run corner café serves the neighborhood's best bagels, plus pastrami, corned beef, and other deli classics. Order at the counter and eat at one of the few tables in the bright, white-tiled space, or take your bagel to go and picnic in McCarren Park, just a block away. **Known for:** Greenpoint's best bagels; Jewish deli specialties; welcoming, nostalgic shop. *Average main: $13* ✉ *631 Manhattan Ave., Greenpoint* ☎ *718/389-2302* ⊕ *frankelsdelicatessen.com* Ⓜ *G to Nassau Ave.*

★ Ovenly

$ | **Bakery.** This tiny bakery has made a name for itself with standouts like vegan salted chocolate-chip cookies, pistachio agave cookies, and currant-rosemary scones. The seasonal specials are equally mouthwatering—just try to resist the bourbon-maple-pecan pie made for Thanksgiving. In warm weather, take your goodies up the block to WNYC Transmitter Park for a picnic that will make everyone jealous. **Known for:** mouthwatering cookies and cakes; homegrown ethos; vegan options. *Average main: $6* ✉ *31 Greenpoint Ave., Greenpoint* ☎ *347/689-3608* ⊕ *www.oven.ly* Ⓜ *G to Greenpoint Ave.*

Peter Pan Donut & Pastry Shop

$ | **Café.** This doughnut shop looks like a 1950s lunch counter because it was one, and the current owners preserved the original decor—the servers even wear 1950s-style uniforms. Old-fashioned doughnuts, bagels, and egg sandwiches are made fresh daily. You'll find all the classics, from glazed and cake doughnuts to coconut cream and red velvet. You can order your doughnuts to go, or grab a seat for counter service. Everything is inexpensive and delicious. **Known for:** doughnuts; breakfast sandwiches; 1950s style. *Average main: $6* ✉ *727 Manhattan Ave., Greenpoint* ☎ *718/389-3676* ⊕ *www.peterpandonuts.com* ⊟ *No credit cards* Ⓜ *G to Nassau Ave.*

★ Van Leeuwen Artisan Ice Cream

$ | **Café.** Renowned for all-natural ice cream and exotic flavors like sorrel blackberry crumble and matcha green tea, Van Leeuwen has established a small ice-cream empire in New York City. Everything is made in-house from the highest-quality ingredients: special flavors like pumpkin are available seasonally, and vegan ice cream is especially popular. Greenpoint was the first brick-and-mortar shop, although its current location is down the street from the pint-size original. In warm weather, get a cone to go and stroll through nearby McCarren Park. **Known for:** all-natural ice cream; vegan and gluten-free options; cute shop. *Average main: $6 ⊠ 620 Manhattan Ave., Greenpoint ☎ 347/987-4774 ⊕ www.vanleeuwenicecream.com Ⓜ G to Nassau Ave.*

⍢ Dining

Adelina's Fraschetta Romana

$$ | **Italian.** Neapolitan-style fried pizza—made with imported Italian flour, San Marzano tomato sauce, house-made mozzarella, and various toppings—is the highlight of the menu at this rustic Italian trattoria. Charmingly mismatched furniture conveys a low-key vibe. Start with the *arancini* (Sicilian rice balls stuffed with pesto, mushrooms, or sausage and fried) or an antipasto plate. Bonus: Oak barrels behind the bar hold "natural wines," made from sustainably grown organic grapes, on tap. **Known for:** fried pizza; natural wines on tap; rustic vibe. *Average main: $15 ⊠ 159 Greenpoint Ave., Greenpoint ☎ 347/763-0152 ⊕ www.adelinasbk.com ⊙ No lunch Ⓜ G to Greenpoint Ave.*

Cherry Point

$ | **American.** Opened by an alum of April Bloomfield's restaurants, this cozy gastropub with a rustic-chic vibe (think wood paneling, tile floors, marble tables) does comfort food right, from the house-made charcuterie program to the constantly rotating seasonal specials. Don't skip the cheese and charcuterie board, which comes with insanely addictive saltines when you order the smoked whitefish or beet-cured arctic char. The team put the utmost care into every detail, from the intriguing wine list to the cheese on the grass-fed beef burger. **Known for:** house-made charcuterie; talented chef; cozy gastropub. *Average main: $24 ⊠ 664 Manhattan Ave., Greenpoint ☎ 718/389-3828 ⊕ www.cherry-pointnyc.com ⊙ Closed Mon. Ⓜ G to Nassau Ave.*

Five Leaves

$$ | **Bistro.** Tattooed servers wait tables at this prime spot on the corner opposite McCarren Park where chefs take fanciful (and successful) liberties with traditional bistro fare. Popular dishes include the Five Leaves burger with pickled beets and harissa mayo, truffle fries, and ricotta pancakes served at weekend brunch, which can be a mob scene but worth braving if you can't get here early. The stylish place was inspired by actor Heath Ledger, a Greenpoint fixture who had plans to start a restaurant with the owners before his untimely death; funding from his estate went toward opening it. The sidewalk tables are excellent for people-watching. **Known for:** hipster hot spot; truffle fries; long wait times. *Average main: $20 ⊠ 18 Bedford Ave., Greenpoint ☎ 718/383-5345 ⊕ www.fiveleavesny.com Ⓜ G to Nassau Ave.*

★ Glasserie

$$ | Middle Eastern. Its past as a glass factory inspired Glasserie's warm, romantic atmosphere, and details like rare light fixtures and prints of original electric bulbs abound. Owner Sara Conklin spent her childhood in the Middle East, and her experiences there influence the farm-to-table cuisine. Pair the Persian Gold cocktail (a gin and tonic with saffron) with the phyllo pastries, then order a few more small plates to share. **Known for:** warm, intimate atmosphere; Middle Eastern small plates; great cocktails and wine list. *Average main: $20 ⊠ 95 Commercial St., Greenpoint ☎ 718/389-0640 ⊕ www.glasserienyc. com Ⓜ G to Greenpoint Ave.*

★ Karczma

$$ | Polish. Of all the Polish restaurants in this Polish neighborhood, family-run Karczma is the best, so dig in and order the pierogis—fried, not boiled—and one of the Polish, Czech, or German beers served in giant glasses. The farmhouse-style tavern is easygoing and fun, with oversized picnic tables, camping lanterns hanging from the ceiling, and waitresses wearing traditional folk dresses from the mountain region in southern Poland. This restaurant is a great value for the price, so come hungry and prepare to feast. **Known for:** Polish cuisine; fun atmosphere; great value. *Average main: $13 ⊠ 136 Greenpoint Ave., Greenpoint ☎ 718/349-1744 ⊕ www.karczmabrooklyn.com Ⓜ G to Greenpoint Ave.*

Milk & Roses

$$ | Italian. With hundreds of books lining the built-in wood shelves, candlelit marble tables, red leather booths, and a piano, it doesn't get much cozier than this. The Italian food is good, but the relaxed atmosphere and old-world ambience make this a true haven. The back garden is magical in spring and summer. **Known for:** cozy, weathered atmosphere; secret garden; dependable Italian food. *Average main: $24 ⊠ 1110 Manhattan Ave., Greenpoint ☎ 718/389-0160 ⊕ www. milkandrosesbk.com ▭ No credit cards Ⓜ G to Greenpoint Ave.*

★ Paulie Gee's

$$ | Pizza. When it comes to pizza there's stiff competition, but Paulie Gee's serves outstanding gourmet pies with all kinds of creative toppings—the idea to put Mike's Hot Honey on pizza is just one of many strokes of genius. The extensive list of offerings includes the "Anise and Anephew" (Paulie Gee's personal favorite) made with braised fennel, Berkshire guanciale, and fresh mozzarella, plus a full page of vegan pies. The handmade wood-fired oven is from Naples's famed ovenmaker Stefano Ferrara. The average wait time for a table on Friday or Saturday night is an hour. **Known for:** wood-fired pizza; ample vegan options; cozy farmhouse design. *Average main: $16 ⊠ 60 Greenpoint Ave., Greenpoint ☎ 347/987-3747 ⊕ www.pauliegee.com ◷ No lunch Ⓜ G to Greenpoint Ave.*

Sauvage

$$$ | Bistro. Run by the team behind Williamsburg's award-winning cocktail bar Maison Premiere, this European-style bistro occupies a prime location overlooking McCarren Park. As you'd expect, they make a killer martini, which pairs well with updated bistro classics like oysters and a burger with smoked cheddar and Dijon mustard. An art nouveau–inflected design sets the tone for a romantic date or a fun evening with friends. **Known for:** cocktails from team behind Maison Premiere; art nouveau design; updated bistro classics. *Average main: $25 ⊠ 905 Lorimer St., Greenpoint ☎ 718/486–6816 ⊕ sauvageny.com Ⓜ G to Nassau Ave.*

★ Selamat Pagi

$$ | Indonesian. Warm and intimate Selamat Pagi brings a little Bali to Brooklyn. The exotic flavors of Kaffir lime leaf, coconut oil, lemongrass, and chili transform local organic produce and proteins into *nasi goreng* (vegetable fried rice), coconut curry, chili glazed chicken wings, and other palate-tingling delights. Banana-leaf wallpaper and a DIY design set a rough-around-the-edges yet romantic tone that makes this a great casual date spot—as long as the object of your affection likes spicy food. **Known for:** Balinese cuisine; tropical meets Brooklyn DIY design; plenty of vegetarian options. *Average main: $16 ⊠ 152 Driggs Ave., Greenpoint ☎ 718/701–4333 ⊕ www.selamatpagibrooklyn.com ⊗ No lunch weekdays Ⓜ G to Nassau Ave.*

★ 21 Greenpoint

$$$ | American. Co-owned by Homer Murray (actor Bill Murray's son), this restaurant gained notoriety when it relaunched with a legendary event featuring the older Murray tending bar. But it's worth a visit, with or without Bill, for chef Sean Telo's creative menus that aim to make tasty dishes while sourcing sustainably and reducing food waste; from tempura-coated shishito peppers to wood-fired pizzas, it's always fun to see what he'll come up with. The urban-rustic design (white subway tiles, wooden tables, hanging plants) is equally welcoming for weekend brunch or a romantic dinner by candlelight. **Known for:** owned by Bill Murray's son; creative menu; dedication to sustainability. *Average main: $25 ⊠ 21 Greenpoint Ave., Greenpoint ☎ 718/383–8833 ⊕ www.21greenpoint.com ⊗ No lunch weekdays Ⓜ G to Greenpoint Ave.*

⟨Y⟩ Bars and Nightlife

Alameda

Sophisticates perch on stools at the striking U-shaped bar for creative yet approachable cocktails like the Little Red Book, which blends vodka with strawberries, elderflower, chervil, parsley, Benedictine, and lime. Small plates change frequently, but the grass-fed beef cheeseburger is a constant and there's always a seasonal open-face tartine. *⊠ 195 Franklin St., Greenpoint ☎ 347/227–7296 ⊕ www.alamedagreenpoint.com Ⓜ G to Greenpoint Ave.*

Bar Matchless

Friends and strangers belt it out at karaoke; crack up at comedy shows; play pool, foosball, or darts; listen to live music; and dance at this former auto repair shop by the Williamsburg border. It's a high-energy hot spot on the weekends but chill during the week. Savvy *Girls* watchers might recognize this as the spot where Hannah had her 25th birthday party and Marnie dragged her up onstage to sing. ✉ *557 Manhattan Ave., Greenpoint* ☎ *718/383–5333* ⊕ *www.barmatchless.com* Ⓜ *G to Nassau Ave.*

The Brooklyn Barge

This scrappy, seasonal bar on a barge floating in the East River draws crowds from all over New York City for the low-key vibe and unbeatable views of the Manhattan skyline. Bring your friends and order a pitcher of craft beer with a side of nachos to be savored alfresco as the sun sets. It's also a popular spot for day drinking on the weekends. ✉ *3 Milton St., Greenpoint* ☎ *929/377–7212* ⊕ *www.thebrooklynbarge.com* Ⓜ *G to Greenpoint Ave.*

The Diamond

The regulars come to this unpretentious bar for two reasons: beer and shuffleboard. You can order wine if you must, but the well-curated beer list is the real crowd-pleaser. Eight taps feature a rotating selection of craft beers, from the hyperlocal Greenpoint Beer & Ale Company to Belgian De Dolle Brouwers. ✉ *43 Franklin St., Greenpoint* ☎ *718/383–5030* ⊕ *www.thediamondbrooklyn.com* Ⓜ *G to Greenpoint Ave. or Nassau Ave.*

★ Diamond Lil

Locals flock to this low-key neighborhood spot for great cocktails at affordable prices by a bartender who trained in the Milk & Honey school developed by the late, legendary bartender Sasha Petraske (the man responsible for New York's speakeasy craze). The sophisticated art nouveau–inspired design—complete with embossed wallpaper and a beaded lamp—gives the place a warm, Prohibition-era vibe. Settle into one of the forest green booths and sample tipples like the Frozen Painkiller or the Valparaiso Sour (made with pisco, Campari, lemon, and strawberry). ✉ *179 Nassau Ave., Greenpoint* ⊕ *www.diamondlilbar.com* Ⓜ *G to Nassau Ave.*

The Drift

You might be surprised to find this ski-themed bar on a busy thoroughfare beside the Brooklyn-Queens Expressway. But once inside, you'll discover cushy seating and a laid-back scene with affordable drinks, indulgent bar snacks, and a small patio out back. ✉ *579 Meeker Ave., Greenpoint* ☎ *718/504–7776* Ⓜ *G to Nassau Ave.; L to Graham Ave.*

★ Goldie's

Entering this buzzy bar feels a bit like stepping into a 1970s Vegas coke den. There are gold glitter tabletops, red leather booths, portraits of jungle animals and dead celebrities, and a pool table in the back. Contrary to what you might expect, you'll find a great selection of craft beers and cocktails, including a couple of frozen drinks.

Pro tip: Free bowls of Goldfish crackers are available upon request. ✉ *195 Nassau Ave., Greenpoint* ☎ *718/389-2348* Ⓜ *G to Nassau Ave.*

The Good Room

DJs spin tunes while a cool crowd dances under the disco ball at this happening nightclub, which made a cameo on Aziz Ansari's hit Netflix series, *Master of None*. The bar is adjacent to the dance floor, and there's a smaller side room if you want a breather. ✉ *98 Meserole Ave., Greenpoint* ☎ *718/349-2373* ⊕ *www.goodroombk.com* Ⓜ *G to Nassau Ave.*

The Gutter

Dark and spacious, with rock music, pitchers of beer, and happy hour specials, this is the perfect dive bar/bowling alley. You can play pool in the main room or bowl at the eight lanes in the side room ($7 per game or $40–$45 per hour; $3 shoe rental; bowling is cash only). Bowling leagues meet Monday through Thursday, which tend to be quieter than weekends, when bands play live music. ✉ *200 N. 14th St., Greenpoint* ☎ *718/387-3585* ⊕ *www.thegutterbrooklyn.com* Ⓜ *G to Nassau Ave.*

Ramona

This big, polished, inviting cocktail bar is a favorite of Greenpointers seeking inventive craft drinks. Feeling classic? Consider a nice barrel-aged negroni or rye old-fashioned. Prefer daring? Maybe a frozen, salted watermelon rosé or spicy absinthe concoction will suit you. Just don't miss the sweet weekday happy hour deals. ✉ *113 Franklin St., Greenpoint* ☎ *347/227-8164* ⊕ *ramonabarnyc.com* Ⓜ *G to Nassau Ave.*

Saint Vitus

Hidden behind an unmarked black door, this warehouse music venue named for a Black Sabbath song has a Gothic design, with red votive candles that cast a glow over the black walls, massive mahogany bar, and relics from old churches. Bands play heavy metal and rock music most nights. ✉ *1120 Manhattan Ave., Greenpoint* ⊕ *www.saintvitusbar.com* Ⓜ *G to Greenpoint Ave.*

Spritzenhaus 33 Bierhall

There are 25 taps worth of excellent craft and imported beers, as well as wines served by the carafe, at this massive, lively beer hall. Seating is at long communal tables, which encourage mingling, and there are board games and Jenga to play. The garage-style windows are open in summer, in winter, there's a fireplace. ✉ *33 Nassau Ave., Greenpoint* ☎ *347/987-4632* ⊕ *www.spritzenhaus33.com* Ⓜ *G to Nassau Ave.*

Sunshine Laundromat

You don't need to bring your dirty laundry to enjoy this combo laundromat-bar. Just head to the back for quality beer at good prices and, as if brews and washers weren't enough, enjoy one of the borough's best assortments of pinball machines to tickle your inner arcade lover. ✉ *860 Manhattan Ave., Greenpoint* ☎ *718/475-2055* ⊕ *sunshinelaundromat.com* Ⓜ *G to Nassau Ave.*

★ Tørst

Beer aficionados adore Tørst, a craft-beer bar that takes its design cues from Denmark. A marble bar and several hues of wood come together in a way that feels very of-the-moment, and the offerings from 21 taps progress from light to dark. Drafts come in three sizes, so you can get small glasses if you want to taste a few. ⊠ *615 Manhattan Ave., Greenpoint* ☎ *718/389–6034* ⊕ *www. torstnyc.com* Ⓜ *G to Nassau Ave.*

Warsaw

This Polish community center serves as Greenpoint's top concert venue, hosting a wide variety of bands befitting the tagline "where pierogis meet punk." There's a neighborhood bar attached, and the main performance space offers excellent sight lines and acoustics; though it might be the throwback decor that best sets apart this spot from other NYC halls. ⊠ *261 Driggs Ave., Greenpoint* ☎ *718/387–0505* ⊕ *www.warsawconcerts.com* Ⓜ *G to Nassau Ave.*

🛏 Hotels

Box House Hotel

$$ | **Hotel.** Adventurous travelers are drawn to this all-suites hotel, formerly a door factory, in industrial northern Greenpoint, where suites feel like stylish New York City apartments, with kitchens, living rooms, and homey touches like shelves lined with books (some also have terraces). **Pros:** exciting, developing neighborhood; huge suites with kitchens and living rooms; free neighborhood transportation. **Cons:** functional bathrooms not particularly luxurious; no black-out curtains; isolated location in industrial area isn't for everyone. *Rooms from: $349* ⊠ *77 Box St., Greenpoint* ☎ *646/396–0251* ⊕ *www.thebox-househotel.com* ⇆ *56 suites* ⊚ *No meals* Ⓜ *G to Greenpoint Ave.*

4

Bushwick and East Williamsburg

Greenpoint

EAST WILLIAMSBURG

Williamsburg

BUSHWICK

Bedford-Stuyvesant

The sense of change is palpable in the largely industrial areas of Bushwick and East Williamsburg, two diverse neighborhoods south and east of central Williamsburg. Buildings splashed with vibrant street art stand alongside factories that make everything from plastic bags to wontons and tortillas. Roberta's pizzeria was a force of transformation when it opened in 2008, serving top-quality casual food in a space reclaimed from what felt like an industrial wasteland. Now, a remarkably short time later, some of Brooklyn's most exciting restaurants, bars, and cafés draw a varied international clientele. The bustle of creativity in evidence here brings an inevitable tension, but also represents a major resurgence for an area that rose high in the 19th century as a center of glass, chemical, and beer production but then experienced a 20th-century decline with low points that included widespread rioting and looting during New York City's July 1977 blackout. These two diverse neighborhoods are home to many Puerto Ricans, who, drawn by work at Brooklyn Navy Yard, first started arriving in the 1940s. Immigrants from the Dominican Republic and Central America have also settled here in large numbers and maintain a vital presence. Flushing Avenue, which runs roughly east–west, is the dividing line between Bushwick and East Williamsburg. Bushwick Avenue runs north–south through both neighborhoods.—*Updated by Carly Fisher*

◉ Sights

★ The Bushwick Collective

For evidence of art's ability to transform lives, visit this colorful outdoor street-art gallery curated by Joseph Ficalora, a Bushwick native who came of age during the neighborhood's period of decline and channeled his grief over losing both of his parents into a space where street artists create temporary works of art. Pixel Pancho of Turin and Baltimore-based Gaia are among the established artists featured at this urban street-arts destination. ⊠ *Troutman St., Bushwick* ⊕ *thebushwickcollective. com* Ⓜ *L to Jefferson St.*

56 Bogart (The BogArt)

Many young Bushwick galleries showcase edgy and experimental work—visiting this converted warehouse is an easy way to see a lot of art in one shot. The BogArt contains large studios and more than a dozen galleries. Standouts include Robert Henry Contemporary, Theodore:Art, David & Schweitzer Contemporary, and Fuchs Project. ■TIP→ Gallery hours vary, but the best time to visit is on Friday and weekends, when most of them are open. ⊠ *56 Bogart St., Bushwick* ☎ *718/599-0800* ⊕ *www.56bogartstreet.com* Ⓜ *L to Morgan Ave.*

Luhring Augustine
Probably the neighborhood's most established gallery, this annex of the Chelsea original is worth a stop to see whatever show is up and to appreciate the soaring space and its cantilevered ceiling. ⊠ *25 Knickerbocker Ave., Brooklyn* ☎ *718/386-2746* ⊕ *www.luhringaugustine.com* ⊙ *Closed Mon.–Wed. Sept.–June and Sun.–Tues. July and Aug.* Ⓜ *L to Morgan Ave.*

Moore Street area street art
Bushwick and East Williamsburg have become synonymous with street art, and there are some impressive, constantly changing murals over by Roberta's restaurant. Start on White Street, at Seigel Street, then head south on White to Moore Street, east on Moore to Bogart Street, then north on Bogart and east on Grattan Street. ⊠ *Moore St., Brooklyn* Ⓜ *L to Morgan Ave.*

 Shopping

Beacon's Closet. Branch location at 23 Bogart St. *See Chapter 3, Greenpoint, or Chapter 8, Park Slope and Prospect Park, for full listing.*

★ **Better Than Jam**
Stocked with clothes, jewelry, accessories, art, local zines, bath products, and housewares

all handmade in New York's five boroughs, this store, attached to the Shops at the Loom, is the perfect place to find distinctive gifts and souvenirs. The space also doubles as a communal art studio, with workshops, classes, and open hours available to the public. It's closed Tuesday–Thursday. ⊠ *20 Grattan St., Brooklyn* ☎ *929/441-9596* ⊕ *www.betterthanjamnyc.com* Ⓜ *L to Morgan Ave.*

Catland
If you're looking for books about mystical traditions, incense, oils, candles, crystals, tarot cards, or other esoteric tools and talismans, this is the place to go. Even if you don't buy anything, it's definitely worth a look. The large event space is available to rent for rituals, workshops, or other needs. ⊠ *987 Flushing Ave., Bushwick* ☎ *718/418-9393* ⊕ *www.catlandbooks.com* Ⓜ *L to Morgan Ave.*

Chess and the Sphinx
With a canny collection of clothing and accessories from the 1940s through the 1990s and beyond, this shop has quality designer items at very reasonable prices. Browse the racks and you might find vintage

pieces from Azzedine Alaïa, Chanel, Dior, Diane Von Furstenberg, and Yves Saint Laurent amid the lower-profile labels. ✉ *252 Knickerbocker Ave., Bushwick* ☎ *718/366–2195* ⊕ *www.chessandthesphinx.com* Ⓜ *L to Jefferson St.; M to Central Ave.*

Fine & Raw Chocolate

On a mission "to save the world through silliness and chocolate," this company makes its products with organic ingredients and low-heat techniques that help maintain flavors. The chocolate bars, in fun packaging fashioned from recycled, nontoxic materials, make great presents. The loft space has a glass wall, so you can watch chocolate being made. A small café serves hot chocolate that's nicely thick, and, unlike most places, unsweetened. ✉ *288 Seigel St., Brooklyn* ☎ *718/366–3633* ⊕ *www.fineandraw.com* Ⓜ *L to Morgan Ave.*

Friends NYC

Do you dig Bushwick's quirky-artsy vibe and want to dress like a local? Swing by this basement boutique, featuring funky handpicked clothing and accessories from indie designers, stellar vintage finds, and home goods and gifts, along with a few random inflatable flamingos and fidget spinners for good measure. ✉ *56 Bogart St., Brooklyn* ☎ *718/386–6279* ⊕ *www.shopfriend-snyc.com* Ⓜ *L to Morgan Ave.*

Material World Records

Browse metal, techno, indie, rap, and punk recordings, many by locals, at this small shop packed with vinyl, cassettes, CDs, DVDs,

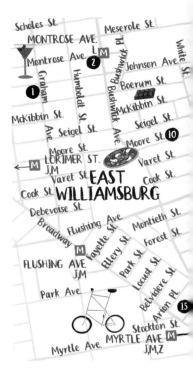

and books. You won't find too many mainstream artists here, but it's the perfect place to acquaint yourself with the booming Bushwick music scene. ✉ *184 Noll St., Bushwick* ☎ *718/381–5703* ⊕ *materialworldre-cords.com* Ⓜ *L to Morgan Ave.*

Shops at the Loom

This renovated textile mill is Bushwick's take on a minimall, with more than 20 businesses including a yoga studio, a bike shop, and a tattoo parlor. You can pick up a coffee at Kave Espresso Bar, take a DIY craft class at Brooklyn Creative Studio, or pick up head-turning

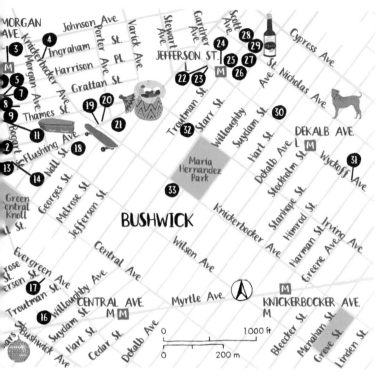

club wear at House of La Rue. If the weather's fine, sip your drink in the urban-landscaped courtyard and access the free Wi-Fi. ✉ *1087 Flushing Ave., Brooklyn* 🕾 *718/417–1616* ⊕ *www.shopsattheloom.com* Ⓜ *L to Morgan Ave.*

☕ Coffee and Quick Bites

AP Café
$ | Café. Conveniently located amid the street-art murals of the Bushwick Collective, this minimalist café has expansive windows perfect for art- and people-watching—though most of the crowd is busy staring at their laptops. Grab expertly pulled coffee on the go or stick around for Instagram-worthy healthy sandwiches, soups, and brunch dishes. **Known for:** healthy food; coworking space; great coffee. *Average main: $8* ✉ *420 Troutman St., Bushwick* 🕾 *347/404–6147* ⊕ *www.apcafenyc.com* Ⓜ *L to Jefferson St.*

★ Dillinger's
$ | Eastern European. The Soviet-era childhoods of its two owners inspired the food and decor of this casual coffeehouse that has impressed the neighborhood with its Russian-inflected lunch and brunch fare. Popular dishes include the buckwheat-and-kale salad and the avocado toast, both topped with a fried egg if desired. **Known for:** Cheburashka sweetened coffee; health-forward brunch dishes with a Russian slant; large back patio. *Average main: $7* ✉ *146 Evergreen Ave., Brooklyn* 🕾 *718/484–3222* ⊘ *No dinner* Ⓜ *J, M, Z to Myrtle Ave.*

> ### ART GALLERIES
>
> More than 50 galleries show art in Bushwick and East Williamsburg. Work tends to be edgy and interesting, though hit or miss. Check out ⊕ *www.bushwickgalleries. com*, ⊕ *www.freewilliamsburg.com*, and ⊕ *www.wagmag.com* to find out what's happening.

Dun-Well Doughnuts
$ | Café. Doughnuts have become a national obsession, and dedicated shops have opened up all over New York City and Brooklyn. This retro-cool shop has an extra edge: all the doughnuts are vegan, and they also come in more than 200 flavors. **Known for:** great option for vegans; wild daily flavors from blueberry–chunky peanut butter to mac 'n' cheese; horchata latte. *Average main: $3* ✉ *222 Montrose Ave., Brooklyn* 🕾 *347/294–0871* ⊕ *www. dunwelldoughnuts.com* ▭ *No credit cards* Ⓜ *L to Montrose Ave.*

★ Little Skips
$ | Café. Artwork by local artists, some of them customers, hang on the wall at this popular hangout space that lures a large contingent of freelancers typing away on their laptops. The sandwiches are excellent, and gluten-free substitutes are available for an additional charge. **Known for:** signature coffee drinks, like maple-sweetened latte and dirty chai latte; solid hot-pressed sandwiches and grilled cheese; baked goods from local artisans. *Average main: $8* ✉ *941 Willoughby Ave., Bushwick*

☎ 718/484-0980 ⊕ littleskips.nyc
Ⓜ J, M, Z to Myrtle Ave.

Tortilleria Mexicana Los Hermanos

$ | **Mexican.** You'd be hard-pressed to find a more authentic taquería than this one, in the front room of a tortilla factory. Meals are inexpensive and delicious (the spicy chorizo taco is a popular option), which means the place gets busy, especially on weekend nights, when the handwritten order tickets sometimes vaporize amid the busy crowd. **Known for:** cheap tacos, taquitos, tostadas, and tortas; fresh tortillas made made on-site; no-frills, BYOB restaurant. *Average main: $8* ⊠ *271 Starr St., Bushwick* ☎ *718/456-3422* ▭ *No credit cards* Ⓜ *L to Jefferson St.*

🍴 Dining

Arepera Guacuco

$ | **South American.** *Arepas* are griddled corn patties filled with meats and cheeses and sometimes vegetables; at this casual Venezuelan restaurant you watch them being freshly patted into shape and griddled, right behind the bar. Start with an order of *tajadas* (sweet plantains topped with shredded cheese) or the *tequeños* (fried green plantains). **Known for:** over a dozen authentic Venezuelan arepas; one of New York's top-rated Venezuelan restaurants; solid weekend brunch. *Average main: $7* ⊠ *44 Irving Ave., Bushwick* ☎ *347/305-3300* ⊕ *www.areperaguacuco.com* Ⓜ *L to Jefferson St.*

Bunna Cafe

$ | **Ethiopian.** The best way to sample the diverse flavors, many quite spicy, of Ethiopian cuisine at this stellar restaurant are the combination platters—for one or to share—though you can also order individual dishes. If the delicious, seasonal *duba wot* (spiced pumpkin) is available, definitely include it in your platter. **Known for:** shareable plates; traditional Ethiopian coffee ceremony and teas; live music events featuring Ethiopian artists. *Average main: $11* ⊠ *1084 Flushing Ave., Bushwick* ☎ *347/295-2227* ⊕ *bunnaethiopia.net* Ⓜ *L to Morgan Ave.*

★ Ichiran

$$ | **Ramen.** Eating at this ramen restaurant can be incredibly awkward or a total blessing, depending on how you view solo dining. Famed for its top-notch noodles (get the classic tonkatsu with spicy red chili sauce) and bizarre cubicle-style private seating, the popular Japanese chain chose Bushwick, with its quirky vibe, as a fitting first U.S. location. **Known for:** isolated solo dining booths; authentic Japanese ramen; noodles delivered within 15 seconds after cooking. *Average main: $15* ⊠ *374 Johnson Ave., Brooklyn* ☎ *718/381-0491* ⊕ *en.ichiran.com* Ⓜ *L to Morgan Ave.*

Montana's Trail House

$$ | **American.** Comfort food leads the menu at the coolest barn in Bushwick, which started life in Kentucky before being reassembled on Troutman Street and deco-

rated with deer heads and other Americana. The "Appalachian-influenced" food translates into fried chicken, brisket, and hot turkey sandwiches. **Known for:** serious cocktails, often including local spirits; sweet tea–brined fried chicken; switchel-based cocktails. *Average main: $20 ⊠ 455 Troutman St., Bushwick* ☎ *917/966–1666* ⊕ *www.montanastrailhouse. com* ☉ *No lunch weekdays* Ⓜ *L to Jefferson St.*

983 Bushwick's Living Room

$$ | American. This popular spot on Flushing Avenue, near some of East Williamsburg's most-frequented shops and restaurants, is best known for lunch and brunch comfort food, and also stays open for dinner. Sandwiches are the big thing—the Philly cheesesteak, marinated artichoke, and crispy buffalo chicken are among the standouts—though there's a bit of everything on the menu, and breakfast is served all day. **Known for:** dining until midnight or later most nights; all-day breakfast and American pub grub; works by local artists on walls. *Average main: $14 ⊠ 983 Flushing Ave., Bushwick* ☎ *718/386–1133* ⊕ *www.983bk.com* Ⓜ *L to Morgan Ave.; J, M to Flushing Ave.*

★ Roberta's

$$ | Pizza. A neighborhood groundbreaker since it opened in 2008, this restaurant in a former garage is a must-visit, especially for pizza connoisseurs. The menu emphasizes hyperlocal ingredients—there's a rooftop garden—and the wood-fired pizzas

have innovative combinations of toppings like fennel, pork sausage, and pistachio. **Known for:** award-winning, nationally recognized pizza; seasonal patio with outdoor tiki bar; impressive beverage menu includes curated coffee program. *Average main: $17 ⊠ 261 Moore St., Bushwick* ☎ *718/417–1118* ⊕ *www. robertaspizza.com* Ⓜ *L to Morgan Ave.*

Sally Roots

$$ | Caribbean. Only a few years ago, you'd have to travel to Crown Heights for solid Caribbean cuisine. The trend has migrated north-east to Bushwick at this tropical restaurant featuring dishes from across the islands, including spicy jerk ribs, mojo pork, akee (a fruit) and salt fish, and tostones. **Known for:** gorgeous seasonal back patio; impressive cocktail menu; good pick for lunch or brunch. *Average main: $20 ⊠ 195 Wyckoff Ave., Bushwick* ☎ *347/425–0888* ⊕ *www. sallyroots.com* Ⓜ *L to Dekalb Ave., M to Myrtle–Wyckoff Aves.*

⛾ Bars and Nightlife

Bizarre

Live music and theatrical performances at this appropriately named bar range from burlesque to circus to all kinds of quirky performance art. Even when there's no show going on, the dance floor fills up on weekend nights thanks to the cheap drinks and fun tunes; there's even a disco ball in the bathroom. Burgers, pastas, crepes, and other standards are served for lunch and dinner, and there's a weekend brunch. ✉ *12 Jefferson St., Bushwick* ☎ *347/915–2717* ⊕ *www.bizarrebushwick.com* Ⓜ *J, M, Z to Myrtle Ave.*

The Cobra Club

Locals love this multifaceted hangout from early morning to late at night: it's a fun cocktail bar in the evening, with karaoke, dance parties, live music, and movie screenings. During the day it's a café and yoga studio, including an infamous metal yoga class (vinyasa practice backed by doom metal music). ✉ *6 Wyckoff Ave., Bushwick* ☎ *917/719–1138* ⊕ *www.cobraclubbk.com* Ⓜ *L to Jefferson St.*

★ Featherweight

The cocktail list at this small spot is full of the hits you'd expect at a bar run by the experts behind the two Weather Up spaces in Manhattan and Prospect Heights. Part of the allure, though, is that bartenders will mix a cocktail to your precise specifications. Prime time here is late night. Finding the entrance is part of the fun: look for the painted feather and the three-story-tall mural of a boxer. ✉ *135 Graham Ave., Brooklyn* ☎ *202/907–3372* ⊕ *www.featherweightbk.com* Ⓜ *J, M to Lorimer St.; L to Montrose Ave.*

★ House of Yes

Aerial burlesque performers, neon-clad ravers, or glittery galactic princesses are just the average attendees you'll find at this experimental performance venue on any given night. Highly coveted, themed events often sell out quickly and range from roller disco parties and drag cabarets to acid trip–inspired dance parties. Expect to show up late and dance until the sun comes up. ✉ *2 Wyckoff Ave., Bushwick* ⊕ *houseofyes.org* Ⓜ *L to Jefferson St.*

Left Hand Path

It won't have the frills of typical Bushwick bars as far as dancing, performances, or kitschy events, but Left Hand is always guaranteed to have a solid craft beer list and seasonal backyard patio perpetually packed with locals. Late night, the bar serves hot dumplings from Flushing's Dumpling Galaxy until 2 am, just when drunk bar-goers need 'em. ✉ *89 Wyckoff Ave., Bushwick* ☎ *718/417–1262* ⊕ *www.lefthandpathbk.com* Ⓜ *L to Dekalb Ave.*

Lot 45

A sleek warehouse space, this loungelike affair bills itself as a "local living room," and that's definitely the vibe, though the cocktails and food are of a higher than casual caliber. DJs keep the dance floor crowded, and the spacious outdoor area has plush couches when you need a breather. ✉ *411*

Troutman St., Bushwick ☎ 347/505–9155 ⊕ www.lot45bushwick.com Ⓜ L to Jefferson St.

Pearl's Social and Billy Club

Emblematic of the new Bushwick, this chill spot looks cool and has a laid-back personality as well as patrons who have lots of interesting things to say. The expertly mixed cocktails are served in mason jars. Locals love Pearl's for day drinking; nighttime can rock until 4 am. *✉ 40 St. Nicholas Ave., Bushwick ☎ 347/627–9985 ⊕ www.pearlssocial. com Ⓜ L to Jefferson St.*

Pine Box Rock Shop

In a former coffin ("pine box") factory, this bar and performance space is best known for its beer selection, though the specialty vegan cocktails are worth checking out, too. Weekly trivia, karaoke, and live-music events take place, and every month or so the space hosts a Saturday "vegan shop-up" with vendors selling crafts and notably fine vegan food. *✉ 12 Grattan St., Brooklyn ☎ 718/366–6311 ⊕ www.pineboxrockshop.com Ⓜ L to Morgan Ave.*

 Performing Arts

★ Syndicated Bar Theater Kitchen

Trying to squeeze in dinner before a show can be rough, which is why this one-stop-shop lets you do both. A hybrid 60-seat movie theater and massive bar, Syndicated screens a rotating calendar of films ranging from award-winning classics to indie flicks at cheaper prices than the big-screen blockbusters. The best part? You can order bar and craft beverages from your seat without missing a moment. *✉ 40 Bogart St., Brooklyn ☎ 718/386–3399 ⊕ syndicatedbk.com Ⓜ L to Morgan Ave.*

5

Bedford-Stuyvesant and Crown Heights

Williamsburg

Bushwick

BEDFORD-
STUYVESANT

Clinton
Hill

Prospect
Heights

CROWN
HEIGHTS

Prospect
Park

Brownsville

Prospect Lefferts
Gardens

Bedford-Stuyvesant (known as Bed-Stuy) and Crown Heights, two large, exciting, and diverse neighborhoods south of Williamsburg and southwest of Bushwick, are noteworthy for their deep African American roots, landmarked architecture, and dynamic mix of ethnic restaurants, cool bars and cafés, and stylish shops. Starting in the 1870s, many residences, storefronts, and churches were erected to accommodate an influx of middle- and upper-middle-class white families, who were then joined, and mostly replaced by, African Americans from the South, black West Indian immigrants, Italians, and Orthodox Jews. In Bed-Stuy's Stuyvesant Heights district and on Dean Street in Crown Heights, it's a sheer delight to encounter whole blocks of beautifully preserved Italianate brownstones, or to experience the grandeur of a Romanesque Revival church or a Renaissance Revival apartment house. Bed-Stuy and Crown Heights prospered into the 1960s but experienced periodic race riots and subsequent high crime that lasted into the 1990s. It's easiest to sense the area's reboot in booming, youthful Crown Heights, where most of the new action is concentrated along Franklin Avenue north of Eastern Parkway, the main drag. Bed-Stuy, whose main artery is Bedford Avenue, which runs north–south, is more spread out, and gritty blocks are interspersed with inviting pockets of restaurants and shops.—*Updated by Carly Fisher*

Sights

Brooklyn Botanic Garden.
Entrances at 990 Washington Ave. and 150 Eastern Pkwy. *See Chapter 7, Prospect Heights, for full listing.*

Brooklyn Children's Museum
What's red, yellow, and green, and shaped like a spaceship? The Brooklyn Children's Museum, an interactive space where kids can run, touch and play with abandon. Exhibits range from a working greenhouse to art experiences.

The cornerstone is World Brooklyn, a warren of rooms dedicated to various NYC cultures that includes an Italian pizza shop, Hispanic bakery, and a replica MTA bus. ⊠ *145 Brooklyn Ave., Crown Heights* ☎ *718/735–4400* ⊕ *www.brooklynkids. org* ⊷ *$11* ⊙ *Closed Mon.* Ⓜ *C to Kingston–Throop Aves.; 3 to Kingston Ave.; A, C to Nostrand Ave.*

Dean Street
Few residential streets in Crown Heights are as beautiful as Dean Street (especially between Bedford

and New York avenues). Unique brownstones reflect Italianate, Edwardian, Victorian, and Renaissance Revival styles. Walking east from Bedford, take note of several wood-frame houses starting at No. 1208, which date back to the 1860s. At the corner of Dean and New York Avenue, compare the two churches across the street from one another: the neo-Byzantine Hebron French-speaking Seventh-day Adventist Church and the redbrick Union United Methodist Church. ⊠ *Dean St., Crown Heights* Ⓜ *A, C to Nostrand Ave.*

Grant Square

Surrounded by imposing buildings like the Union League Club and the former Chatelaine Hotel at the intersection of high-trafficked roads, Grant Square was the center of the area's social life in the early 20th century. William Ordway Partridge's bronze statue of Ulysses S. Grant was unveiled in 1896. The original Loews Bedford Theatre, which opened in the early 1900s, is on the western side of the plaza at 1372 Bedford Avenue; the building was converted into a church. ⊠ *Between Rogers Ave., Bedford Ave., and Bergen St., Crown Heights* Ⓜ *A, C to Nostrand Ave.*

★ Herbert Von King Park

This 7.8-acre park is one of Brooklyn's oldest idylls—a leafy expanse with a playground, baseball field, dog run, and an amphitheater that serves as a venue for SummerStage and Bed-Stuy Pride. ⊠ *Between Marcy and Tompkins Aves., from Lafayette Ave. to Greene Ave., Brooklyn* ⊕ *www.nycgovparks.org/parks/herbert-von-king-park* Ⓜ *A, C to Nostrand Ave.; G to Bedford–Nostrand Aves. or Myrtle–Willoughby Aves.*

Richard Beavers Gallery

Nestled between a bodega and a barber shop on Marcus Garvey Boulevard, this small fine-arts gallery displays work by international artists tackling urban and inner-city themes in various genres, from abstract art to realism, photography, street art, and more. ⊠ *408 Marcus Garvey Blvd., Brooklyn* ☎ *347/663–8195* ⊕ *richardbeavers-gallery.com* ☉ *Closed Mon.; open Tues.–Fri. by appointment only* Ⓜ *C to Kingston–Throop Aves.*

★ Stuyvesant Heights

More than 8,000 Victorian brownstones and row houses line the streets of Bed-Stuy, 825 of which fall in the landmarked historic district of Stuyvesant Heights. MacDonough Street and Stuyvesant Avenue are highlights. You can see some of the best buildings if you stroll east on MacDonough, starting at Lewis Avenue. Pass the 1860s Italianate brownstone that's now Akwaaba Luxury B&B (347 MacDonough) and turn right onto Stuyvesant Avenue. Just south of Bainbridge Street, on the west side, are two gorgeous white mansions. ⊠ *Lewis Ave. at MacDonough St., Brooklyn* Ⓜ *A, C to Utica Ave.*

23rd Regiment Armory

At Atlantic and Bedford, the 23rd Regiment Armory is one of Brooklyn's most imposing and

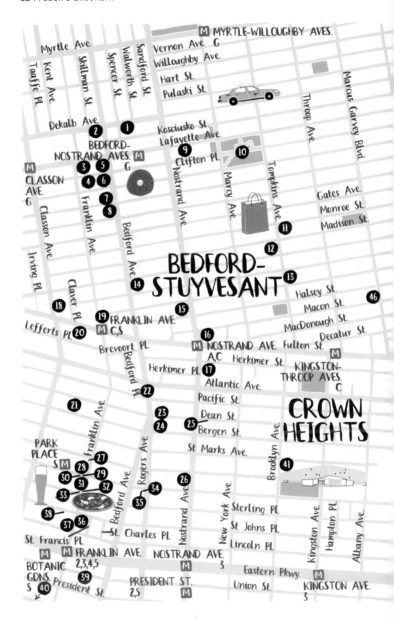

important landmarks: an almost full-block Romanesque Revival building by architects Fowler & Hough that dates back to 1895. The building—much of it restored, from the crenelated towers to the arched windows—now serves as a homeless shelter, which means that the nearby blocks can feel a bit dodgy. During the day it's safe, though, with people milling about—just be smart. ✉ *1322 Bedford Ave., Crown Heights* Ⓜ *A, C to Nostrand Ave.; C, S to Franklin Ave.*

Weeksville Heritage Center

Honoring the history of the 19th-century African American community of Weeksville, one of the first communities of free blacks in New York (founded by James Weeks), this Crown Heights museum comprises an industrial-modern building by Caples Jefferson Architects, botanical gardens, and three houses that date as far back as 1838. The restored homes, along historic, gravel Hunterfly Road, are now period re-creations depicting life in the 1860s, 1900s, and 1930s. Tours ($8) are Tuesday, Thursday, and Friday at 3 pm. ✉ *158 Buffalo Ave., Crown Heights* ☎ *718/756-5250* ⊕ *www.weeksvillesociety.org* 🎫 *$8 house tours; grounds free* 🕐 *Closed Sat.–Mon.* Ⓜ *A, C to Utica Ave.; 3, 4 to Crown Heights–Utica Ave.*

 Shopping

Calabar Imports

As Bed-Stuy and Crown Heights seemingly shift in the direction of gentrification, Calabar Imports

GETTING HERE

Many major subway lines cross the large area occupied by Bed-Stuy and Crown Heights. Utica Avenue and Crown Heights–Utica Avenue stops on the A and C trains are closest to Weeksville Heritage Center. To stroll Crown Heights' architectural highlights, get out at the Nostrand Avenue A and C stop. Find most of the restaurants, shops, and bars just off the Franklin Avenue 2, 3, 4, and 5 stop.

remains a distinctively authentic stalwart, with locations in both neighborhoods and in Harlem. Mother-and-daughter duo Heloise Annette Oton and Atim Annette Oton specialize in importing unique clothing, accessories, and home goods from Africa, Asia, and South America that you'll be hard-pressed to find anywhere else. ✉ *351 Tompkins Ave., Brooklyn* ☎ *718/638-4288* ⊕ *www.calabar-imports.com* 🕐 *Closed Tues.* Ⓜ *2, 3, 4, 5 to Franklin Ave.*

Harold & Maude

Whether you're shopping for yourself, your eclectic friend, your favorite kid, or your grandparent, add this funky vintage store to your hit list. Clothing and accessories for all seasons and all ages are sourced from across the United States and Japan, with the store's cofounders creating their own original line, too, mostly out of vintage Japanese textiles. ✉ *592 Lafayette Ave., Brooklyn* ⊕ *www.haroldandmaudevintage.com* 🕐 *Closed Tues.* Ⓜ *G to Classon Ave.*

Marché Rue Dix

Paris is all about the concept stores, so it's little surprise that owners Nilea Alexander and Lamine Diagne retained some francophone flair for this offshoot of their popular French-Senegalese restaurant, Café Rue Dix, located just next door. Blending stunning vintage duds, emerging indie design, handpicked home goods, and natural apothecary products, there's always something unique to discover at this boutique. ⊠ *1453 Bedford Ave., Brooklyn* ☎ *347/414–5436* ⊕ *www. marcheruedix.com.*

Peace & Riot

Run by Bed-Stuy native and interior decorator Achuziam Maha-Sanchez and her husband, Lionel Sanchez, this design shop stocks stylish items for the home, such as funky wood coasters, Brooklyn-theme umbrella holders, and colorful items from North and West Africa. Brooklyn tote bags and geometric photo frames make great souvenirs. ⊠ *401–403 Tompkins Ave., Brooklyn* ☎ *347/663–6100* ⊕ *www.peaceandriot.com* Ⓜ *A, C to Nostrand Ave.*

Sincerely, Tommy

This avant-garde womens-wear shop isn't typical of this neighborhood, but the items in stock—funky sheer and cutout tops, a gotta-have-it bright-red coat, cool bags—are attention grabbing anywhere in town. The white-draped dressing rooms are a nice touch, as is the quaint coffee shop: it's surely the first place east of Bedford Avenue to serve Balthazar pastries. ⊠ *343 Tompkins Ave., Brooklyn* ☎ *718/484–8484* ⊕ *www.sincerelytommy.com* Ⓜ *C to Kingston–Throop Aves.; G to Bedford–Nostrand Aves.*

Suzette Lavalle

An indie boutique run by a former fashion stylist might make you think triple-dollar signs, but Suzette Lavalle manages to keep her eponymous boutique shockingly budget-friendly. Lavalle vets on-trend clothing, accessories, home goods, and gifts, with most items under $50. She hasn't left her styling days behind entirely; you can still book a consultation and personal shopping trip for $75 an hour. ⊠ *726 Franklin Ave., Crown Heights* ☎ *646/281–4129* ⊕ *www. suzettelavalle.com* Ⓜ *2, 3, 4, 5, C train to Franklin Ave.*

☕ Coffee and Quick Bites

A&A Bake & Doubles

$ | Caribbean. Inside this tiny shop, the "King of Doubles" whips up Trinidad and Tobago's classic breakfast sandwich called a "doubles" (always plural): fried bread filled with chickpea curry and tamarind, apple, and mango chutneys. Choose your hot-sauce heat level (mild, slight, or plenty) and grab some napkins and maybe a Solo sparkling apple or banana juice to go. **Known for:** top-notch Trinidadian doubles; Caribbean specialties like salt fish and aloo pie; some of the best cheap eats you'll find. *Average main: $2* ⊠ *481 Nostrand Ave., Brooklyn* ☎ *718/230-0753* ⊘ *Closed Sun. No dinner* ⊟ *No credit cards* Ⓜ *A, C to Nostrand Ave.*

Alice's Arbor

$$ | American. The rustic vibe at this mellow eatery comes partly from the barn and pallet wood repurposed for its décor and furnishings, and partly from the all-natural dishes gracing its menu. Locals love trying seasonal foods sourced from farms within 800 miles of Brooklyn, be they fresh oysters, cheeses, breads, or natural wines, beers, and spirits. **Known for:** farm-to-table fare; rustic interior; tasty, healthful ingredients. *Average main: $20* ⊠ *549 Classon Ave., Brooklyn* ☏ *718/399–3003* ⊕ *alicesarborbk.com* Ⓜ *A, C, S at Franklin Ave.*

Baron's

$$ | American. Don't let the parquet floors and houseplants fool you—Baron's is a restaurant, not somebody's oversized dining room. Though the menu is on the simple side, its creative, veggie-forward takes deliver tantalizing weekday-dinner and weekend-brunch choices, complemented by classic cocktails, beer, and imported wine. **Known for:** New American dishes; balanced cocktails; homey décor. *Average main: $20* ⊠ *564 Dekalb Ave., Brooklyn* ☏ *718/230–7100* ⊕ *www.barons-brooklyn.com/* Ⓜ *G at Bedford-Nostrand Aves.*

Brooklyn Kolache Co

$ | Café. Sure, doughnuts are all the rage, but for something a little different, head to this cozy bakery-café near Pratt Institute for the renowned Czech (via Texas; the owner is from Austin) *kolaches,* pillowy pastries filled with sweet and savory ingredients like lemon curd, strawberry and sweet cheese, or sausage and cheese. There can be more than 20 varieties to choose from at any one time. **Known for:** sweet and savory kolaches; vegan and gluten-free options; backyard garden patio. *Average main: $8* ⊠ *520 DeKalb Ave., Brooklyn* ☏ *718/398–1111* ⊕ *www.brooklynkolacheco.com* Ⓜ *G to Bedford–Nostrand Aves.*

David's Brisket House Deli

$ | Deli. This storefront deli doesn't look like much, but several things make it a standout. One is the pastrami, available as a sandwich or with eggs for breakfast; another is the fact that you can order a "small" sandwich—definitely enough for average appetites—rather than the typical oversize versions that you get at places like Katz's. **Known for:** generously sized Jewish deli sandwiches; smoked brisket and pastrami with cult-following status; pastrami and brisket combo. *Average main: $11* ⊠ *533 Nostrand Ave., Brooklyn* ☏ *718/789–1155* ⊕ *www.davidsbriskethouseinc. com* ⊙ *Closed midday Fri.* Ⓜ *A, C to Nostrand Ave.*

★ Dough

$ | Bakery. Ask the baker at Dough which doughnut you should try, and you may get this answer: "The only thing better than the chocolate salted caramel is life itself." That may be true, but the cinnamon, original glazed, and more unusual flavors like the passion fruit and hibiscus are also unforgettably delicious—good luck choosing. The doughnuts are as big as a man's hand, and they're fried in batches throughout the day to ensure freshness. **Known for:** legendary meal-size yeast doughnuts; the doughka, a cross between a doughnut and babka; salted chocolate caramel is the standby, but hibiscus is the underdog. *Average main: $2 ⊠ 448 Lafayette Ave., Brooklyn ☎ 347/533-7544 ⊕ www.doughbrooklyn.com Ⓜ A, C to Nostrand Ave.; C, S to Franklin Ave.; G to Classon Ave.*

🍴 Dining

★ Barboncino

$$ | Pizza. Settle in with the after-work crowd, and you'll feel like a Crown Heights local at this beloved neighborhood pizza parlor. Here, friends meet for specialties like the standout Neapolitan pizza (order the "Arugula") and the famous veal-and-pork meatballs topped with Parmesan, and for the convivial late-night drink specials. **Known for:** excellent wood-fired Neapolitan-style pizzas; happy hour deals after work and late at night; Tuesday-night live jazz. *Average main: $15 ⊠ 781 Franklin Ave., Crown Heights ☎ 718/483-8834 ⊕ www.barboncinopizza.com ⊘ No lunch weekdays Ⓜ 2, 3, 4, 5 to Franklin Ave.; S to Botanic Garden.*

Berg'n

$ | American. This food and beer hall from the team behind Smorgasburg and the Brooklyn Flea lures visitors from all over Brooklyn and beyond to a warehouse on a formerly nondescript street. The massive space, often filled and sometimes completely jammed, has a 40-foot antique bar and a handful of Smorg's favorite vendor stands including Mighty Quinn's Barbecue, Lumpia Shack, and LandHaus. **Known for:** rotating pop-up food vendors with something for everyone; communal seats filled with families and groups; beer snob–approved draft list, with local brews on tap. *Average main: $10 ⊠ 899 Bergen St., Crown Heights ⊕ www.bergn.com ⊘ Closed Mon. Ⓜ S to Park Pl.; C to Franklin Ave.; 2, 3, 4, 5 to Franklin Ave.*

★ BKW by Brooklyn Winery

$$ | American. Believe it or not, wine is being made in Brooklyn, and it is actually legit. BKW, the restaurant offshoot of Brooklyn Winery, lets you taste the portfolio of grapes from New York State and beyond with handpicked seasonal dishes that run the gamut from approachable pan-roasted chicken breast with sun-dried tomato couscous to inventive barbacoa-braised short ribs with parsnip puree, yuzu cream, and apple slaw. **Known for:** signature-label wines produced in New York State, solid specials, including two happy hours; great brunch menu with excellent scones and Bloody Marys. *Average main: $18 ⊠ 747 Franklin Ave., Crown Heights ☎ 718/399-1700 ⊕ www.bkwnyc.com ⊘ No lunch weekdays Ⓜ S to Park Pl.; 2, 3, 4, 5 to Franklin Ave.*

Café Rue Dix

$$ | French Fusion. Whether it's the rhythmic African music, the aromatic Ataya tea, or the stylish diners from all parts of Brooklyn, be prepared for this romantic Senegalese-French fusion bistro to steal your heart (and stomach). The charming knickknacks in this vibrant, intimate space create an authentic backdrop for dishes straight from the owners' kitchen in Dakar, such as the hearty Thiebou Jen (stewed fish and vegetables over rice; the national dish of Senegal) and Fataya (beef empanadas with Senegalese hot sauce). **Known for:** authentic Senegalese and French fusion cuisine; Wednesday-night three-course prix-fixe menu; traditional Cafe Touba Senegalese coffee and Ataya gunpowder green tea. *Average main: $17* ⊠ *1451 Bedford Ave., Crown Heights* ☎ *929/234–2543* ⊕ *www.caferuedix.com* Ⓜ *2, 3, 4, 5 to Franklin Ave.; S to Park Pl.*

★ Chavela's
$$ | Mexican. Open Chavela's wrought-iron doors and you'll find a boisterous Mexican restaurant with a colorfully tiled bar, where diners order margaritas and micheladas by the pitcher. Pair your drink with the Plato Don (a substantial dish of steak, chicken, or veggies, plus rice, beans, guac, tortillas, pico de gallo, and queso fresco) or the *especiales del día*. **Known for:** pitchers of quality house margaritas and sangrias on draft; weekday happy hour deals on tacos and drinks; prix-fixe weekend brunch special is even more popular than Friday night. *Average main: $14* ⊠ *793 Franklin Ave., Crown Heights* ☎ *718/622–3100* ⊕ *www.chavelasnyc.com* Ⓜ *2, 3, 4, 5 to Franklin Ave.; S to Park Pl.*

★ Glady's
$$ | Caribbean. Paying homage to the area's Caribbean roots, Glady's is a cool tropical place with hanging plants, a funky sound track, and chalkboard menus. Start with a handcrafted tiki cocktail and an order of jerk fried wings, and then move on to the curry goat, oxtail stew, or peppered shrimp before finishing off with house-made coconut sorbet. **Known for:** legit jerk-seasoned dishes with chicken, pork, seitan, or lobster; spicy curried goat and peppered shrimp tamed with sweet plantains or bok choy; Instagram-worthy cocktails, including frozen slushies. *Average main: $13* ⊠ *788 Franklin Ave., Crown Heights* ☎ *718/622–0249* ⊕ *www.gladysnyc.com* Ⓜ *2, 3, 4, 5 to Franklin Ave.; S to Botanic Garden.*

Mayfield
$$ | Modern American. For a mix of standard American comfort food (such as a burger and fries) and dishes that are more inventive (like steak tartare with horseradish yogurt or buttermilk fried quail with spoonbread), head to Mayfield. The attention to detail stands out, from the carefully chosen local ingredients to the vintage bowling-lane-topped tables. **Known for:** daily $1 oyster happy hour; upscale tavern food with market-fresh ingredients; approachable curated wine list and inventive craft cocktails. *Average main: $22* ⊠ *688 Franklin Ave., Crown Heights* ☎ *347/318–3643* ⊕ *www.mayfieldbk.com* ⊙ *No lunch weekdays* Ⓜ *S to Park Pl.*

★ Peaches HotHouse

$$ | Southern. Fried chicken is nearly ubiquitous in Bed-Stuy, but no one does it better than Peaches HotHouse, sister restaurant to Peaches, just a few blocks east. One look at your crispy, juicy "hot chicken"—a specialty in Nashville, made with a spice rub either before or after it's breaded—and it's clear you're in for a delicious meal. **Known for:** hot chicken with Southern sides like grits, slaw, or mac and cheese; hoppin' weekend brunch; great craft cocktails and weekday happy hours. *Average main: $13* ⊠ *415 Tompkins Ave., Brooklyn* ☎ *718/483-9111* ⊕ *www.bcrestaurantgroup.com/hothouse* Ⓜ *C to Kingston-Throop Aves.*

Pilar Cuban Eatery

$$ | Cuban. Though the Cuban community hasn't yet found Bed-Stuy, a stellar Cuban restaurant will be waiting when it does. White walls with splashes of bright turquoise have a definitively retro art deco vibe of Havana, matched by Caribbean staples like the pressed roast pork and ham Cuban sandwich, house-cured chorizo, garlic-sautéed shrimp, and tender pernil (slow-roasted pork shoulder), or modern riffs like Cuban nachos with plantain chips. **Known for:** authentic Cuban dishes, including tostones, pernil, and maduros; good vegan options like stewed okra cooked with tomatoes, sofrito, and chickpeas; best Cuban café con leche outside of Miami. *Average main: $18* ⊠ *397 Greene St., Brooklyn* ☎ *718/623-2822* ⊕ *www.pilarny.com* Ⓜ *G to Bedford-Nostrand Aves.*

★ Saraghina

$$ | Italian. The owner of this pizzeria has declared his obsession with pizza, and the classic Neapolitan-style pies that come out of the wood-burning oven have, in turn, inspired local diners to obsess about this restaurant. The menu includes several house-made pastas, meatballs, salads, breakfast and lunch panini, and weekend brunch. **Known for:** Neapolitan-style pizzas with super-fresh ingredients; coveted backyard patio; evening tapas bar for a drink and snack. *Average main: $15* ⊠ *435 Halsey St., Brooklyn* ☎ *718/574-0010* ⊕ *www.saraghinabrooklyn.com* ▭ *No credit cards* Ⓜ *A, C to Utica Ave.; C to Kingston-Throop Aves.*

Silver Rice

$ | Japanese. This pocket-size "sushi roll shop" may not look like much, but one bite of the Unagi Silver Rice Cup and you'll be jonesing for more. Daily specials served on Japanese-style wooden plates seem almost too delicate for Crown Heights, including the Fisherman's Bowl, piled high with sashimi, roe, pickled daikon, and cucumber. **Known for:** chirashi rice bowls piled with fresh fish; underrated sake list with picks straight from Japan; ice creams, particularly the signature Saikyo miso flavor. *Average main: $12* ⊠ *638 Park Pl., Crown Heights* ☎ *718/398-8200* ⊕ *www.silverrice.com* ⊗ *No lunch weekdays* Ⓜ *2, 3, 4, 5 to Franklin Ave.; S to Park Pl.*

Stonefruit Espresso + Kitchen

$ | Café. If avocado toast and grain bowls are your jam, Stonefruit is a must. Part café, part plant shop and apothecary, this sunny corner spot is a popular daytime stop-off for fancy, health-centric farm-to-table fare like smoked whitefish with fresh greens on locally made sourdough, or grass-fed yogurt with house-made apricot rose granola. **Known for:** exceptional fresh-baked seasonal goods; notable specialty coffees and teas; great coworking space in back, with plants and ceramics you can purchase. *Average main: $10* ✉ *1058 Bedford Ave., Brooklyn* ☎ *718/230–4147* ⊕ *stonefruitespresso.com* Ⓜ *G to Bedford–Nostrand Aves.*

🍸 Bars and Nightlife

Bedford Hall

A loungy bar and restaurant with leather sofas, a billiards table and performance space in back, several flat-screen TVs, and a front room set up like a library, Bedford Hall is a local favorite for just about everyone. It's relaxed late afternoon, with Brooklynites working on laptops, but dinner and brunch get busy. Late at night, beneath photos memorializing iconic Bed-Stuy residents, dressed-to-the-nines partygoers dance to live DJs until the sun comes up. ✉ *1177 Bedford Ave., Brooklyn* ☎ *347/461–9854* ⊕ *www.bedfordhall.com* Ⓜ *A, C to Nostrand Ave.; C, S to Franklin Ave.*

Bed-Vyne Brew

A corner bar with outdoor seating is rare in these parts, which makes Bed-Vyne's deck a summertime favorite. Inside the cozy space, decorated with wood reclaimed from barns in upstate New York, chatty bartenders pour wine, pints of handcrafted seasonal brews, and growlers to go. Bed-Vyne Spirits, the sister outpost around the corner at 305 Halsey Street, serves cocktails as well. Come late (after 9 pm) for DJ sets, or Tuesday for live music. ✉ *370 Tompkins Ave., Brooklyn* ☎ *347/915–1080* ⊕ *brew.bed-vyne. com* Ⓜ *A, C to Nostrand Ave.; C to Kingston–Throop Aves.*

Butter & Scotch

Because dessert is always a little sweeter with booze, Allison Kave and Keavy Blueher opened this bakery-bar hybrid concept in 2015 to serve the best of both worlds. By day, the bakery offers a small lunch menu of biscuit sandwiches and savory hand pies, but it comes to life at night with boozy shakes, floats, sundaes, pies, and cake for the perfect nightcap. ✉ *818 Franklin Ave., Crown Heights* ☎ *347/350–8899* ⊕ *www.butterandscotch.com* Ⓜ *2, 3, 4, 5 to Franklin Ave.; S to Botanic Park.*

★ Casablanca Cocktail Lounge

It's easy to see why seemingly the whole neighborhood has embraced this latest incarnation of Casablanca—there's been a bar with that name on this spot since the 1940s. Quality bartenders, reasonably priced drinks, and cool DJs mean that weekend nights get crowded with dancing and good times. ✉ *300 Malcolm X Blvd., Brooklyn* ☎ *718/221-2272* ⊕ *www. casablancabrooklyn.com* Ⓜ *A, C to Utica Ave.*

C'mon Everybody

Just like the name suggests, this Bed-Stuy bar and music venue has a broad appeal thanks to its roomy seating areas and busy event calendar. There are storyteller nights, comedy, Saturday LGBT tea dances, burlesque shows, and plenty of sociable patrons lending the club still more fun and flirtation daily. ✉ *25 Franklin Ave., Brooklyn* ⊕ *www.cmoneverybody.com* Ⓜ *G to Classon Ave.*

Crown Inn

Any night of the week, a chill crowd convenes at this simple neighborhood bar with exposed brick walls for drink specials ($5 Kirin), cocktails, several wines by the glass, and craft brews like Bell's Two Hearted Ale, a hoppy choice from Michigan's Upper Peninsula. In warmer months, the back patio is a neighborhood favorite. There are occasional pop-up food vendors, too. ✉ *727 Franklin Ave., Crown Heights* ☎ *347/915-1131* Ⓜ *S to Park Pl.; 2, 3, 4, 5 to Franklin Ave.*

Do or Dive

Former occupants Do or Dine pioneered the Bed-Stuy hipster dining scene. As a tongue-in-cheek nod, the current owners spray painted the letter "V" over "dine," preserving its legacy, now in the form of a late-night dive bar. The seasonal backyard patio opens for day drinking, serving up "that frozen coffee thing" (a boozy coffee slushy with bourbon and brandy), fresh watermelon margaritas, and cheap beers for hanging out with garage rock tunes blasting late in the evening. ✉ *1108 Bedford Ave., Brooklyn* ☎ *347/406-8241* Ⓜ *G to Bedford–Nostrand Aves., A to Nostrand Ave.*

Doris

The unassuming yellow door is the first indication of the cheery vibe that is Doris. Southwestern-style accents, DJs spinning vinyl, and an absolutely charming backyard translate to a fun Bed-Stuy drink spot that many would agree is the local favorite. On summer nights the outdoor space fills up with Brooklynites sipping craft cocktails and draft beers that are just $5 during happy hour, which is daily from 5 to 8 pm. ✉ *1088 Fulton St., Brooklyn* ☎ *347/240-3350* Ⓜ *C, S to Franklin Ave.*

Dynaco

Duck inside this unassuming bar on busy Bedford Avenue for a strong cocktail or craft beer, and you might feel transported to a mountain lodge, complete with wood finishes, low lighting, and a fireplace. The brothers who founded Dynaco used reclaimed materials for a cozy, warm vibe, even repurposing the name from an old-school Hi-Fi speaker brand. Cash only. ✉ *1112 Bedford Ave, Brooklyn* Ⓜ *G to Bedford–Nostrand Aves.*

Franklin Park (and Dutch Boy Burger)

This two-room bar and burger restaurant resides in a converted garage. Seasonal beers are on tap—including brews from Sixpoint and Smuttynose—and courtyard tables draw crowds in warm weather. On-site Dutch Boy Burger keeps slightly different hours, including brunch (try the hangover burger, topped with a fried egg and American cheese). On the second Monday of every month, follow the literary crowd to Franklin Park for their award-winning reading series, which often spotlights rising stars. ✉ *618 St. Johns Pl., Crown Heights* ☎ *718/975-0196* ⊕ *www.franklinparkbrooklyn.com* Ⓜ *S to Park Pl.; 2, 3, 4, 5 to Franklin Ave.*

Glorietta Baldy

Don't be afraid to ask for a taster at this craft beer and cocktail bar—the specialty tap list changes so frequently that even locals can't keep up. You'll find lots of New York state wines, rare spirits, and curated craft brews at this small, dimly lit bar. Happy hour is good for quieter conversation, but expect crowds around the bar during weekend evening prime times when the bar lights up until 4 am. ✉ *502 Franklin Ave., Brooklyn* ☎ *347/529-1944* ⊕ *www.gloriettabaldy.com* Ⓜ *C, S to Franklin Ave.*

King Tai

A throwback art deco Miami concept might seem out of place in Bed-Stuy, but somehow it all feels right as rain after a couple of the inventive cocktails here. The limited drink menu changes seasonally, featuring tropical-inspired sippers with a decidedly unique edge (think mezcal, sherry, Aperol, and lemon). Empanadas or other light appetizers are usually available, but the bar doesn't mind if you bring your own snacks. ✉ *1095 Bergen St., Brooklyn* ☎ *718/513-1025* ⊕ *www.kingtaibar.com* Ⓜ *A, C to Nostrand Ave.*

★ Super Power

Make sure your phone's battery is charged up, because the cocktails at this tiki bar are ridiculously Instagram-worthy. Steering away from the super-sugary well drinks of the past, these colorful punches are loaded with fresh ingredients, solid spirits, and crafted toppers like orchids and umbrellas that will give you liquid courage. During summer, head to the back patio covered with tropical flora. ✉ *722 Nostrand Ave., Brooklyn* ☎ *718/484-0020* ⊕ *superpowerbrooklyn.com* Ⓜ *A, C, 2, 3, 4, 5 to Nostrand Ave.*

6

Fort Greene and Clinton Hill

Dumbo

Williamsburg

Downtown Brooklyn

CLINTON HILL

Bed-Stuy

FORT GREENE

Boerum Hill

Park Slope

Prospect Heights

Crown Heights

C ultural and educational institutions, flatteringly lit cafés, and showstopping architecture make today's Fort Greene and Clinton Hill irresistible in many ways. Wedged between the Brooklyn Navy Yard to the north and Atlantic Avenue to the south, Fort Greene has leafy streets and an illustrious past: everyone from Walt Whitman to Spike Lee has called this area home, though the neighborhood has been through ups and downs. Significant landmarks in African American history occurred here, including the opening of Brooklyn's first African American school, in 1847, after slavery was abolished in New York State. The Brooklyn Navy Yard brought prosperity, and then decline in the middle of the 20th century. Crime and poverty impacted the area through the 1960s, '70s, and '80s, but by the 1990s, the neighborhood was reinvigorated once again. Fulton Street and DeKalb Avenue, for shopping and dining respectively, are important thoroughfares, and off Fulton on Lafayette Avenue is a neighborhood cultural mainstay, the Brooklyn Academy of Music. Mostly residential Clinton Hill nestles comfortably between Fort Greene to the west and Bedford-Stuyvesant to the east. Here, tree-lined Clinton and Washington avenues please the eye with their pretty streets and 19th-century mansions in various architectural styles.—*Updated by Caroline Trefler*

◉ Sights

BLDG 92

There's so much history in the 300 square acres of the Brooklyn Navy Yard, and you can get a good glimpse of it with a visit to this free museum, which has a small selection of permanent and rotating exhibits about what happened here, what was made here, and what's going on now. Historic, photography, ecology, and architectural tours ($24–$30) are offered, too—some by bus, some by bicycle. Check the website for details. ⊠ *63 Flushing Ave., Fort Greene* ☎ *718/907–5992* ⊕ *www.bldg92.org* ☉ *Closed Mon. and Tues.* Ⓜ *F to York St., G to Clinton–Washington Aves., A or C to High St.–Brooklyn Bridge.*

BRIC Arts Media House

The organizers of renowned arts festival Celebrate Brooklyn! (*see Best Brooklyn Events in Chapter 1*) operate this 40,000-square-foot gallery, television studio, and performance space between the Brooklyn Academy of Music (BAM) and Downtown Brooklyn. The gallery specializes in Brooklyn-based artists, and the artwork also spills over into the café and hallways. Upstairs, the UrbanGlass studio has classes for all ages, as well as a shop/showcase on the first floor with jewelry, housewares, and objets d'art. ✉ *647 Fulton St., Fort Greene* ☎ *718/855-7882* ⊕ *www. bricartsmedia.org* ⊙ *Galleries closed Mon.* Ⓜ *2, 3, 4, 5 to Nevins St.; B, Q, R to DeKalb Ave.; G to Fulton St.; C to Lafayette Ave.*

★ Clinton Hill Architecture Walk

Part of the National Register of Historic Places, the buildings along Clinton and Washington avenues were originally lavish summer homes for turn-of-the-20th-century industrialists like Charles Pratt. Federal, French Second Empire, Romanesque Revival, Greek Revival, Gothic Revival, and neo-Grec mansions line the streets, serving as university buildings, community centers, and private residences. There are also quintessentially Brooklyn brownstones and Italianate row houses, with mansard roofs as far as the eye can see. ✉ *Clinton and Washington Aves., Brooklyn* Ⓜ *C, G to Clinton–Washington Aves*

Comandante Biggie Mural

On the South Portland Avenue side of a corner lot nicknamed the Brooklyn Love Building, graffiti artist Cern One, with Jorge Garcia and Lee Quiñones, created a brightly hued mural of Brooklyn rapper The Notorious B.I.G. ("Biggie"). The structure's Fulton Street facade is home to street-level shops, but its second story is tagged with lyrics from Biggie's 1994 single "Juicy." It

reads "Spread Love It's the Brooklyn Way" in tall lettering. ✉ *Brooklyn Love Bldg., 690–694 Fulton St., Fort Greene* ⊕ *www.brooklynlovebuilding. wordpress.com* Ⓜ *2, 3, 4, 5, B, D, N, Q, R to Atlantic Ave.–Barclays Ctr.; C to Lafayette Ave.; G to Fulton St.*

★ Fort Greene Park

With 30 acres of green hills, Brooklyn's oldest park is the unofficial nucleus of the neighborhood. It served as a military fort during the Revolutionary War and again during the War of 1812. At its center, the Prison Ship Martyrs Monument commemorates American war prisoners. Although it predates them, landscape architects Olmsted and Vaux (known for designing Central Park and Prospect Park) designed the current layout of Fort Greene Park. ✉ *DeKalb and Myrtle Aves., Fort Greene* ☎ *718/722-3218* ⊕ *www. nycgovparks.org/parks/fort-greene-park* Ⓜ *B, Q, R to DeKalb Ave.; G to Fulton St.; C to Lafayette Ave.; 2, 3, 4, 5 to Nevins St.*

Museum of Contemporary African Diaspora Arts

(*MoCADA*) Since 1999, MoCADA has been showcasing emerging artists, sociocultural and political installations, and exhibitions relating to peoples of African descent. MoCADA also sponsors dance performances and children's programming throughout Brooklyn. Check their website for details on upcoming events. ✉ *80 Hanson Pl., Fort Greene* ☎ *718/230-0492* ⊕ *www.mocada.org* ✉ *$8* ⊙ *Closed Mon. and Tues.* Ⓜ *2, 3, 4, 5, B, Q, to Atlantic Ave.–Barclays Ctr.; C to Lafayette Ave.; G to Fulton Ave.*

FORT GREENE

N. Portland Ave.

Myrtle Ave.

Adelphi St.

Clermont Ave.

Clinton Ave.

Waverly Ave.

Willoughby St.

Washington Park

Fort Greene Park

Vanderbilt Ave.

DEKALB AVE.
B,Q,R

Rockwell Pl.

Dekalb Ave.

Carlton Ave.

Lafayette Ave.

NEVINS ST.
2,3,4,5

Ashland Pl.

St. Felix St.

Fort Greene Pl.

S. Elliott Pl.

S. Portland Ave.

S. Oxford St.

Cumberland St.

Greene Ave.

FULTON ST.
G

LAFAYETTE
C

State St.

ATLANTIC AVE.
BARCLAYS CTR.
B,Q,2,3,4,5

Hanson Pl.

ATLANTIC AVE.
BARCLAYS CTR.
D,N,R

Pacific St.

BARCLAY'S CENTER

4th Ave.

Dean St.

Bergen St.

5th Ave.

St. Marks Ave.

Prospect Pl.

Park Pl.

BERGEN ST.
2,3

6th Ave.

Pacific St.

Dean St.

Carlton Ave.

Atlantic Ave.

0   1000 ft
0   200 m

CLINTON

HILL Willoughby Ave.

Ryerson St.
Grand Ave.
Steuben St.
Washington Ave.

Dekalb Ave.

28

CLINTON-
WASHINGTON AVES.
G Ⓜ

Hall St.
Clifton Pl.

27

25

26 →

24

23

Waverly Ave

St James Pl.
Cambridge Pl.
Grand Ave.

Gates Ave.

22

20 CLINTON-
WASHINGTON AVES.
G Ⓜ Fulton St. Putnam
Ave.

21

Lefferts Pl.

19

★ Pratt Institute Sculpture Park

One of New York City's largest sculpture gardens is free to the public and houses installations by students, faculty, and alumni of the Pratt Institute, an arts and architecture school founded in 1887. The 50-plus-piece collection changes slightly from year to year, spanning the 25-acre campus. ⊠ *200 Willoughby Ave., Brooklyn* ☎ *718/636–3600* ⊕ *www.pratt.edu* Ⓜ *C, G to Clinton–Washington Aves.*

Shopping

Bird

Look for the vintage laundromat sign that reads "French Garment Cleaners" and you'll have found the Fort Greene outpost of this minichain of sophisticated clothing shops. The racks are stocked with low-key statement pieces, the jewelry cases are filled with delicate accessories, and the staff is eager to help you find whatever you might be looking for. ⊠ *85 Lafayette Ave., Fort Greene* ☎ *718/858–8667* ⊕ *www.birdbrooklyn.com* Ⓜ *C to Lafayette Ave.; G to Fulton St.*

Feliz

This elegantly cozy boutique sells everything you never knew you always wanted. The shelves are filled with handmade jewelry, international textiles, scents by local perfumeries, candles, and whimsical children's toys. It's the perfect place to pick up unusual gifts, though it's hard to resist a little something for yourself. ⊠ *185 DeKalb Ave., Fort Greene* ☎ *718/797–*

GETTING HERE

The Brooklyn Academy of Music is located around the corner from Atlantic Avenue–Barclays Center subway stop, a major hub accessed by multiple lines. For central Fort Greene's brownstone streets, the Clinton–Washington Avenues station is your best bet, though any of the exits here makes a good starting point.

1211 ⊕ *www.felizbrooklyn.blogspot.com* Ⓜ *B, Q, R to DeKalb Ave.; C to Lafayette Ave.; G to Fulton St.*

Gnarly Vines

If only every neighborhood had a devoted wine store like this one, with tasting notes written out for just about every wine in the shop. Owner Brian Robinson is passionate about wine, and his shop is well stocked with budget-friendly bottles as well as rare finds, with an emphasis on family winemakers. Paintings by local artists line the walls, and tastings by local importers, microdistillers, and international labels imbue the space with relaxed, convivial energy. ⊠ *350 Myrtle Ave., Brooklyn* ☎ *718/797–3183* ⊕ *www.gnarlyvines.com* Ⓜ *G to Clinton–Washington Aves.*

★ Greenlight Bookstore

If you build it, they will read. Popular demand—and some vocal attendees of a 2008 community board meeting—augured the opening of this independent bookstore. It now hosts readings by popular national and international authors as well as local book club meetings. The shelves are well stocked with contemporary titles and the staff are eager to help. The children's section in the rear of the store hosts weekly storytelling events. ⊠ *686 Fulton St., Fort Greene* ☎ *718/246-0200* ⊕ *www.greenlightbookstore.com* Ⓜ *C to Lafayette Ave.; G to Fulton St.*

☕ Coffee and Quick Bites

Bittersweet
$ | Café. Tight on space but long on taste, this slim café is named for its two primary menu categories: coffee and desserts. Baristas know most customers both by sight and by their La Colombe coffee beverage of choice. **Known for:** small space; across from the park; neighborhood vibe. *Average main: $3* ⊠ *180 DeKalb Ave., Fort Greene* ☎ *718/852-2556* ⊕ *www.bittersweetbk.com* Ⓜ *C to Lafayette Ave.; G to Fulton St.*

Choice Market
$ | Café. If you're planning a picnic at the Pratt Institute Sculpture Park or looking for a low-key meal, this take-out counter and café will do you right. Prepared salads, sandwiches, and excellent pastries are pricier than your average corner deli, but then again, most bodegas don't have farro salad, salmon burgers, or pear brûlée cheesecake on the menu. **Known for:** top-quality pastries; hot breakfast prepared to order; don't expect fast service. *Average main: $8* ⊠ *318 Lafayette Ave., Brooklyn* ☎ *718/230-5234* ⊕ *market.choicebrooklyn.com* Ⓜ *C to Clinton–Washington Aves.; G to Classon Ave.*

★ Peck's
$ | Deli. Theo Peck's eponymous gourmet shop descends from New York culinary royalty: Peck cut his teeth as a chef at Michelin-starred restaurant Blue Hill at Stone Barns, and his great-grandfather co-owned Ratner's kosher dairy, once a Lower East Side institution. The narrow store sells deli meats and cheeses, an impressive selection of beer, and goods from Brooklyn purveyors. **Known for:** Brooklyn-made products; sandwiches; great prepared food. *Average main: $10* ⊠ *455A Myrtle Ave., Brooklyn* ☎ *347/689-4969* ⊕ *www.peckshomemade.com* Ⓜ *G to Clinton–Washington Aves.*

🍴 Dining

★ Aita
$$ | Italian. Don't let the unassuming air at this intimate restaurant on a leafy, largely residential block fool you: there is some serious cooking going on here. Case in point: any of the house-made pastas (perhaps cavatelli topped with shaved Parmesan and black truffles); bright, seasonal salads (maybe peach, arugula, and goat cheese); or any of the fish or meat main dishes, like lamb chops *milanese* or roasted chicken. **Known for:** unpretentious neighborhood spot; laid-back brunch; excellent cocktails. *Average main: $22* ⊠ *132 Greene Ave., Brooklyn* ☎ *718/576-3584* ⊕ *www.aitarestaurant.com* ⊗ *No lunch Mon.* Ⓜ *C, G to Clinton–Washington Aves.*

★ Emily

$$ | **Pizza.** When this small, narrow restaurant opened in early 2014, it quickly became a sensation for the roster of innovative and delicious pizzas (the Colony, with pepperoni, pickled jalapeños, and honey hits perfect notes of sweet, salty, and spicy), as well as the standout (though pricey) Emmy burger. It's still really hard to choose, so bring a friend and share both. **Known for:** the Emmy burger; thin-crust pizzas; the first of a minichain of Emily restaurants. *Average main: $20* ⊠ *919 Fulton St., Brooklyn* 🕾 *718/844–9588* ⊕ *www.pizzalovesemily.com* Ⓜ *C to Clinton–Washington Aves.*

Habana Outpost

$ | **Latin American.** If the hearty Cuban sandwich and spicy Mexican corn on the cob don't win you over, the exceptionally potent margarita slushies will. An indoor–outdoor party scene with democratic appeal and crowd-pleasing Latin American fare, Habana Outpost occupies a spacious corner lot that is popular with families, first dates, and the occasional raucous-but-friendly group of revelers. **Known for:** family-friendly; party atmosphere on the patio; movie nights. *Average main: $9* ⊠ *757 Fulton St., Fort Greene* 🕾 *718/858–9500* ⊕ *www. habanaoutpost.com* ⊟ *No credit cards* Ⓜ *C to Lafayette Ave.; G to Fulton St.*

★ Locanda Vini e Olli

$$$ | **Italian.** Tucked behind a 150-year-old pharmacy facade on a quiet residential block, this convivial restaurant feels like a large family farmhouse in Tuscany. The menu skews hearty, in the pastas (perhaps sage-scented pappardelle with braised rabbit), mains (there are usually preparations of beef, lamb, duck, and fish to choose among), and antipasti (the chicken liver risotto starter is sublime), with seasonal vegetables showcased as well. **Known for:** hearty Italian fare; upscale family spot; seasonal wine dinners. *Average main: $25* ⊠ *129 Gates Ave., Brooklyn* 🕾 *718/622–9202* ⊕ *www.locandany.com* ⊘ *No lunch* Ⓜ *C, G to Clinton–Washington Aves.*

Mettā

$$ | **Argentine.** The corner location with an elegant interior and giant front windows looking onto the Fort Greene brownstones and cherry trees make this one of the prettiest restaurants in a neighborhood chock-full of pretty streets, pretty shops, and pretty families. The food is innovative and South American influenced, with an emphasis on cooking with fire, so anything charred stands out. **Known for:**

romantic atmosphere; fire-cooked food; great wine and cocktail list. *Average main: $22 ⊠ 197 Adelphi St., Fort Greene ☎ 718/233–9134 ⊕ www. mettabk.com ⊗ Closed Mon. No lunch Ⓜ C to Lafayette Ave.; G to Fulton St.*

Roman's

$$$ | Italian. Part of an all-star Brooklyn restaurant group that includes Williamsburg favorites Diner and Marlow & Sons, this seasonally focused eatery has an Italian accent. Menus change daily and include farm-fresh fare like wintry fennel salads or pork meatballs *in brodo,* or delicacies like artichoke-studded house-made spaghetti in summer. **Known for:** seasonal menu; hip scene; great for special occasions. *Average main: $26 ⊠ 243 DeKalb Ave., Fort Greene ☎ 718/622–5300 ⊕ www.romansnyc. com ⊗ No lunch Ⓜ C to Lafayette Ave.; G to Clinton–Washington Aves.*

★ Speedy Romeo

$$ | Pizza. The menu at this rustic neighborhood spot features a roster of superb thin-crust pizzas, including the Dangerfield, with mini meatballs, and a St. Louis–style specialty with provel cheese (a combination of cheddar, Swiss, and provolone cheeses), pepperoni, and pickled chilies. Still, you'd be remiss if you didn't explore the offerings from the wood-fired grill, if only for an appetizer. **Known for:** inventive thin-crust pizzas; grill specials; St. Louis provel cheese. *Average main: $21 ⊠ 376 Classon Ave., Brooklyn ☎ 718/230–0061 ⊕ www.speedy-romeo.com Ⓜ G to Classon Ave.*

Walter's

$$ | American. A sister restaurant to Williamsburg's Walter Foods, this buzzy bistro has a menu of upscale comfort food, a comely crowd, and rosy-hued lighting that gives the space a glamorous vibe. Stop in for a cocktail after a day in Fort Greene Park, or come for a heartier repast courtesy of Walter's raw bar, satisfying main dishes (fried chicken with garlic mashed potatoes is a winner), and market-fresh veggie sides. **Known for:** fun bar scene; upscale comfort food; great cocktails. *Average main: $20 ⊠ 166 DeKalb Ave., Fort Greene ☎ 718/488–7800 ⊕ www. walterfoods.com/walters Ⓜ B, Q, R to DeKalb Ave.; C to Lafayette Ave.; G to Fulton St.*

🍸 Bars and Nightlife

Frank's Cocktail Lounge

A local institution, Frank's has live jazz bands, hip-hop DJs, R&B-centric karaoke, and a crowd that joins Barclays- and BAM-goers with dapper neighborhood denizens in throwback fedoras. There's usually a cover charge weekends, but drinks are modestly priced (cash only) and immodestly potent—all the better to fortify patrons heading for the dance floor. ⊠ *660 Fulton St., Fort Greene ☎ 718/399–2240 Ⓜ 2, 3, 4, 5, B, Q, D, N, R to Atlantic Ave.–Barclays Ctr.; G to Fulton St.; C to Lafayette Ave.*

★ Hot Bird

A barbecue-chicken joint was the previous tenant of this laid-back bar with a large patio on an industrial stretch of Atlantic Avenue—hence the name. Stake out a picnic table for a group of friends, or just hit it up as a casual date spot. There's a small menu of tacos to go with the drinks, which is good, because once you're here, you won't want to leave. ⊠ *546 Clinton Ave., Brooklyn* ☎ *718/230–5800* Ⓜ *C to Clinton–Washington Aves.*

Karasu

Tucked away behind Walter's restaurant, this dimly lit, refined spot specializes in creative cocktails, sake, shochu (a Japanese rice liquor), and Japanese whiskey. The vibe is clubby but calm, and the relatively small menu includes a few raw dishes, delicious *karaage* (Japanese fried chicken), and several other items that make a perfect shared dinner. ⊠ *166 DeKalb Ave., Fort Greene* ☎ *347/223–4811* ⊕ *www.karasubk.com* Ⓜ *B, Q, R to DeKalb Ave.; C to Lafayette Ave.; G to Fulton St.*

The Mayflower

Tiny, candlelit, and discreet, this attitude-free cocktail den is equally suited to a romantic tryst, casual nightcap, or predinner drink while awaiting your table at Aita, the owners' Italian restaurant next door. The bar is located in a carriage house and, unlike many other watering holes in the neighborhood, usually stays open until 2 or 3 am. ⊠ *132 Greene Ave., Brooklyn* ☎ *718/399–2240* ⊕ *www.aitarestaurant.com* Ⓜ *C, G to Clinton–Washington Aves.*

Sisters

Walk into this airy skylit space, all wood and white with soaring ceilings, and you can't help but fall a little bit in love. The cocktails are well executed, food is served all day (starting with coffee and pastries in the morning, then lunch, weekend brunch, and dinner), and there's live music in the back room a few times a week, too. ⊠ *900 Fulton St., Brooklyn* ☎ *347/763–2537* Ⓜ *C to Clinton–Washington Aves.*

 Performing Arts

★ Brooklyn Academy of Music (BAM)

Founded in 1861 and operating at its current location since 1908, BAM is a multidisciplinary performing arts center that has grown to span three edifices, including the Beaux Arts, seven-story Peter Jay Sharp building. It's known for innovative performances of many types, and the facilities include an unadorned "black box" theater, dance venues, a four-screen movie theater, an opera house, a ballroom, and a café. ⊠ *Peter Jay Sharp Bldg., 30 Lafayette Ave., Fort Greene* ☎ *718/636–4100* ⊕ *www.bam.org* Ⓜ *2, 3, 4, 5, B, D, N, Q, R at Atlantic Ave.–Barclays Ctr.; G to Fulton St.; C to Lafayette Ave.*

Prospect Heights

Fort Greene

Clinton Hill

PROSPECT HEIGHTS

Park Slope

Crown Heights

Prospect Park

A small neighborhood bordered by several larger ones, Prospect Heights feels like Brooklyn in microcosm. Historic brownstones and longtime attractions such as the Brooklyn Museum and Brooklyn Botanic Garden anchor the neighborhood physically and psychically, while the Barclays Center sports and entertainment arena, which debuted in 2012, looms large as a harbinger of further expansion. Since the early 2000s, Prospect Heights has progressed from Park Slope's sleepy northeastern satellite into an appealing, magnetic enclave with a distinct identity. A 21-block historic district, north of Grand Army Plaza between Flatbush and Washington avenues (the neighborhood's western and eastern borders) has helped keep development in Prospect Heights relatively modest, attractive, and largely chain-free. Both Washington Avenue and Vanderbilt Avenue, the main drags, are lined with shops, restaurants, and bars. The Barclays Center dominates the neighborhood's northwestern corner, but so far the blockbuster venue and its events haven't spoiled the neighborhood's overall mellow vibe, and touches like the Barclays's 135,000-square-foot rooftop garden, installed in 2015, represent an attempt to integrate the behemoth into the surrounding environment. With hundreds of arena-affiliated housing units being built or on the way, though, it remains to be seen how long the status quo will be maintained.—*Updated by Emily Saladino*

Sights

Barclays Center

This rust-tinted spaceship of an arena houses two sports franchises—basketball's Brooklyn Nets and ice hockey's New York Islanders—and hosts events from rock concerts to circuses. With a capacity rivaling Madison Square Garden's, Barclays also has plenty of room to offer concessions courtesy of local restaurateurs, including Williamsburg Pizza, Paisano's Burger, and Calexico.

✉ *620 Atlantic Ave., Prospect Heights* ☎ *917/618–6100* ⊕ *www.barclays-scenter.com* Ⓜ *2, 3, 4, 5, B, D, N, Q, R to Atlantic Ave.–Barclays Ctr.; G to Fulton St.; C to Lafayette Ave.; LIRR to Atlantic Terminal.*

★ Brooklyn Botanic Garden

A verdant 52-acre oasis, the BBG charms with its array of "gardens within the garden," including an idyllic Japanese hill-and-pond garden, a stunning rose garden, and a Shakespeare garden. The Japanese cherry arbor turns into

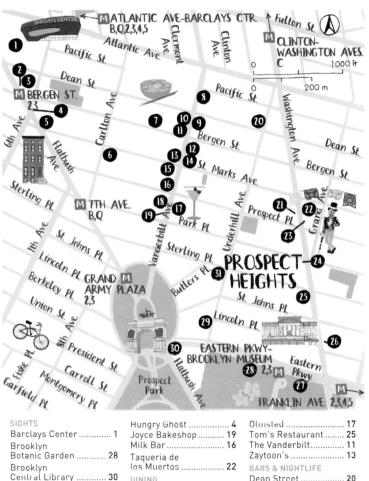

a breathtaking cloud of pink every spring, and the Sakura Matsuri two-day cherry blossom festival is the largest public-garden event in America. There are multiple entrances, and a variety of free garden tours are available with admission; check the website for seasonal details. ✉ *150 Eastern Pkwy., Prospect Heights* ☎ *718/623–7200* ⊕ *www.bbg.org* ✑ *$15* ⊙ *Closed Mon. except major holidays* Ⓜ *2, 3 to Eastern Pkwy.–Brooklyn Museum; 2, 3, 4, 5 to Franklin Ave.; S to Botanic Garden; B, Q to Prospect Park.*

Brooklyn Central Library

This celebrated art deco edifice is a neighborhood anchor, its monumental facade resembling an open book with bronze panels. Inside, this cathedral to knowledge houses more than a million catalogued books, magazines, and multimedia materials, and serves as a respite for those requiring quiet study, free Wi-Fi, or a quick bite from the café by local pie maker Four & Twenty Blackbirds. ✉ *10 Grand Army Plaza, Prospect Heights* ☎ *718/230–2100* ⊕ *www.bklynpubliclibrary.org* Ⓜ *2, 3 to Grand Army Plaza or Eastern Pkwy.–Brooklyn Museum; B, Q to 7th Ave.*

★ Brooklyn Museum

Spanning 560,000 square feet of exhibition space, this beaux arts behemoth is New York's second-largest museum and houses one of the world's most impressive collections of Egyptian art, as well as important African, pre-Columbian, Native American, feminist, and contemporary collections. Monthly

GETTING HERE

The Barclays Center, at the northern end of Prospect Heights, sits above the Atlantic Avenue–Barclays Center station. To visit the Brooklyn Botanic Garden or the bars and restaurants on Washington Avenue, get off at Eastern Parkway–Brooklyn Museum. For Vanderbilt Avenue, start at 7th Avenue or Grand Army Plaza.

(except September) First Saturday nights offer free entry and a neighborhood party vibe with music and cash bars. ✉ *200 Eastern Pkwy., Prospect Heights* ☎ *718/638–5000* ⊕ *www.brooklynmuseum.org* ✑ *$16 suggested donation, $25 combo ticket with Brooklyn Botanic Garden* ⊙ *Closed Mon. and Tues.* Ⓜ *2, 3 to Eastern Pkwy.–Brooklyn Museum.*

Cook Space

Culinary confidence, Vietnamese street food, and pasta 101 are among the topics of classes offered at this beautifully restored, postindustrial space in a former widget warehouse. Founded by a Brooklyn restaurateur and former Danny Meyer line cook, this studio also hosts after-school children's programs and private events. Check the website for class schedules. ✉ *603 Bergen St., Suite 202, Prospect Heights* ☎ *718/230–8400* ⊕ *cookspacebrooklyn.com* Ⓜ *2, 3 to Bergen St.; C to Clinton–Washington Aves.; B, Q to 7th Ave.*

Shopping

Kith Brooklyn

The Brooklyn flagship of this cult New York City sneaker label (with its own shop within Bergdorf Goodman) stocks highly coveted footwear and sportswear in a mod, sophisticated space. Kith Treats, a proprietary ice cream and cereal bar within the store, occupies a window-facing front corner and has a sidewalk takeout window. ⊠ *233 Flatbush Ave., Prospect Heights* ☎ *347/889–6114* ⊕ *kith.com* Ⓜ *2, 3 to Bergen St.; 4, 5 to Atlantic Ave.–Barclays Ctr.*

Unnameable Books

This tiny, beloved bookstore is jam-packed with poetry, fiction, art books, comics, and all sorts of esoteric titles. ⊠ *600 Vanderbilt Ave., Prospect Heights* ☎ *718/789–1534* Ⓜ *B, Q to 7th Ave.*

 Coffee and Quick Bites

Ample Hills Creamery. Branch at 623 Vanderbilt Ave. *See Chapter 9, Gowanus, for full listing.*

Bergen Dean Sandwich Shop

$ | American. Tucked a block behind the Barclays Center, this no-frills takeout gem has a small menu anchored by a slow-cooked, aromatic porchetta sandwich that is large enough to share (though you won't want to), as well as soups, snacks, and desserts. Other sandwich stars include chicken schnitzel, pork rib, and kimchi-spiced barbecue chicken. **Known for:** sandwiches; takeout; quick, casual service. *Average main: $9* ⊠ *64 6th Ave., Prospect Heights* ☎ *347/463–9191* ⊕ *www.bergendean.com* Ⓜ *2, 3 to Bergen St.; 2, 3, 4, 5, B, D, N, Q, R to Atlantic Ave.–Barclays Ctr.*

Hungry Ghost

$ | Café. One of Brooklyn's mini-chains, Hungry Ghost fuels the borough with coffee, teas, and snacks in sleek, mid-century-modern environs. The beans are from Oregon's cult label Stumptown, and the sandwiches and many baked goods are made in-house. **Known for:** artisanal coffee; snacks; sandwiches. *Average main: $8* ⊠ *235 Flatbush Ave., Prospect Heights* ☎ *718/483–8666* ⊕ *www.hungryghostbrooklyn.com* Ⓜ *2, 3 to Bergen St.*

Joyce Bakeshop

$ | Café. The neighborhood's friendliest place for a cuppa joe (locally roasted Gorilla coffee) is known for its exceptional pastries—from French *macarons* to scones to whoopie pies—baked fresh on the premises. Table seating is available in the bright, airy room. **Known for:** pastries; Gorilla coffee; friendly atmosphere. *Average main: $7* ⊠ *646 Vanderbilt Ave., Prospect Heights* ☎ *718/623–7470* ⊕ *www.joycebake-shop.com* Ⓜ *2, 3 to Grand Army Plaza; B, Q to 7th Ave.*

Milk Bar

$ | Café. The veggie-friendly menu at this snug, Australian-accented corner café includes avocado toast, egg dishes, sandwiches, and salads, plus coffee and tea. There's table seating inside and outdoor chairs when the weather's warm. **Known for:** light fare; vegetarian options; coffee. *Average main: $9 ⊠ 620 Vanderbilt Ave., Prospect Heights ☎ 718/230–0844 ⊕ www.milkbar-brooklyn.com ◷ No dinner ⊟ No credit cards Ⓜ 2, 3 to Grand Army Plaza; B, Q to 7th Ave.*

★ Taqueria de los Muertos

$ | **Mexican.** Casual and unassuming, this taquería with Day of the Dead decor serves what are arguably the neighborhood's best tacos, as well as burritos, nachos, and tostadas with a variety of fillings and four types of beans. Just a few blocks north of the Brooklyn Museum, it's among the best options for a quick, low-fuss meal (there's no table service on weekdays). There are brunch options on weekends. **Known for:** great tacos; quick bite; four types of beans. *Average main: $7 ⊠ 663 Washington Ave., Prospect Heights ☎ 718/484–0310 ⊟ No credit cards Ⓜ 2, 3 to Eastern Pkwy.–Brooklyn Museum; C to Clinton–Washington Aves.; S to Park Pl.*

 Dining

Alta Calidad

$$ | **Mexican.** Specializing in modern Mexican creations and craft cocktails, this buzzy spot occupies a snug, bright corner space with large picture windows. Crowds flock for seasonally inspired menu items as varied as Mexican Coca-Cola lamb ribs, vegetarian tacos, and creative brunch fare. **Known for:** modern Mexican dishes; buzzy scene; cock-tails and South American wines. *Average main: $21 ⊠ 552 Vanderbilt Ave., Prospect Heights ☎ 718/622–1111 ⊕ altacalidadbk.com Ⓜ 2, 3 at Bergen St.; B, Q at 7th Ave.*

Amorina Cucina Rustica

$$ | **Italian.** This homey pizza-and-pasta restaurant splits the difference between sophisticated artisanal fare for adults and simpler, kid-friendly options. While thin-crust pies are available with just sauce and cheese (this is Brooklyn, so the tomatoes are organic and the mozzarella farm-fresh), Amorina shines when it comes to unusually topped pizzas, such as Gorgonzola and fruit with figs, or a sauce-free potato pie with caramelized onions. **Known for:** unusual pizza toppings; family-friendly fare; classic pastas. *Average main: $14 ⊠ 624 Vanderbilt Ave., Prospect Heights ☎ 718/230–3030 ⊕ www.amorinapizza.com ◷ No lunch ⊟ No credit cards Ⓜ 2, 3 to Grand Army Plaza; B, Q to 7th Ave.*

Cheryl's Global Soul

$$ | **International.** Breezy and casual, this place serves internationally inspired comfort foods like Creole barbecue shrimp and Korean bibimbap, plus sandwiches, egg dishes at brunch, and a kids' menu. Local families and gallerists at the nearby Brooklyn Museum convene in the slim space, where the wine list is similarly globally minded, and cocktails range from traditional (margarita, rum punch) to inventive (a stinger made with Brazilian cane liquor and homemade gingerade). **Known for:** international comfort food; cocktails; family-friendly dining. *Average main: $18* ✉ *236 Underhill Ave., Prospect Heights* ☎ *347/529-2855* ⊕ *cherylsglobalsoul. com* ◷ *No dinner Mon.* Ⓜ *2, 3 to Grand Army Plaza; B, Q to 7th Ave.*

Chuko

$$ | Japanese. A small, reliably tasty menu of signature ramen headlines this Prospect Heights institution for noodle bowls, buns, gyoza, beer, and sake. Long waits for a table have (slightly) abated since the operation moved in 2016 to this (slightly) larger location offering 20 more seats, but expect crowds, especially during winter months. **Known for:** ramen; very popular; lines. *Average main: $14* ✉ *565 Vanderbilt Ave., Prospect Heights* ☎ *718/576-6701* ⊕ *www. barchuko.com* Ⓜ *2, 3 to Bergen St.; A, C to Clinton-Washington Aves.; B, Q to 7th Ave.*

El Atoradero

$$ | Mexican. A Bronx transplant, this bright, cheery nook turns out superlative Mexican dishes ranging from crowd-pleasing tacos and flautas to regional specialties such as tender roasted rabbit, all at affordable prices. The cozy space has a backyard garden and bar seating; those seeking additional libations can head a few doors down to the proprietors' agave-centric bar, Madre Mezcaleria. **Known for:** authentic Mexican cooking; friendly service; affordable prices. *Average main: $18* ✉ *708 Washington Ave., Prospect Heights* ☎ *718/399-8226* ⊕ *elatoraderobrooklyn.com* Ⓜ *2, 3 to Grand Army Plaza; B, Q to 7th Ave.*

James

$$ | American. Part of the charm of this acclaimed New American eatery is its jewel-box location on a corner of two otherwise residential brownstone blocks. The menu features fresh takes on comforting staples like tender sautéed skate, Angus beef burgers (arguably the neighborhood's best), flavorful roast chicken, and creative brunch dishes. **Known for:** upscale American favorites; cozy, stylish space; Angus beef burger. *Average main: $22* ✉ *605 Carlton St., Prospect Heights* ☎ *718/942-4255* ⊕ *www.jamesrestaurantny.com* ◷ *No lunch weekdays* Ⓜ *2, 3 to Bergen St.; B, Q to 7th Ave.*

Mitchell's Soul Food

$ | Southern. A no-frills neighborhood institution, Mitchell's offers soul food classics like fried and smothered chicken, collard greens, and superlative corn bread to locals, including families and a smattering of solo diners, at tables and booths or via takeout service. What it lacks in curb appeal, it makes up for in durability—Mitchell's has been dishing out the good stuff since the 1970s. **Known for:** soul food; casual atmosphere; corn bread. *Average main: $11* ✉ *617A Vanderbilt Ave., Prospect Heights* ☎ *718/789-3212* ◷ *Closed Sun. and Mon.* Ⓜ *A, C to Clinton-Washington Aves.; 2,3 to Bergen St.; B, Q to 7th Ave.*

Morgan's Brooklyn Barbecue

$$ | Barbecue. This Texas-style BBQ joint a couple blocks south of the Barclays Center pairs well with a night of hoops or beats. A friendly spot with urban-roadhouse decor, a large bar area, and a serious custom oak smoker, Morgan's scores with its array of well-tenderized meats sold by the pound—beef or pork ribs, pulled pork, smoked chicken—and anchored by exceptional slow-roasted brisket (order it; you won't regret it). **Known for:** indoor-outdoor seating; hearty barbecue; great slow-roasted brisket. *Average main: $18 ⊠ 267 Flatbush Ave., Prospect Heights ☎ 718/622–2224 ⊕ www. morgansbrooklynbarbecue.com M 2, 3 to Bergen St.; 2, 3, 4, 5, B, D, N, Q, R to Atlantic Ave.–Barclays Ctr.; B, Q to 7th Ave.*

★ Olmsted

$$ | American. The accolades keep rolling in for this elegant, perennially packed farm-to-table restaurant serving seasonal, creative fare alongside cocktails, wine, and desserts including house-made strawberry-rhubarb soft serve. The twinkling rear garden has bench seating and a kitchen garden, plus a warbling live quail. **Known for:** elegant, seasonal menus; twinkling year-round garden; reservations needed well in advance. *Average main: $22 ⊠ 659 Vanderbilt Ave., Prospect Heights ☎ 718/552–2610 ⊕ olmstednyc.com ⊘ No lunch M B, Q to 7th Ave.; 2, 3 to Grand Army Plaza.*

Tom's Restaurant

$ | Diner. Lines form down the block every weekend around midday for a spot at this snug, old-school counter spot with straightforward diner food such as scrambled eggs, deli sandwiches, and standout lemon-ricotta flapjacks (ask for flavored butters). The legend of Tom's may outstrip the reality (contrary to myth, Suzanne Vega's hit "Tom's Diner" is *not* named for the place), but at least staffers offer the folks in line coffee, orange slices, and bacon or sausage bites while they wait. **Known for:** straightforward diner favorites; long waits but friendly service; lemon-ricotta flapjacks. *Average main: $8 ⊠ 782 Washington Ave., Prospect Heights ☎ 718/636–9738 ⊕ www. tomsbrooklyn.com ⊘ No dinner ▭ No credit cards M 2, 3 to Eastern Pkwy.–Brooklyn Museum; 2, 3, 4, 5 to Franklin Ave.; S to Botanic Garden.*

The Vanderbilt

$$ | Modern American. The mellowest of longtime Brooklyn chef Saul Bolton's several restaurants in the borough, the Vanderbilt offers a broad menu in a large space. Comfort food like meatballs, chicken, and pork chops are joined by creative small plates, a charcuterie menu, a well-chosen craft-beer menu, cocktails, and brunch specialties (including delicious shrimp and grits). **Known for:** large, varied menu; spacious interior; craft beer. *Average main: $16 ⊠ 570 Vanderbilt Ave., Prospect Heights ☎ 718/623–0570 ⊕ www.thevanderbiltnyc.com ⊘ No lunch weekdays M 2, 3 to Bergen St.; C to Clinton–Washington Aves.; B, Q to 7th Ave.*

Zaytoons

$ | Lebanese. Offering excellent Middle Eastern standards (think salads, hummus, falafel, shawarma, and kebabs) at reasonable prices, Zaytoons is a longtime local favorite, especially in warmer months when the spacious outdoor garden is open. Service is quick and friendly and dishes are consistently well spiced, fresh, and delicious. **Known for:** BYOB Tuesdays with $5 corkage fee; big garden open in warm weather; Lebanese dips, falafel, and shawarma pitza. *Average main: $10 ⊠ 594 Vanderbilt Ave., Prospect Heights ☎ 718/230-3200 Ⓜ 2, 3 to Bergen St.; A, C to Clinton–Washington Aves.; B, Q to 7th Ave.*

Bars and Nightlife

Dean Street
This sizable, stalwart neighborhood spot does double duty as both a local watering hole and a casual, New Orleans–style eatery whose offerings could be termed pub-menu-plus (gumbo, chicken and dumplings, shrimp po'boy). Weekend brunch draws families and couples for a stick-to-your-ribs menu, while the nighttime crowd is solidly local and unpretentious, whether enjoying the game on TV or shooting the breeze over a bite. ⊠ *755 Dean St., Prospect Heights ☎ 718/783-3326 ⊕ www.deanstreetbrooklyn.com Ⓜ A, C to Clinton–Washington Aves.; B, Q to 7th Ave.*

Gold Star Beer Counter
A rotating list of craft brews spanning 16 taps and 50-plus bottles and cans attracts a friendly, low-key crowd of hops heads and casual revelers to this mod, narrow space with counter stools, a standing bar, and a few small tables. The kitchen turns out coffee and pastries by day and elevated pub grub by night, and there is a sidewalk window for on-the-go growler purchases. ⊠ *176 Underhill Ave., Prospect Heights ⊕ goldstarbeercounter.com Ⓜ 2, 3 to Grand Army Plaza; B, Q to 7th Ave.*

★ Tooker Alley
Knowledgeable bartenders mix drinks from a multipage, Roaring '20s–style cocktail menu at this bar that takes pride in reinventing old staples with local themes, such as the Manhattanite and a Crown Heights negroni made with local Sorel liqueur. It also offers a small menu of snacks like stuffed dates and smoked trout on toast points. The staff are friendly and solicitous, and the backyard is open in summer. ⊠ *793 Washington Ave., Prospect Heights ☎ 347/955-4743 ⊕ www.tookeralley.com Ⓜ 2, 3 to Eastern Pkwy.–Brooklyn Museum; 2, 3, 4, 5 to Franklin Ave.; S to Botanic Garden.*

Washington Commons
With more than a dozen taps and many more bottles and cans, the rotating craft-beer selection is one of two major attractions at this friendly pub. The other is its large, concrete beer-garden space out back—ample summer seating for you, a slew of friends, and a bag of takeout (there is no kitchen, but outside food is welcome). ⊠ *434 Park Pl., Prospect Heights ☎ 718/230-3666 Ⓜ 2, 3 to Eastern Pkwy.–Brooklyn Museum; B, Q to 7th Ave.; S to Park Pl.*

The Way Station

Unabashed geeks flock to this cocktail bar–cum–performance space known for live music, cozy banquettes, a vaguely steampunk theme, and the Dr. Who–style Tardis bathroom (seriously). The actual barroom is small but welcoming, and you can bring your cocktail over to the ample side room to watch everything from local folkies to burlesque. ⊠ *683 Washington Ave., Prospect Heights* ☎ *347/627–4949* Ⓜ *2, 3 to Eastern Pkwy.–Brooklyn Museum; B, Q to 7th Ave.; S to Park Pl.*

★ Weather Up

A classy speakeasy-style bar with an unmarked door and an amber-lit interior framed by subway tile, Weather Up is an excellent date spot. Good drinks come to those who wait, and on a busy night it can take a few minutes for your painstakingly well-crafted cocktail to arrive. The list changes seasonally, and the leafy backyard opens in summer. ⊠ *589 Vanderbilt Ave., Prospect Heights* ☎ *212/766–3202* ⊕ *www.weatherupnyc.com* Ⓜ *2, 3 to Bergen St.; A, C to Clinton–Washington Aves.; B, Q to 7th Ave.*

Park Slope and Prospect Park

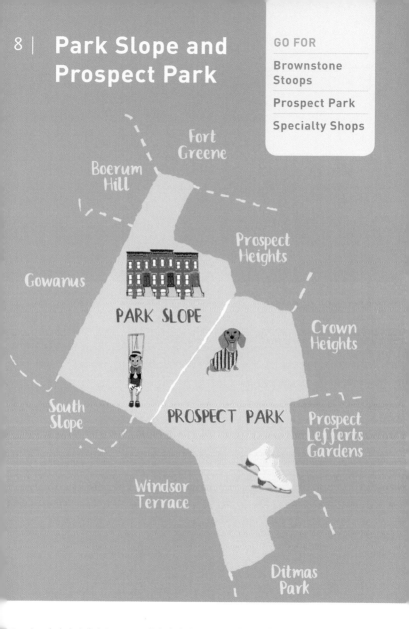

Fort Greene

Boerum Hill

Prospect Heights

Gowanus

PARK SLOPE

Crown Heights

South Slope

PROSPECT PARK

Prospect Lefferts Gardens

Windsor Terrace

Ditmas Park

Park Slope can feel more like a liberal arts college town than a neighborhood in Brooklyn—one filled with literary luminaries and thriving shops and restaurants. It's hard to miss the neighborhood's focus on families—double-wide strollers and kid-friendly activities and businesses abound, especially along the main drags of 5th and 7th avenues. On Park Slope's eastern edge, bordering Prospect Heights and Prospect Park, gorgeous 19th-century architecture built for the well-to-do casts a glow of civility in the form of Queen Anne and Renaissance Revival row houses, oriel and bay windows, and elegant stoops framed by cast-iron rails. By the middle of the 20th century, many of the wealthy denizens who had built up the area had been lured away to the New York City suburbs, and the neighborhood became more working class. In the 1960s and 1970s many of the homes here were bought inexpensively and renovated—not coincidentally, the *Old-House Journal*, a magazine about fixing up old houses, was first published in Park Slope in 1973. Today Park Slope is prime real estate, encompassing Brooklyn's largest historic district and the lovely expanse of Prospect Park, which provides greenery and endless diversions, among them the world-class summer performance festival Celebrate Brooklyn! —*Updated by Christina Knight*

◉ Sights

Lefferts Historic House
A visit to this Dutch Colonial farmhouse, built in 1783 and moved from nearby Flatbush Avenue to Prospect Park in 1918, is a window into how Brooklynites lived in the 19th century, when the area was predominantly farmland. Rooms are furnished with antiques and reproductions from the 1820s, when the house was last redecorated. ✉ *452 Flatbush Ave., Prospect Park* ☎ *718/789–2822* ⊕ *www.prospectpark.org/lefferts* 💲 *$3 suggested donation* ⊗ *Closed weekdays* Ⓜ *B, Q, S to Prospect Park.*

LeFrak Center at Lakeside
The highlight of this 26-acre space in Prospect Park is the all-season ice- and roller-skating rink. The walkways, the esplanade near the lake, and the Music Island nature reserve are—all part of the original Olmsted and Vaux plans—make for a pleasant stroll. Themed roller-skating night takes place on Friday, April through October; in winter, the rink hosts hockey and curling clinics for all ages. The Bluestone

Café offers sunny outdoor seating year-round. ⊠ *171 East Dr., Prospect Park* ☎ *718/462–0010* ⊕ *www. lakesidebrooklyn.com* ⊠ *Skating $6 weekdays, $9 weekends; rentals $6–$7* ⊙ *Rink: closed days vary by season* Ⓜ *B, Q, S to Prospect Park; Q to Parkside Ave.*

Old Stone House

This reconstructed Dutch farm-house dating to 1699, played a central role in the Battle of Brooklyn, one of the largest battles of the Revolutionary War, and survived until the 1890s. The small museum here focuses on the Revolutionary era in Brooklyn from 1776 until 1783. Art exhibits, concerts, plays, and other commu-nity events take place year-round, including a ball game to celebrate the Brooklyn Baseball Club, which started here and gave rise to the Brooklyn Dodgers. ⊠ *Washington Park/J.J. Byrne Playground, 336 3rd St., Park Slope* ☎ *718/768 3195* ⊕ *www.theoldstonehouse.org* ⊠ *$3 suggested donation* ⊙ *Closed Mon.–Thurs.* Ⓜ *R to Union St.; F, G, R to 4th Ave.–9th St.*

Park Slope Historic District

Stretching over 33 beautiful resi-dential blocks, Park Slope's historic district, the largest in Brooklyn, is mostly between St. John's Place and 15th Street, and between 7th Avenue and Prospect Park West. Prospect Park West, Carroll Street, and Montgomery Place have some of the neighborhood's most elegant homes, representing the area's architectural styles: Queen Anne, Romanesque Revival, Italianate, French Second Empire, Neo-Grec. Notable buildings that stand out from the row houses are the Montauk Club (built in 1899), at the corner of 8th Avenue and Lincoln Place, designed by Francis Kimball to resemble a famous Gothic palace in Venice; and the three 19th-century churches on the corners of 7th Avenue and St. John's Place. Take an hour or so and stroll around. The Park Slope House Tour (*see Best Brooklyn Events in Chapter 1*), held every May, is a chance to see inside some of the gorgeous homes in the area. ⊠ *Park Slope* Ⓜ *2, 3 to Grand Army Plaza; B, Q to 7th Ave.; F, G to 7th Ave. or Prospect Park.*

★ Prospect Park

Brooklyn residents are passionate about Prospect Park, and with good reason: lush green spaces, gently curved walkways, summer concerts, vivid foliage in autumn, and an all-season skating rink make it a year-round getaway. In 1859 the New York Legislature decided to develop plans for a park in the fast-growing city of Brooklyn. After landscape architects Frederick Law Olmsted and Calvert Vaux completed the park in the late 1880s, Olmsted remarked that he was prouder of Prospect Park than of any of his other works—Manhattan's Central Park included. ⊠ *450 Flatbush Ave., Prospect Park* ☎ *718/965–8951* ⊕ *www.prospectpark.org* ⊠ *Carousel: $2* ⊙ *Carousel: closed Mon.–Wed.* Ⓜ *2, 3 to Grand Army Plaza; F, G to 7th Ave. or 15th St.–Prospect Park; B, Q to 7th Ave.*

Atlantic Ave.

Pacific St.

Dean St.

Bergen St.

St. Marks Ave.

Prospect Pl.

Park Pl.

Sterling Pl.

Washington Ave.

PROSPECT HEIGHTS

Grand Army Plaza

EASTERN PKWY.-BROOKLYN MUSEUM
2,3 Ⓜ

Flatbush Ave.

Botanic Gardens

Washington Ave.

PROSPECT PARK

48

47

44

PROSPECT PARK
B,Q,S Ⓜ

45

49

46

Prospect Park Audubon Center

Built in 1904 and styled after the grand 16th-century National Library of St. Mark's, in Venice, the center sits opposite the Lullwater Bridge, making it an idyllic spot for watching swans, ducks, and wedding photo sessions. Interactive exhibits, park tours, and programs for kids revolve around nature education. Sign up for a bird-watching tour to see some of the 200 species spotted here. ⊠ *101 East Dr., Prospect Park* ☎ *718/287–3400* ⊕ *www.prospectpark.org/audubon* ☉ *Closed Mon.–Wed.; Jan.–Mar., hrs vary (call ahead)* Ⓜ *B, Q, S to Prospect Park.*

Prospect Park Zoo

Of the 1,000 inhabitants and 170 species at the small, engaging zoo, playful sea lions and busy meerkats are the standout entertainers for kids. An outdoor discovery trail has a simulated prairie-dog burrow, a duck pond, and creatures such as red pandas and emus in habitat. A café serves lunch. ⊠ *450 Flatbush Ave., Prospect Park* ☎ *718/399–7339* ⊕ *www.prospectparkzoo.com* ⤳ *$8* Ⓜ *2, 3 to Eastern Pkwy.; B, Q S to Prospect Park.*

★ Smorgasburg

More than a hundred of New York City's best and brightest cooks and culinary artisans unite in Prospect Park (replacing the Brooklyn Bridge Park Pier 5 location) every Sunday to form the city's hottest foodie flea market. An offshoot of the Brooklyn Flea, this food bazaar extravaganza has launched countless culinary crazes (ramen burger,

GETTING HERE

The Grand Army Plaza station on the 2, 3 line is right outside the main entrance to Prospect Park and the Brooklyn Museum. The 7th Avenue stop on the B/Q is best for Park Slope's main shopping and dining arteries and the Prospect Park Bandshell. Any train that serves Atlantic Avenue–Barclay's is convenient to bustling 5th Avenue, as is the 2, 3 to Bergen Street.

anyone?), and most vendors are small-scale, homegrown operators. Lines can grow long and vendors can sell out as the afternoon goes on, so head over early in the day if possible. There is also an outpost on the Williamsburg waterfront (between Kent Avenue and North 7th Street) on Saturdays, as well as smaller Smorgasburgs in Queens, at Coney Island, at the South Street Seaport, and at Central Park SummerStage events. The latest addition to this grub empire is a collaboration with the Winter Flea, held weekends year-round at Industry City in Sunset Park. The larger Smorgasburgs are seasonal and generally take place from May through October, but check the website to confirm. ⊠ *Breeze Hill, Prospect Park* ⊕ *www.brooklynflea.com* Ⓜ *Q, S to Prospect Park; F, G to 15th St.–Prospect Park.*

Shopping

A. Cheng
Owner Alice Cheng curates a lovely selection of elegant women's clothing. Choose from her own A. Cheng line, Sessùn from France, or Local from Italy. Ace&jig's hand-woven designs speak to palpable comfort. Featherweight cashmere, silk mock turtlenecks, and loose dresses are perfect for work or play. ⊠ 466 Bergen St., Park Slope ☎ 718/783–2826 ⊕ www.achengshop.com Ⓜ 2, 3 to Bergen St.

★ Annie's Blue Ribbon General Store
The perfectly giftable, Brooklyn-made products at this variety store include Apotheke candles and diffusers, Bellocq teas, Claudia Pearson's hand-drawn tea towels, Brooklyn Slate, and Bocce's Bakery birthday-cake treats for your favorite canine. Brooklyn-themed tchotchkes, ecofriendly cleaning supplies (including a Common Good Refill station), stationery, and toys round out the selection. ⊠ 202 5th Ave., Park Slope ☎ 718/522–9848 ⊕ www.blueribbongeneralstore.com Ⓜ R to Union St.

Barnes & Noble
Two floors of books, a vast and varied selection of magazines, and an extensive collection of travel information for New York City and beyond welcome browsers at this busy location of the national chain. Popular storytelling events for children take place Saturday mornings. ⊠ 267 7th Ave., Park Slope ☎ 718/832–9066 Ⓜ F, G to 7th Ave.

★ Beacon's Closet, Park Slope
Of the four secondhand clothing shops in a two-block stretch, this one's the best. The well-organized local chain carries vintage and modern styles for men and women. The racks are updated daily, thanks to area fashionistas who sell their cast-offs here. Most threads cost $11 to $23 (the latter for, say, a nearly new Paul Smith jacket from a season or three ago, or an Italian Sisley wool coat). If secondhand isn't your thing, the shop also sells brand-new costume jewelry, hosiery, journals, and hand-poured Paddywax candles in a wide variety of scents and packaging. ⊠ 92 5th Ave., Park Slope ☎ 718/230–1630 ⊕ www.beaconscloset.com Ⓜ 2, 3 to Bergen St.

Bhoomki
At designer Swati Argade's women's boutique, every handmade piece of jewelry or pair of shoes, hand-blocked silk shirt or woven scarf has a story that reflects sustain-ability, fair trade, and artisan traditions. That's true whether the dress, accessory, or staple item comes from Peru, Mexico, or India. Argade's own Bhoomki studio designs most of the textiles, which are custom-made by weavers and block printers. Other ethical labels include KowTow (all organic cotton), Kordal, and Rujuta Sheth. ⊠ 158 5th Ave., Park Slope ☎ 718/857–5245 ⊕ www.bhoomki.com Ⓜ R to Union St.

Bird. Branch location at 316 5th Ave. *See Chapter 13, Carroll Gardens, for full listing.*

★ Brooklyn Superhero Supply Co.

If you can't crack a smile in this store—where all proceeds from superhero costumes, gear, and secret identity kits benefit 826NYC's writing and tutoring programs for kids—step immediately into its Devillainizer cage. Once cleansed, browse the invisibility, dark matter, and cloning tools sold in plastic jugs and fake paint cans. The clever labels listing "ingredients" and "warnings" are worth every ounce of the tongue-in-cheek superpower products. Hours are daily 11–5 but the volunteer staff must sometimes answer the call of duty elsewhere; call ahead when making a special visit. ✉ *372 5th Ave., Park Slope* ☎ *718/499–9884* ⊕ *www.superherosupplies.com* Ⓜ *F, G to 4th Ave.; R to 9th St.*

The Clay Pot

Family-owned since 1969, this Park Slope stalwart carries glassware, ceramics, jewelry, and wedding rings, nearly all made in the United States and in limited numbers. Ceramics include potbelly mugs, platters silk-screened with illustrations from nature, and etched vases. Other gift items include intricately carved refillable candles, wallets made from Cadillac leather, Davin & Kesler woodworked cuff links and business card holders, and jewelry by designers such as Christina Stankard (beadwork) and Adel Chefridi (metals). ✉ *162 7th Ave., Park Slope* ☎ *718/788–6564* ⊕ *www.clay-pot.com* Ⓜ *F, G to 7th Ave.; B, Q to 7th Ave.*

Community Bookstore

In a neighborhood known for its large population of authors, editors, and bloggers, it's fitting to have a bookstore where pride of place goes to literature. Works in translation are well represented among the staff picks, and there's a whole section devoted to small presses including New Directions, Europa Editions, and NYRB Classics. Local authors are prominently featured and readings take place two or three times a week. ✉ *143 7th Ave., Park Slope* ☎ *718/783–3075* ⊕ *www. communitybookstore.net* Ⓜ *2, 3 to Grand Army Plaza; B, Q to 7th Ave.; F, G to 7th Ave.*

Den

Men and women get equal rack space at this hip newcomer highlighting independent labels and local designers who cut their teeth and cloth at Parsons School of Fashion. The shop is a creation of the shops Min-k (Park Slope) and Odin (Manhattan). Women can find Min-k, Uzi, Elk, and H. Fredriksson; menswear sways toward Odin, but there are also items by La Paz and Creep. Odin perfumes and a small selection of accessories, women's shoes, and children's clothes round out the offerings. ✉ *360 7th Ave., Park Slope* ☎ *929/250–2062* Ⓜ *F, G to 7th Ave.*

Norman and Jules

Unique toys and dolls from around the world score points with children and their parents at this high-end toy shop. It stocks an excellent selection of wooden toys as well as games and puzzles, household-helper tools, and Tegu magnetic blocks. There are arts and crafts kits and supplies, too. ⊠ *158 7th Ave., Park Slope* ☎ *347/987–3323* ⊕ *www.normanandjules.com* Ⓜ *2, 3 to Grand Army Plaza; F, G to 7th Ave.*

Otto
Splurge on Anni Kuan's New York–made designs, Catherine André's limited-edition knits, and clothing by other European designers like Anne Willi, Niu, Bitte Kai Rand, and Schella Kann at this carefully curated women's shop that still carries the Bondi Bather bathing suits and lingerie it began with in 1989. New to the bathing mix are Amara Felice's vintage cuts, handmade in Brooklyn. Woolens from Europe and handbags by Alfred Stadler and Hobo are a few of the other luxurious items. ⊠ *354 7th Ave., Park Slope* ☎ *718/788–6627* ⊕ *www.ottobrooklyn.com* Ⓜ *F, G to 7th Ave.*

powerHouse Arena. Branch location at 1111 8th Ave. *See Chapter 10, DUMBO, for full listing.*

Stories Bookshop + Storytelling Lab
This compact children's bookstore enthralls with its selection of beautifully illustrated contemporary titles and graphic novels, for infants to adolescents, and there are classics for your nostalgia, too. Titles that encourage confidence and curiosity about the world are easily found and the staff is adept at recommending books for your listener or reader. Gauge your tot's interests at the weekday story time

and meet authors at the readings every Sunday. ⊠ *458 Bergen St., Park Slope* ☎ *718/369–1167* ⊕ *www. storiesbk.com* Ⓜ *2, 3 to Bergen St.*

★ V Curated
Designer Vanessa Vallarino's motto for her cooperative of 38 emerging designers is one-of-a-kind, and handmade in the United States. Aesthetics lean toward eye-catching but also simple and clean women's wear and accessories. The silk tops, pants, and dresses with soft colors and gently blurred patterns come from Vallarino's on-site studio. ⊠ *456 Bergen St., Park Slope* ☎ *347/987–4226* ⊕ *www.vcurated.com* Ⓜ *2, 3 to Bergen St.*

☕ Coffee and Quick Bites

Café Grumpy. Branch location at 383 7th Ave. *See Chapter 3, Greenpoint, for full listing.*

★ Cafe Regular
$ | Café. A charming European atmosphere and a focus on top-quality products like La Colombe coffee, Jacques Torres hot chocolate, and Dona chai (hand-brewed in Brooklyn) make the two tiny locations in Park Slope feel like a special-occasion getaway. Snacks are few but the relatively new red banquettes make it comfy to linger longer. **Known for:** cold brew; running out of pastries; its interior wall mural. *Average main: $5* ⊠ *158a Berkeley Pl., Park Slope* ☎ *718/783–0673* ⊕ *www.caferegular.com* ⊗ *No dinner* Ⓜ *2, 3 to Grand Army Plaza; B, Q to 7th Ave.*

The Chocolate Room

$ | Café. Chocolate from Belgium and France fills the molten, moist, frosty, frothy, and gooey desserts made at this cozy, sit-down dessert café founded by a Park Slope couple in 2005. The main event is dessert— warm chocolate chip almond cake, flourless chocolate cake with raspberry framboise, a black chocolate stout float, or any of the seasonal or weekend-only specials. **Known for:** brownie sundae; date night; chocolate gift boxes. *Average main: $9* ✉ *51 5th Ave., Park Slope* ☎ *718/783–2900* ⊕ *www.thechocolateroombrooklyn. com* Ⓜ *2, 3 to Bergen St.*

Colson Patisserie

$ | Café. Expertly baked pastries like croissants, tarts, turnovers, macaroons, and financiers are the darling showpieces at this Belgian-inspired bakery, though the soups, salads, and sandwiches are also delicious. There are tiny self-service tables and, in good weather, sidewalk seats. **Known for:** being Bill De Blasio's favorite coffee spot; tight seating at peak weekend hours. *Average main: $8* ✉ *374 9th St., Park Slope* ☎ *718/965–6400* ⊕ *www.colson-pastries.com* Ⓜ *F, G to 7th Ave.*

Du Jour Bakery

$ | Café. This unpretentious café is owned by TJ and Vera Obias, husband-and-wife pastry chefs who make everything on premises "du jour"—some of the delectable classic French and American baked goods are even made fresh twice a day. Breakfast, brunch, and lunch menus include frittatas, melts, and salads. **Known for:** custom-made

cakes; pastry selection. *Average main: $9* ✉ *365 5th Ave., Park Slope* ☎ *347/227–8953* ⊕ *www.dujourbakery. com* ☾ *No dinner* Ⓜ *R to 9th St.; F, G to 4th Ave. or 7th Ave.*

★ Gorilla Coffee

$ | Café. This popular Brooklyn-based brand has fueled Park Slope since 2002 with its specially blended roasts and beans from direct-trade and family farms. There's a pour-over menu with the concise descriptions you'd expect on a fine-wine menu. **Known for:** Espresso-a-go-go blend; signature Sunrise drink of cold brew, plus OJ and dash of vanilla syrup; great location outside the Bergen Street subway station. *Average main: $5* ✉ *472 Bergen St., Park Slope* ☎ *347/987–3766* ⊕ *www.gorillacoffee.com* Ⓜ *2, 3 to Bergen St.*

Kulushkät

$ | Middle Eastern. At this excellent falafel joint, the falafel balls (classic, spicy, or with spinach and mushrooms) are fried to order and everything is made fresh daily. Run by a family of Jewish-Moroccan heritage, the shop serves mostly takeout, but there are a few stools. **Known for:** thick-cut, not shaved shawarma; pickled red cabbage. *Average main: $10* ✉ *446C Dean St., Park Slope* ☎ *347/799–1972* ⊕ *www. kulushkat.com* Ⓜ *2, 3 to Bergen St.*

Nacho Macho Taco

$ | Mexican. This family-run, cheerful hole-in-the-wall brings flavors from the owners' Mexican roots to Tex-Mex-style tacos, burritos, and enchiladas. Meats are marinated for days and the flourishes of pico de gallo, mole, and avocado sauce with tomatillo are made fresh daily (sometimes twice) and are amazing. **Known for:** quick and friendly service; fresh and varied ingredients; sauces. *Average main: $8 ⊠ 82 5th Ave., Park Slope ☎ 718/622-8282 Ⓜ 2, 3 to Bergen St.*

SkyIce Sweet and Savory

$ | Thai. The taste-bud-popping ice creams and sorbets made by this corner Thai spot are served by the scoop and pint. Flavors include durian, black sesame seaweed, and Thai tea and coffee; sorbets like lychee rose and raspberry cilantro taste like they came straight from a garden. **Known for:** 12-flavor ice-cream sampler; family recipes. *Average main. $10 ⊠ 63 5th Ave., Park Slope ☎ 718/230-0910 ⊕ www. skyice.net ⊗ No lunch Tues. Ⓜ 2, 3 to Bergen St.*

⅄ Dining

★ al di là Trattoria

$$$ | Italian. Roughly translated as "the great beyond," al di là has been consistently packed since it opened in 1998, and it's easy to understand why: perfectly prepared dishes from northern Italy in a cozy atmosphere. The warm farro salad with seasonal ingredients and goat cheese is perfectly al dente; the hand-pinched ravioli are delicious; and meatier entrées like braised rabbit, pork loin scaloppine, and charcoal-grilled young Bo Bo chicken are highlights. **Known for:** knowledgeable servers; ragus; not taking reservations.

Average main: $26 ⊠ 248 5th Ave., Park Slope ☎ 718/783-4565 ⊕ www. aldilatrattoria.com Ⓜ R to Union St.

★ Convivium Osteria

$$$ | Italian. The rustic Italian farmhouse decor, Mediterranean wines, and candlelight at this renowned neighborhood restaurant will transport you to another land even before you try the food. The menu is inspired by Italy, with hints of Spain and Portugal, and organic ingredients and naturally raised, free-range meats are used in dishes like braised rabbit or pine nut-crusted rack of lamb. **Known for:** romantic ambience; coveted wine cellar seating; antipasti selection. *Average main: $27 ⊠ 68 5th Ave., Park Slope ☎ 718/857-1833 ⊕ www. convivium-osteria.com ⊗ No lunch Ⓜ 2, 3 to Bergen St.*

Fonda

$$ | Mexican. Authentic and flavorful contemporary Mexican food, perfectly mixed cocktails, and amiable staff define this cozy restaurant—the first of three in New York City overseen by award-winning chef and cookbook author Roberto Santibanez. It's tempting to order by sauce alone: enchiladas with mole, scallops and shrimp with avocado serrano sauce, and poblano peppers with roasted-tomato chipotle sauce. **Known for:** happy hour at the bar; duck zarape; tight seating when crowded. *Average main: $24 ⊠ 434 7th Ave., Park Slope ☎ 718/369-3144 ⊕ www.fondarestaurant.com ⊗ No lunch weekdays Ⓜ F, G to 7th Ave. or 15th St.–Prospect Park.*

Hugo + Sons

$$ | Italian. Executive chef/owner and neighborhood resident Andrea Taormina pays homage to his homeland of Sicily and the Park Slope vibe in this sunny corner spot with red leather banquettes. The individual pizzas, "land" and "sea" items change seasonally, but the kids menu and wagyu beef burger are steadies, as are the gluten-free options. **Known for:** mix of Italian and French cuisine; $1 oysters at the bar; great light through plate- glass windows. *Average main: $21* ✉ *367 7th Ave., Park Slope* ☎ *718/499–0020* ⊕ *www.hugoandsons.com* ⊗ *No lunch weekdays* Ⓜ *F, G to 7th Ave.*

Piccoli Trattoria

$$ | Italian. Homemade pastas, an enthusiastic and knowledgeable staff, and the steady hand of a chef who's been with the trattoria from the start in 2011 make this a neighborhood Italian favorite worth a trip. The risottos are creamy with aged Parmesan and surprising pairings like cauliflower and anchovies pangrattato; the black spaghetti Calabrese with shrimp and chorizo is authentic with roasted tomatoes and Calabrian chili. **Known for:** bang for your buck; flexibility on substitutions; the osso-buco special. *Average main: $18* ✉ *522 6th Ave., Park Slope* ☎ *718/788–0066* ⊕ *www.piccoliny.com* ⊗ *No lunch weekdays* Ⓜ *F, G to 15th St.*

Rose Water

$$$ | American. The delicious combinations of tastes and textures at this small restaurant stand out for creativity. Seasonal dishes range from venison to duck breast to scallops, and the accompaniments hit the mark, whether grilled squid with aji dolce and bronze fennel, or fingerling potato with trout roe and crème fraîche. **Known for:** $32 three-course menu Sunday–Thursday; $60 five-course menu Friday, Saturday with off-menu items; posting the dinner menu daily online. *Average main: $26* ✉ *787 Union St., Park Slope* ☎ *718/783–3800* ⊕ *www.rosewaterrestaurant.com* ⊗ *No lunch weekdays* Ⓜ *R to Union St.*

Stone Park Cafe

$$$ | Modern American. Park Slope natives own this elegant restaurant where the New American menus change seasonally, but the scallop and marrow tacos appetizer always star on the menu, along with homemade pastas. Main courses like veal flank steak with Jersey asparagus and scallops with green gazpacho as well as the pastry chef's desserts are plated with finesse. **Known for:** $39 three-course menu Monday–Thursday; great sidewalk seating across from the park that holds the Stone House. *Average main: $27* ✉ *324 5th Ave., Park Slope* ☎ *718/369–0082* ⊕ *www.stoneparkcafe.com* ⊗ *No lunch Mon.* Ⓜ *R to Union St. or 9th St.*

Sugarcane

$$ | Caribbean. Pan-Caribbean cuisine favoring Trinidad has made this restaurant a hit since 2002. Hands-down winners are seafood dishes with Trinidadian curry; braised oxtails with sweet peppers and dark rum; and jerk chicken with

Red Stripe barbecue sauce. **Known for:** authentic dishes; tight space; loud music. *Average main: $24* ⊠ *238 Flatbush Ave., Park Slope* ☎ *718/230–3954* ⊘ *No lunch* Ⓜ *2, 3 to Bergen St.*

Sun-in-Bloom
$$ | **Vegetarian.** Those seeking vegan, gluten-free, or macrobiotic sustenance fill the tables at this bright, rustic eatery. Favorites include the "live" (uncooked) Bloom burger with sunflower dill dressing, the lasagna layered with butternut squash and roasted tomato, smoky shiitake bacon BLT wrapped in collards, the Reuben with marinated tempeh, and just about any of the desserts. **Known for:** the vegetable lasagna; selection of prepackaged to-go items. *Average main: $14* ⊠ *460 Bergen St., Park Slope* ☎ *718/622-4303* ⊕ *www.suninbloom.com* ⊘ *No dinner weekends* Ⓜ *2, 3 to Bergen St.*

Talde
$$ | **Asian Fusion.** *Top Chef* alumnus Dale Talde throws bold flavors into Asian-American comfort foods at this casual restaurant where seating at the chef's counter and antique mahogany carvings add touches of showbiz. Favorite dishes include Korean fried chicken with a kimchi-yogurt sauce cooled by sliced grapes, fried oyster and bacon pad thai, and pretzel pork and chive dumplings. **Known for:** unusual flavor pairings; piecemeal service style. *Average main: $24* ⊠ *369 7th Ave., Park Slope* ☎ *347/916-0031* ⊕ *www.taldebrooklyn.com* Ⓜ *F, G to 7th Ave.*

🍸 Bars and Nightlife

★ Barbès
Outstanding regulars like the Django Reinhardt mantle-bearer Stephane Wrembel, western-swingers Brain Cloud, and Slavic Soul Party spin threads of folk and "ethnic" into 21st-century music, while the Erik Satie Quartet keeps Satie, Britten, and other classical composers relevant. Performances take place in the back room, where a pitcher is passed to collect the $10 suggested cover. Up front, the somewhat musty bar has a laid-back vibe and a full cocktail menu. ⊠ *376 9th St., Park Slope* ☎ *347/422-0248* ⊕ *www.barbesbrooklyn.com* Ⓜ *F, G to 7th Ave.*

★ Blueprint
Homemade bitters, syrups, and ginger beer make every carefully made cocktail here all the more tasty. Try the house favorite Smoky Mary's, with chipotle tequila, agave, and an alderwood smoked salt rim. The warm atmosphere is mid-century modern meets old Western hotel, and in summer you can sip your tiki-style drink on the back patio. An impressive menu of small dishes is served until 2 am. All breads and desserts are made in-house. ⊠ *196 5th Ave., Park Slope* ☎ *718/622-6644* ⊕ *www.blueprint-brooklyn.com* Ⓜ *R to Union St.*

Brookvin
This cozy wine bar owned by the Big Nose Full Body wine store on the same block has knowledgeable staff who are happy to help you choose, and offer tastes, from the selection of wines by the glass, half bottle,

or bottle. Friends who want beer or cocktails have options, too. The food menu includes shareable options like cheese and charcuterie plates, pâtés, meatballs with polenta, or mac 'n' cheese. Happy hour lasts until 7 pm on weekdays and until 5 pm on weekends. There's a pleasant back patio. ⊠ *381 7th Ave., Park Slope* ☎ *718/768–9463* ⊕ *www. brookvin.com* Ⓜ *F, G to 7th Ave.*

The Gate

The corner patio makes The Gate, now in its third decade, the best spot to drink outdoors in the Slope. The menu is all about the rotating selection of craft beers—about 25 on tap at any given time—and hard-to-find bottles and cans. There's also a full bar. Trivia, television show viewing parties, and open-mike nights keep the neighborhood vibe alive. ⊠ *321 5th Ave., Brooklyn* ☎ *718/768–4329* ⊕ *www.thegatebrooklyn.com* Ⓜ *F, G to 4th Ave.; R to 9th St.*

Union Hall

This neighborhood standby has something going on just about every night. On the main floor, two bocce courts and a library nook with couches and fireplace are popular hangouts; downstairs, there are smart comedy shows featuring *Daily Show* and *Saturday Night Live* regulars, eclectic talks, or DJs spinning. The outdoor patio is open in good weather. The menu of perfectly tasty burgers, sandwiches, and bar snacks (the beer cheese is a highlight) means the patrons tend to settle in for the evening. Events are either free or have a modest cover ($5 to $20). ⊠ *702 Union St.,*

Park Slope ☎ *718/638–4400* ⊕ *www. unionhallny.com* Ⓜ *R to Union St.*

Wolf & Deer

The stylish, U-shape bar says it all: bars should be a social spot to meet your neighbors, people-watch, and showcase how a busy bartender works under pressure. Cocktails are taken so seriously, the menu is a bound book through which you can also leaf to hearty and well-made bar food. If the great happy hour doesn't draw you in, the view through the wide-open window will. ⊠ *74 5th Ave., Park Slope* ☎ *718/398–3181* ⊕ *www. wolfanddeerbrooklyn.com.*

 Performing Arts

Puppetworks

Marionette puppets have been enacting classic fairy tales like *Beauty and the Beast, Goldilocks and the Three Bears, Jack and the Beanstalk,* and *Pinocchio* for children at this storefront theater since 1990. A friendly puppeteer preps the young audience on theater etiquette before each performance. Afterward, theater education continues with a Q&A. Public performances are given on weekends only; call or email for reservations. ⊠ *338 6th Ave.* ☎ *718/965–3391* ⊕ *www.puppetworks. org* 🎟*$11* Ⓜ *F, G to 7th Ave.*

Boerum Hill

Cobble Hill

Carroll Gardens

GOWANUS

PICKLES

Park Slope

Red Hook

South Slope

seeing ★★☆☆☆ | Shopping ★☆☆☆☆ | Dining ★★★★☆ | Nightlife ★★★★☆

A former center of industrial and shipping activity and home to the stevedores who worked the waterfront, Gowanus has become known for its innovative maker spaces, cool bars and restaurants, experimental performance venues, and funky design shops. Bordered by the long-established neighborhoods of Carroll Gardens to the northwest and Park Slope to the northeast, Gowanus and its spacious warehouses, many of which had been abandoned by the 1970s, began attracting artists and creative businesses during that decade, though redevelopment didn't really begin to gain momentum until the early 2000s. Brooklyn Boulders lures a community of rock climbers and gives a West Coast feel to the neighborhood. Make no mistake, Gowanus is still up-and-coming: empty lots and the polluted Gowanus Canal, an Environmental Protection Agency Superfund site, present challenges. However, walk along 3rd or 4th Avenue or Union Street and you'll soon run across a coffee bar, cocktail den, or offbeat shop worth investigating, plus casket companies.—*Updated by Christina Knight*

Sights

Brooklyn Boulders

Sprawled across a 22,000-square-foot space, Brooklyn Boulders is the go-to for climbing enthusiasts as well as novices interested in learning the ropes. All visitors must first complete a short safety course before taking to the walls, which vary in size and difficulty. Private lessons and group classes are also available, along with open climbing sessions. Acro yoga is one of several nonclimbing classes offered. ⊠ *575 Degraw St., Brooklyn* ☎ *347/834–9066* ⊕ *www.brooklynboulders.com* Ⓜ *2, 3, 4, 5, B, D, N, Q, R to Atlantic Ave.–Barclays Ctr.; R to Union St.*

Gowanus Canal

Once a bustling commercial waterway serving the neighborhoods of Red Hook, Carroll Gardens, and Park Slope, the nearly 2-mile Gowanus Canal is now one of the most polluted bodies of water in the United States and is designated an Environmental Protection Agency Superfund site. Seven bridges cross the 100-foot-wide canal, which may sometimes smell, but is still photogenic. Juxtapositions of nature and industry—and a wealth of sunlight—make the waterway an urban charmer. The Gowanus Canal Conservancy organization is a nonprofit dedicated to making the canal and its shores a healthy part of the community. ⊠ *Brooklyn*

⊕ *gowanuscanalconservancy.org* Ⓜ *F,
G to Smith–9th Sts.; R to 9th St.*

 Shopping

⭐ Claireware

The hand-thrown, glazed porcelain items made here by Claire Weissberg lean to blues and greens or black and white, and patterns include soft-focus peacock eyes, fish scales and turtle backs, as well as swirls and dots—all aimed to bring some cheer to a kitchen. Call before you come; hours can be flexible. ⊠ *543 Union St., Brooklyn* ☎ *718/875–3977* ⊕ *www.claireware. net* Ⓜ *R to Union St.*

Find Home Furnishings

A visit to Find Home Furnishings has become a pilgrimage for vintage and one-of-a-kind furniture geeks. One reason is the prices, which are considerably lower than at similar high-end Manhattan shops. Popular items include trunks, dining room tables, benches, stools, and desks—ranging in style from mid-century modern to reproductions to Indonesian teak. ⊠ *43 9th St., Brooklyn* ☎ *718/369–2705* ⊕ *www. findhomefurnishings.com* Ⓜ *F, G to Smith–9th Sts.*

⭐ Gowanus Souvenir Shop

Everyone will find a charming or cheeky treasure to covet here. Most items are custom made for the shop by local artists and designers. Riffs on the canal's Superfund status include the Gowanus is Superfun trucker caps and Gowanus Swim Team shirts. Beyond the Mutopia Toy figurines and It Came From the Gowanus comic are rotating fine art works, jewelry, and books. ⊠ *567 Union St.* ☎ *424/888–2869* ⊕ *www.gowanus-souvenir.com* ⊙ *Closed Mon.–Thurs.* Ⓜ *R to Union St.*

The Modern Chemist

International beauty products from Asia, Scandinavia, and beyond (Korean face masks, SachaJuan hair care, Turkish perfumes) as well as hip little gift items fill shelves at this tiny branch of the independent pharmacy. The DUMBO location (62 Water Street) is three times the size, with more offerings. ⊠ *191 4th Ave., Brooklyn* ☎ *718/369–6100* ⊕ *www.themodernchemist.com* Ⓜ *R to Union St.*

Whole Foods

This isn't your average Whole Foods Market. Built to serve the grocery-starved, food-obsessed Brooklyn population and to display the borough's exploding local food scene, the 55,000-square-foot store includes a restaurant, rooftop beer garden with trivia night, and, of course, aisles and aisles of artisanal foodstuffs. Hit the massive salad and prepared-food bar, and take your bounty to the spacious seating area upstairs. ⊠ *214 3rd St., Brooklyn* ☎ *718/907–3622* ⊕ *www. wholefoodsmarket.com* Ⓜ *F, G to 4th Ave.; R to Union St. or 9th St.*

CARROLL GARDENS

Court St.

Hoyt St.

Ⓜ BERGEN ST.
F,G

Carroll Park
Carroll St. Ⓜ

Sackett St.

Bord St.

GOWANUS CANAL

Thomas Greene Playground

CARROLL ST.
F,G Carroll St.

Union St.

President St.

Carroll St.

1st Pl.
2nd Pl.
3rd Pl.

Smith St.
2nd St.
3rd St.
4th St.
5th St.

1st St.

20

18
17
15 16
14
19

13
12
11 10

GOWANUS

8

9
1st St.

3rd St.

3rd Ave.

7

Nevins St.

1

Ⓜ SMITH/9TH STREETS.
F,G

2

2nd Ave.

6

4th Ave.

Hamilton Pl.

10th St.
11th St.
12th St.
13th St.
14th St.
15th St.

3rd Ave.

4

3

5

6th St.
7th St.
8th St.
9th St.

9TH ST. Ⓜ
R

4TH AVE. Ⓜ
F,G

St. Marks Pl.

M

ATLANTIC AVE.
2,3,4,5,B,Q

Warren St.

Baltic St.

4th Ave.

Butler St.

Douglass St.

22

24

23

M

25

BERGEN ST.
2,3

ett St.

Degraw St.

26

27

UNION ST.
M R

5th Ave.

President St.

Carroll St.

Garfield Pl.

0 ———— 1000 ft
0 ———— 200 m

2nd St.

Washington
Park   3rd St.

6th Ave.

4th St.

5th St.

PARK
SLOPE

Ave.

🍵 Coffee and Quick Bites

★ Ample Hills Creamery

$ | Café. Among artisanal ice-cream fans, nobody has earned a more passionate following than Ample Hills, the Prospect Heights creamery started by screenwriter Brian Smith and his wife, Jackie Cuscuna. Their Gowanus branch churns with families and ice-cream aficionados, who pack the second-floor terrace and attend ice-cream-making classes. **Known for:** the dark chocolate–based It Came from Gowanus; rooftop terrace; windows into the production kitchen. *Average main: $5* ✉ *305 Nevins St., Brooklyn* ☎ *347/725–4061* ⊕ *www.amplehills.com* Ⓜ *F, G to Carroll St.; R to Union St.*

★ Four & Twenty Blackbirds

$ | Café. Pie, ordered whole or by the slice, is why you come to this rustic flagship of the Elsen sisters' enterprise. The bakers are experts on the topic, having written a definitive book and appeared in basically every food magazine around. **Known for:** salted caramel apple pie; whole pie orders; seasonal speciality pies. *Average main: $5* ✉ *439 3rd Ave., Brooklyn* ☎ *718/499–2917* ⊕ *www.birdsblack.com* Ⓜ *F, G to 4th Ave.; R to 9th St.*

Root Hill Cafe

$ | Café. This beloved neighborhood café keeps 'em coming with inexpensive and tasty breakfast and lunch, baked goods, and Nobletree Brazilian coffee roasted in Red Hook. Large windows let in lots of light, which is one of the reasons that customers tend to

GETTING HERE

The Carroll Street, Union Street, 9th Street, and 4th Avenue stations are in or within walking distance of Gowanus. You can also walk down 4th Avenue from Atlantic Avenue–Barclays Center to reach the concentration of places to visit between Douglass and Carroll streets.

linger. **Known for:** being serious about closing at 5 pm; hipster vibe; customers working while drinking (coffee). *Average main: $4* ✉ *262 4th Ave., Brooklyn* ☎ *718/797–0100* Ⓜ *R to Union St.*

🍴 Dining

Bar Tano

$$ | Italian. This Italian corner restaurant with a lively bar scene is perfect for a casual meal, happy hour deals at the bar, and a leisurely weekend brunch or a romantic dinner. The menu hits all the high points, from bucatini pesto and carbonara, to a daily whole fish and wine-braised short ribs with polenta. **Known for:** the bar's happy hour pizzettas and snacks; Italian wines at reasonable prices. *Average main: $18* ✉ *457 3rd Ave., Brooklyn* ☎ *718/499–3400* ⊕ *www.bartano.com* Ⓜ *F, G to 4th Ave.; R to 9th St.*

★ Claro

$$ | Mexican. The cuisine of Oaxaca, the Mexican state where chef-owner T.J. Steele lives part-time, gets its most intense dedication in the barbacoa: slow-cooked, marinated

goat served with a consommé.
Known for: chef-owners T.J. Steele and Chad Shaner; El Buho mezcal cocktails; grill-watching from the patio bar. *Average main: $22 ⊠ 284 3rd Ave., Brooklyn ☎ 347/721–3126 ⊕ www.clarobk.com ⊘ No lunch weekdays Ⓜ R to Union St.*

Dinosaur Bar-B-Que
$$ | Barbecue. When this upstate legend opened an outpost in Gowanus, it was if Union Street was anointed barbecue row. With 180 seats, sidewalk picnic tables, and family-style orders, it's good for groups. **Known for:** pulled pork—the dish that put this Syracuse-based chain on the map; live music Friday and Saturday nights. *Average main: $18 ⊠ 604 Union St., Brooklyn ☎ 347/429–7030 ⊕ www.dinosaurbar-bque.com Ⓜ R to Union St.*

Ghenet
$$ | Ethiopian. Laid-back and welcoming Ghenet is where to dig into Ethiopian dishes with *injera*, the slightly spongy sourdough bread, made fresh daily. Use it to scoop up fragrantly spiced dishes like tuna or steak tartare, *kitfo* (finely chopped prime beef, cooked and aggressively seasoned), and the aromatic *doro wett* chicken stew. **Known for:** tej (homemade honey wine); can accommodate gluten-free eaters with advance notice. *Average main: $18 ⊠ 384 Douglass St., Brooklyn ☎ 718/230–4475 ⊕ www.ghenet.com ⊘ No lunch weekdays Ⓜ 2, 3 to Bergen St.; R to Union St.; 2, 3, 4, 5, B, D, N, Q, R to Atlantic Ave.–Barclays Ctr.*

Hey Hey Canteen
$$ | Asian Fusion. The Asian comfort food and creative twists on standard dishes pique curiosity, and with inexpensive pricing, it's possible to try a lot of items in a single visit at this low-key spot. On the unusual side, there's eggplant fries with shallot aioli, a Caesar salad made with chrysanthemum leaves, and green fried rice with spinach and cilantro. **Known for:** closes at 9:30 pm; creative mix of ingredients; Hong Kong fried chicken sandwich. *Average main: $13 ⊠ 400 4th Ave., Brooklyn ☎ 347/987–3830 ⊕ www.heyheycanteen.com ⊘ Closed Mon. No lunch Sat. Ⓜ F, G to 4th Ave.; R to 9th St.*

Insa
$$ | Korean Barbecue. A neon sign beckons those hungry for Korean barbecue and cuisine, thirsty for natural wines and Red Hook–made Tokki soju, and itching to sing karaoke. One door leads to the pine-paneled dining room with 18 mahogany grill tables, beyond which are five karaoke rooms. **Known for:** group dinner or karaoke occasions; hot dates in the bar; craft suju, made in America. *Average main: $24 ⊠ 328 Douglass St., Brooklyn ☎ 718/855–2620 ⊕ www.insabrooklyn.com ⊘ No lunch weekdays Ⓜ R to Union St.*

Littleneck
$$ | Seafood. Diners at this "upscale shack" feel like they've been transported to a beachside New England restaurant, where clams—the eponymous littlenecks are popular—and ice-cold craft

beer are served early and often. Look for a Portuguese chorizo-and-seafood stew and an excellent lobster roll on the menu. **Known for:** happy hour specials; delicious cocktails; clam chowder. *Average main: $22* ⊠ *288 3rd Ave., Brooklyn* ☎ *718/522–1921* ⊕ *www.littleneck-brooklyn.com* ⊗ *Closed Tues. No lunch weekdays* ▭ *No credit cards* Ⓜ *F, G to Carroll St.; R to Union St.*

Pig Beach

$$ | **Barbecue.** Executive chef Matt Abdoo, a top prize winner at the Memphis' World Champion Barbecue contest, brings his four-star restaurant chops (Del Posto) to this breezy indoor/outdoor space where glazed baby back ribs, secret-sauce burgers topped with pulled pork, smoked fried chicken, and a 30-ounce pork chop with peach habanero jam please everyone from families to twentysomething groups. **Known for:** 12–13 guest pitmasters from Memorial Day through December; Ohio State football game viewing; families in the early hours, adult crowd at night. *Average main: $15* ⊠ *480 Union St., Brooklyn* ⊕ *www.pigbeachnyc.com* ⊗ *Closed Mon. No lunch weekdays* Ⓜ *R to Union St.; F, G to Carroll Gardens.*

Runner & Stone

$$ | **Mediterranean.** Day or night, bread—everything from brioche to baguettes to ciabatta and more—and house-made pasta are the main draws at this farm-to-table restaurant, café, and bakery owned by baker Peter Endriss and chef Chris Pizzulli. Mornings mean fresh croissants and breakfast pastries, lunch focuses on sandwiches with choice of side, and dinner features seasonally inspired entrées. **Known for:** house-cured duck pastrami and smoked salmon at brunch; breads and pastries; prize-winning interior design. *Average main: $22* ⊠ *285 3rd Ave., Brooklyn* ☎ *718/576–3360* ⊕ *www.runnerandstone.com* Ⓜ *R to Union St.; F, G to Carroll St.*

🍸 Bars and Nightlife

★ The Bell House

One of the top music venues in the borough, the Bell House hosts big-name rock musicians, cult comedy acts and live podcast recordings, and weekly trivia and karaoke in the bustling front bar area. Brooklynites (and Manhattanites, too) come not only for the performances but also for the excellent beer selection. ⊠ *149 7th St., Brooklyn* ☎ *718/643–6510* ⊕ *www.thebellhouseny.com* Ⓜ *F, G to Smith–9th Sts. or 4th Ave.; R to 9th St.*

Black Mountain Wine House

Tucked away on a residential section of Hoyt Street, Black Mountain nearly hides in plain sight; the outside looks more like a cabin than a wine bar stocked with a long list of wines by the glass (both old and new world), craft beer, and a great food menu. Come in fall or winter, when the fireplace makes the dim space quite cozy. ⊠ *415 Union St., Brooklyn* ☎ *718/522–4340* ⊕ *www.blkmtnwine-house.com* Ⓜ *F, G to Carroll St.*

Canal Bar

Yep, it's a dive bar—and one with a strong connection to Chicago (drink specials during a Cubs or Bears game). Happy hour goes until 8 pm, drinks are cheap, and the bourbon list is better than average, as is the crowd of regulars who hang out here at all hours, quaffing drafts of Goose Island and Revolution Brewing. The bar is small and narrow but it also has a small back patio. ⊠ 270 3rd Ave., Brooklyn ☎ 718/246-0011 ⊕ www. canalbar.com Ⓜ R to Union St.; F, G to Carroll St.

Lavender Lake

Built by a group of set designers who occupy an adjacent studio, Lavender Lake's main draw is its fabulous back patio. When the weather is nice, well-turned-out local residents sip craft beers and excellent cocktails under a string of lights outside; during the day, it's a chill place to read a book or play a board game. The fried brussels sprouts get thumbs up, but the kitchen is hit or miss. ⊠ 383 Carroll St., Brooklyn ☎ 347/799-2154 ⊕ www.lavenderlake.com Ⓜ F, G to Carroll St., R to Union St.

Littlefield

Part gallery, part event space, part late-night club, Littlefield is a place where you can expect the unexpected. The new location on Sackett Street is stylish, still intimate, and has good sight lines. It's only open for events, which are almost nightly: comedy shows (Wyatt Cenac's "Night Train" series), game shows, live music, and storytelling are some of what you'll find on the calendar. ⊠ 635 Sackett St., Brooklyn ⊕ www.little-field.com Ⓜ 2, 3 to Bergen St.; 4, 5, B, D, N, Q, R to Atlantic Ave.–Barclays Ctr.; R to Union St.

Royal Palms Shuffleboard

Could there be anything more Brooklyn than a shuffleboard club with employees cast straight from a Wes Anderson movie (the jumpsuit uniforms!)? Locals head to this massive space after work for league play on Mondays and Tuesdays and cocktails named after shuffleboard legends. Weekends can get crowded, but borrow a board game until you score a waxed concrete lane. Groups of 10 or more can reserve 48 hours in advance for a lane, cabana, and drink packages. ⊠ 514 Union St., Brooklyn ☎ 347/223-4410 ⊕ www. royalpalmsshuffle.com Ⓜ R to Union St.; F, G to Carroll St.

ShapeShifter Lab

Musician Matthew Garrison owns this venue known for its high-quality jazz combos, experimental music, and acoustics. The white brick walled space is large, but the audiences—often musicians and jazz fans in-the-know—are often small, even if the event is one highlighted in the New York Times. There's a simple bar and cover is often $10 or less. ⊠ 18 Whitwell Pl., Brooklyn ⊕ www.shapeshifterlab. com Ⓜ R to Union St.

🛏 Hotels

Hotel Le Bleu

$ | **Hotel.** This hotel provides comfortable, carpeted rooms, some with terraces with views of the Statue of Liberty or Manhattan. **Pros:** close to Park Slope neighborhood attractions; friendly staff; opposite a park. **Cons:** an unappealing block of 4th Avenue; glass door of bathroom lacks privacy. *Rooms from: $239* ⊠ *370 4th Ave., Brooklyn* ☎ *718/625–1500* ⊕ *www.hotellebleu.com* ⤵ *48 rooms* ⦿| *Breakfast* Ⓜ *R to 9th St.; F, G to 4th Ave.*

The Union Hotel

$ | **Hotel.** The subway is just two blocks away from the redbrick building, and some of Brooklyn's best dining and shopping are within an easy stroll. **Pros:** location near the subway; breakfast included at Runner & Stone, beloved for baked goods; near places that locals frequent. **Cons:** very small rooms; showers not completed enclosed; no bedside tables or lamps. *Rooms from: $159* ⊠ *611 Degraw St., Brooklyn* ☎ *718/403–0614* ⊕ *www.unionhotelbrooklyn.com* ⤵ *43 rooms* ⦿| *Breakfast* Ⓜ *R to Union St.*

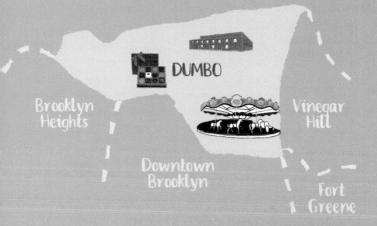

DUMBO

Brooklyn Heights

Vinegar Hill

Downtown Brooklyn

Fort Greene

For sheer jaw-dropping drama, few city walks rival the one along the DUMBO waterfront. The photogenic area pairs turn-of-the-20th-century warehouses and refurbished manufacturing buildings on cobblestone streets with rumbling trains and the Brooklyn and Manhattan bridges overhead. The latter bridge provides the district's name, an acronym of Down Under the Manhattan Bridge Overpass. Across the East River, the Manhattan skyline provides arresting backdrops for wedding proposals, fashion shoots, and innumerable selfies. Long before scenery became a draw, though, this area welcomed tinkerers and their start-ups, among them Robert Gair, who invented the corrugated box nearby and manufactured the product in DUMBO. The humble Brillo soap pad also came of age in these parts. The influx of technology start-ups supplies 21st-century swagger, while galleries and performance hubs imbue the neighborhood with artistic élan. Shops and restaurants pepper the short blocks of this small neighborhood. Head north on Main Street or New Dock Street to reach the waterfront, with its expansive park and the delightful Jane's Carousel. DUMBO's picture-perfect sidewalks and cinematic Manhattan views were no happy accident of urban development.—*Updated by Emily Saladino*

◉ Sights

A.I.R. Gallery

(*Artists in Residence, Inc.*) The country's first all-female, artist-run cooperative was established in 1972. This modern gallery space features hundreds of women artists' work every year and also hosts events, lectures, and creative symposiums. ⊠ *155 Plymouth St., DUMBO* ☎ *212/255–6651* ⊕ *www.airgallery.org* ⊘ *Closed Mon. and Tues.* Ⓜ *F to York St.*

Brooklyn Bridge Park. *See Chapter 11, Brooklyn Heights and Downtown Brooklyn, for full listing.*

DUMBO Walls

Keep an eye out under and around the Manhattan Bridge and the Brooklyn-Queens Expressway, where walls display street art by the likes of CAM, Shepard Fairey, and MOMO. The project is sponsored by the DUMBO Improvement District and Two Trees Management Co., along with the New York City Department of Transportation Urban Art Program and the Jonathan LeVine Gallery. ⊠ *DUMBO* Ⓜ *F to York St.*

★ Empire Stores

Housed in a sparkling renovation of an enormous 19th-century warehouse, this collection of shops and restaurants features a 7,000-square-foot rooftop garden with East River and Manhattan views. It's also home to a 3,200-square-foot exhibition space from the Brooklyn Historical Society that has small displays and a gift shop in a modern, industrial-chic space. Other tenants include area businesses, a luxury automobile showroom, and a West Elm store with a Brooklyn Roasting Company café. ⊠ 53–83 Water St., DUMBO ⊕ empirestoresdumbo.com Ⓜ A, C to High St.; F to Jay St.

Gleason's Gym

Want to be like Mike (Tyson)? Head to this athletic institution dating to 1937, whose illustrious alumni include the likes of Muhammad Ali, Jake LaMotta (the real-life boxer whose life is depicted in the movie Raging Bull), and Brooklyn's own Iron Mike. The gym sells one-day memberships for would-be ringmasters, as well as tickets to amateur boxing and Muay Thai matches. ⊠ 77 Front St., DUMBO ☎ 718/797-2872 ⊕ www.gleasonsgym.net ⓔ $10 one-day spectator; $20 one-day workout Ⓜ A, C to High St.; F to York St.

★ Jane's Carousel

Equal parts architectural marvel and children's plaything, this beautifully restored 1922 carousel twirls within a glass-walled waterfront pavilion designed by Pritzker Prize–winning French architect Jean Nouvel. Situated between the Brooklyn and Manhattan bridges, near the northern reaches of 85-acre Brooklyn Bridge Park and directly across from Manhattan's skyline, the carousel's 48 horses and two chariots are off to the races year-round. ⊠ Brooklyn Bridge Park, DUMBO ☎ 718/222-2502 ⊕ www.janescarousel.com ⓔ $2 ⊘ Closed Tues. year-round and Mon. and Wed. mid-Sept.–mid-May Ⓜ A, C to High St.; F to York St.

Kings County Distillery

New York City's oldest whiskey distillery bottles award-winning craft moonshine, bourbon, and other booze in a 115-year-old building in the sprawling Brooklyn Navy Yard. The distillery is open for 45-minute tours that include tastings and admission to the Boozeum, the spirited on-site museum. Tours are available Tuesday through Sunday at 3 and 5 pm, and on Saturday every half hour from 2 to 5 pm. (last tour at 5 pm). Reservations for weekday tours are recommended. Check the website for special events. ⊠ Brooklyn Navy Yard, 299 Sands St., Bldg. 121, DUMBO ☎ 347/689-4180 ⊕ www.kingscounty-distillery.com ⓔ Tours $14 Ⓜ A, C to High St.; F to York St.

Manhattan Bridge Archway Plaza

In 2008, city planners transformed this industrial storage lot into an 8,000-square-foot venue for seasonal markets, performances, and other events. On Sunday from 10 am to 6 pm from April to October, the soaring space and

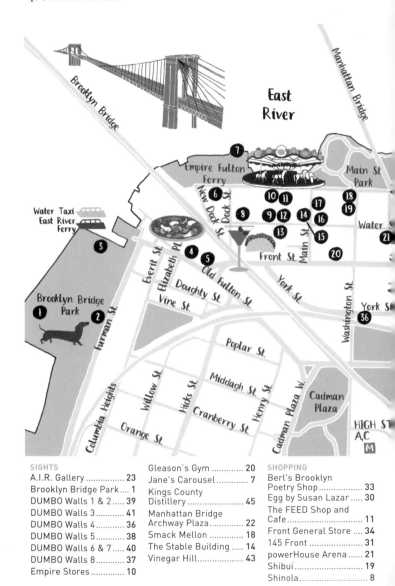

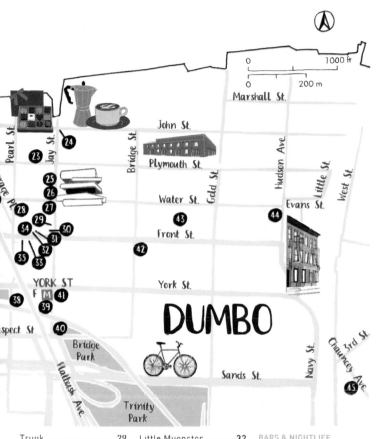

Marshall St.

John St.

Pearl St.

Jay St.

Bridge St.

Plymouth St.

Gold St.

Hudson Ave.

Little St.

West St.

Water St.

Evans St.

Front St.

York St.

DUMBO

Navy St.

3rd St.

Chauncey Ave.

Sands St.

Bridge Park

Trinity Park

Flatbush Ave.

spect St.

York St.

surrounding Pearl Street blocks host approximately 80 vendors and food trucks as part of the Brooklyn Flea. ⊠ *Water St., DUMBO* ☎ *718/237–8700* ⊕ *www.dumbo.is* Ⓜ *F to York St.*

Smack Mellon

The transformation of an industrial boiler house into an edgy arts compound is quintessential DUMBO. This 12,000-square-foot structure now hosts large-scale, avant-garde exhibitions and runs a prestigious residency program. Don't be surprised if you pass a smartphone-clutching event planner on your way in: the 5,000-square-foot gallery here is also a popular wedding venue. ⊠ *92 Plymouth St., DUMBO* ☎ *718/834–8761* ⊕ *www.smackmellon.org* ⊘ *Closed Mon. and Tues.* Ⓜ *A, C to High St.; F to York St.*

★ The Stable Building

Formerly the Galapagos Art Space (it moved to Detroit), this cutting-edge arts destination is now home to four first-floor gallery spaces that were previously part of the 111 Front Street gallery collective. Exhibitions include fine-art photography, mixed-media works, street art, abstract pieces, emerging artists, and more. Gallery hours vary; most are closed Monday. ⊠ *16 Main St., DUMBO* Ⓜ *2, 3 to Clark St.; A, C to High St.; F to York St.*

Vinegar Hill

An architectural anomaly between a ConEdison substation and the 300-acre Brooklyn Navy Yard industrial park, this small DUMBO

GETTING HERE

The picturesque way to get to DUMBO is via NYC Ferry. The neighborhood's two main subway stops, York Street and High Street, are at opposite ends of the area; the latter is also your best bet for Vinegar Hill.

neighborhood, originally settled by Irish immigrants, has pre–Civil War brick and frame houses, Greek Revival buildings, and Federal town houses on its streets. Don't miss the Commandant's House, a 19th-century, Federal-style landmark whose artfully obscured gate lies at Evans Street near Hudson Avenue: now a (rather impressive) private residence, the house is the Navy Yard's oldest surviving structure. ⊠ *Between Bridge St. and the Navy Yard, DUMBO* Ⓜ *F to York St.*

Shopping

Berl's Brooklyn Poetry Shop

The only New York City bookstore dedicated exclusively to poetry, Berl's is a family-run affair. The husband-and-wife owners are alumni of the Brooklyn Flea, and they fill their former gallery space with books by local and national poets, display artwork by up-and-coming talent, and host readings by published poets and Brooklyn-based university students. Note that the shop doesn't open till 2 pm. ⊠ *126A Front St., DUMBO* ☎ *347/687–2375* ⊕ *www.berlspoetry. com* Ⓜ *A, C to High St.; F to York St.*

Egg by Susan Lazar

Those wondering how the children prowling Dumbo's waterfront playgrounds look so chic need search no further: a branch of the designer's Manhattan flagship, this airy boutique stocks luxe, whimsical wares for infants, toddlers, and boys and girls, plus toys and gifts. Egg's prices run on the higher side, but the well-appointed sale rack rarely disappoints. ⊠ 72 Jay St., DUMBO ☎ 347/356-4097 ⊕ egg-baby.com Ⓜ F to Jay St., A, C to High St.

The FEED Shop and Cafe

Set within the Empire Stores development, the brick-and-mortar debut of this philanthropic label founded by former first niece Lauren Bush Lauren sells signature cloth handbags and houses a chic café offering La Colombe coffee and City Bakery snacks. Each food or handbag purchase benefits a hunger-based charity in conjunction with the United Nations World Food Programme, the United Nations Children's Fund, and Feeding America. ⊠ Empire Stores, 55 Water St., DUMBO ☎ 929/397-2716 ⊕ www. feedprojects.com/feed-shop-cafe Ⓜ F to Jay St.; A, C to High St.

Front General Store

Outfitting DUMBO's cool kids since 2011, this shop sells his-and-hers vintage Ralph Lauren blazers, 1940s Royal Stetson hats, and other curated odds 'n' ends, including antique Mexican glassware and Chesterfield-esque leather armchairs. ⊠ 143 Front St., DUMBO ☎ 347/693-5328 ⊕ frontgeneralstore. com Ⓜ A, C to High St.; F to York St.

145 Front

An artist selling hand-carved children's toys and a Japanese tea shop are among the pop-up retailers in this labyrinthine collection of independent microstores. The winding space has entrances on both Front and Pearl streets, and includes the atelier of long-term tenant Yoshi Sekiguchi, whose à la carte Teizo jewelry is also sold at the Guggenheim Museum. ⊠ 145 Front St., DUMBO ☎ 718/928-3970 ⊕ www.facebook.com/ TheShopsat145FrontStreetDumbo Ⓜ A, C to High St.; F to York St.

powerHouse Arena

Edgy art-book publisher power-House is a vision in concrete and steel at this bright showroom that sells illustrated titles, children's books, and works by authors from Joseph Mitchell to Gary Shteyngart. The space also hosts publishing parties, book launches, readings, and discussion groups. ⊠ 28 Adams St., DUMBO ☎ 718/666-3049 ⊕ www. powerhousearena.com Ⓜ A, C to High St.; F to York St.

Shibui

This understated subterranean space specializes in Japanese antiques, including collector-worthy furnishings and tansu chests as well as accessible blue-and-white ceramics, folk textiles, obis and kimonos, tea sets, and flower-arranging accessories. The friendly staff are happy to provide guidance or assistance, and the shop also offers restoration services. It is closed Monday and Tuesday. ⊠ 38 Washington St.,

DUMBO ☎ 718/875–1119 ⊕ www.
shibui.com Ⓜ F to Jay St.; A, C to
High St.

Shinola

The Brooklyn debut of this upscale
Detroit-based retailer occupies a
grand, 5,000-square-foot showroom within the Empire Stores
development. The space offers a
design-your-own-watch bar, handmade bicycles, and chic backpacks
and belts in buttery leather. There's
also an outpost of Manhattan
counter Smile to Go, offering
salads and sandwiches at a few
casual tables in the back. ⊠ Empire
Stores, 49 Water St., DUMBO
☎ 929/395–0099 ⊕ shinola.com Ⓜ F
to Jay St.; A, C to High St.

Trunk

Pieces at this chic indie clothing
boutique may not be one-of-a-
kind, but we doubt shoppers will
see anyone else wearing the same
thing. Founded by three Brooklyn-
based fashion designers in 2007,
Trunk sells women's apparel,
accessories, and jewelry created
by emerging local labels. The
industrial space resembles an
art gallery, with concrete floors
and overhead lighting. ⊠ 68 Jay
St., #101, DUMBO ☎ 718/522–6488
⊕ trunkbrooklyn.blogspot.com Ⓜ A, C
to High St.; F to York St.

☕ Coffee and Quick Bites

Almondine Bakery

$ | Café. Jacques Torres's partner
Herve Poussot bakes Gallic
pastries (think fresh-baked *fraisier*
with fresh strawberries and
mousseline crème) and delectable
quiches and croissants, and serves
sandwiches on award-winning
baguettes, in this spot across the
street from Torres's chocolate
shop. The *petit* storefront's interior
is nothing special, but the staff
are friendly and the seating is
abundant. **Known for:** coffee; great
croissants; sandwiches. *Average
main: $5* ⊠ 85 Water St., DUMBO
☎ 718/797–5026 ⊕ www.almondine-
bakery.com ⊗ No dinner Ⓜ A, C to
High St.; F to York St.

Archway Cafe

$ | Café. Artwork by local artists
lines the walls of this breezy café
that serves soups, salads, and
excellent sandwiches big enough to
share. In warm weather, take your
order to go, and enjoy an alfresco
spread on nearby picnic tables
beneath the Manhattan Bridge.
Known for: sandwiches; salads;
coffee. *Average main: $6* ⊠ 57 Pearl
St., DUMBO ☎ 718/522–3455 ⊕ www.
archwaycafe.com ⊗ No dinner on
weekends Ⓜ A, C to High St.; F to
York St.

Brooklyn Bridge Park Food
Stands

$ | Eclectic. Several of Manhattan's
and Brooklyn's top restaurants—
including the Ace Hotel's No. 7
Sub and the Brooklyn Ice Cream
Factory—have outposts along the
waterfront just north of Pier 1
in Brooklyn Bridge Park. Across
the street, a dine-in branch of
Danny Meyer's global juggernaut
Shake Shack has an entrance on
Old Fulton Street. **Known for:** ice

cream; burgers; casual outdoor dining. *Average main: $6 ⊠ Water St., DUMBO 🚍 No credit cards Ⓜ A, C to High St.; F to York St.*

★ Brooklyn Roasting Company

$ | Café. Artfully disheveled staffers brew coffee from fair-trade and rain-forest alliance–certified beans, while local gallerists and start-up techies flirt over perfectly poured cortados and other beverages at this East River–adjacent café. The loft-style industrial space is filled with antique roasting equipment and ample seating, and also serves pastries and sandwiches. **Known for:** artisanal coffee; industrial architecture; pastries and light snacks. *Average main: $4 ⊠ 25 Jay St., DUMBO 🕿 718/855–1000 ⊕ www. brooklynroasting.com Ⓜ A, C to High St.; F to York St.*

Burrow

$ | Café. It's easy to miss this tiny Japanese café in the lobby of an office building, but it's worth seeking out its superlative pastries (including a knockout cheese-cake), light snacks, coffee, and tea. Pastry chef Ayako Kurokawa worked at The Modern restaurant in Manhattan before opening this DUMBO jewel box, which has an understated aesthetic with glass doors, white walls, and tiled floors. **Known for:** pastries including green tea cookies; carefully sourced tea and coffee; cheese-cake. *Average main: $2 ⊠ 68 Jay St., DUMBO ⊕ burrow.nyc ⊗ Closed weekends. No dinner Ⓜ F to Jay St., A, C to High St.*

Jacques Torres Chocolate

$ | Café. French-born Torres is New York's adopted Willy Wonka. Here, he dishes out drool-worthy truffles and bonbons, and hot chocolate rich enough to make a Swiss miss blush. **Known for:** wide variety of choco-lates; friendly staff. *Average main: $8 ⊠ 66 Water St., DUMBO 🕿 718/875–1269 ⊕ www.mrchocolate.com Ⓜ A, C to High St.; F to York St.*

Little Muenster

$ | American. This tiny, weekday-only storefront serves rib-sticking, soul-satisfying sandwiches, like gooey grilled cheese made with sustainably sourced ingredients. The takeout counter is occasionally taken over by temporary pop-ups like Little Nica', which serves Nicaraguan street food in homage to one of the owners' Latin American heritage. **Known for:** grilled cheese sandwiches; thoughtfully sourced ingredients; pop-ups. *Average main: $10 ⊠ 145 Front St., DUMBO 🕿 646/499–4331 ⊕ www.littlemuen-ster.com ⊗ Closed weekends. No dinner Ⓜ A, C to High St., F to York St.*

One Girl Cookies. Branch location at 33 Main St. *See Chapter 12, Boerum Hill and Cobble Hill, for full listing.*

VHH Foods

$$ | Café. A casual, all-day sibling to DUMBO's Vinegar Hill House, this indoor-outdoor café spills out of Empire Stores near Brooklyn Bridge Park. Families, travelers, and well-dressed locals convene for grab-and-go sandwiches, salads, Meat Hook hot dogs, and coffee, or settle in for table service on the patio. **Known for:** takeout and dine-in options; outdoor seating; Vinegar Hill House sibling. *Average main: $24* ⊠ *Empire Stores, 55 Water St., 1 E, DUMBO* ☎ *718/243–1569* ⊕ *www.vhhfoods.com* Ⓜ *F to Jay St., A, C to High St.*

⅋⅋ Dining

Atrium

$$$ | **American.** The industrial-chic interiors at this bi-level, French-accented New American destination include pendant lamps and a buzzy open kitchen. Seasonal New American dishes such as Long Island duck and market fish are paired with an array of wines by the glass, and the bar pours house cocktails made with local spirits and an array of international piscos, mezcals, and barrel-aged Spanish gins. **Known for:** industrial-chic interior; elegant New American dining; tech and start-up power lunches. *Average main: $26* ⊠ *15 Main St., DUMBO* ☎ *718/858–1095* ⊕ *www.atriumdumbo.com* Ⓜ *A, C to High St.; F to York St.*

Bridge Coffee Shop

$ | **Latin American.** This homespun Latin American diner is the antidote to DUMBO's stilettoed galleristas and hipper-than-thou start-up scene. Neighborhood denizens, Latino expats, and the occasional off-duty mail carrier convene for hearty plates of *pernil* (roast pork), *maduros* (sweet plantains), and exceptional *medianoche* sandwiches. **Known for:** Latin American favorites; casual, no-frills atmosphere;

PICTURE-PERFECT DUMBO

In 1979, controversial New York engineer and developer David Walentas purchased 2 million square feet of real estate in what was then called the Fulton Landing waterfront, and spent the next decade transforming the area now known as DUMBO into an arts haven. He converted dilapidated warehouses into multimillion-dollar galleries, performance venues, and residences, and hand-picked retail tenants like Jacques Torres to imbue the neighborhood with creative credibility. As DUMBO grew, Walentas criticized subsequent developers who installed chain retailers on the neighborhood's southern border. Art versus commerce, Brooklyn-style.

affordable prices. *Average main: $8* ⊠ *73 Bridge St., DUMBO* ☎ *718/797–0825* Ⓜ *A, C to High St.; F to York St.*

★ Cecconi's

$$$ | **Italian.** A sophisticated addition to Empire Stores' dining scene comes courtesy of this sprawling Italian restaurant with glittering chandeliers, tiled flooring, and a marble bar where white-jacketed bartenders pour several negroni and spritz variations, plus beer and wine. The menu features classics (vitello tonnato, rigatoni Bolognese) as well as seasonal plates such as wood-fired pizzas with black truffles and squash blossoms. **Known for:** Manhattan skyline views; upscale Italian fare; marble bar. *Average main: $25* ⊠ *Empire Stores, 55 Water St., DUMBO* ☎ *718/650–3900* ⊕ *cecconisdumbo. com* Ⓜ *F to Jay St., A, C to High St.*

Gran Eléctrica

$$ | Mexican. Few restaurants are equally suited to neighborhood families and trendy twenty-somethings, but Gran Eléctrica's street-food-centric Mexican menu pleases all palates. In addition to multiregional tacos and small plates (try the chipotle-scented meatballs known as *albóndigas de Juana*), the buzzy, stylish space has an impressive tequila list and pours balanced cocktails. **Known for:** multiregional Mexican dishes; balanced cocktails and diverse tequilas; buzzy space that's family-friendly. *Average main: $14* ✉ *5 Front St., DUMBO* ☎ *718/852–2700* ⊕ *www.granelectrica.com* ⊗ *No lunch weekdays* Ⓜ *A, C to High St.; F to York St.*

Juliana's

$$ | Pizza. This bright, bustling spot is the locals' favorite for classic white and margherita pizzas, homemade soups, and Brooklyn Ice Cream Factory desserts. The lines aren't half as long as at Brooklyn pioneer Patsy Grimaldi's neighboring eponymous institution—and since Patsy himself has severed ties with Grimaldi's, Juliana's is arguably the most authentic pie on the block. **Known for:** authentic Brooklyn pizza; family-friendly dining; crowds. *Average main: $20* ✉ *19 Old Fulton St., DUMBO* ☎ *718/596–6700* ⊕ *www.julianaspizza.com* Ⓜ *2, 3 to Clark St.; A, C to High St.; F to York St.*

Vinegar Hill House

$$$ | Modern American. Outfitted with candlelit tables and a twinkling rear patio, this romantic destination is well worth the sloping walk up from the waterfront. Seasonal menus include inventive New American fare and crowd-pleasing brunch dishes; wait times can be considerable, but the cozy bar pours potent cocktails, local beer, and wine by the glass. **Known for:** romantic space with a twinkling backyard; seasonal, sustainably sourced New American dishes; weekend brunch. *Average main: $25* ✉ *72 Hudson Ave., DUMBO* ☎ *718/522–1018* ⊕ *www.vinegarhillhouse.com* ⊗ *No lunch* Ⓜ *F to York St.*

🍸 Bars and Nightlife

Olympia Wine Bar

The tables are candlelit and the flowers are fresh at this neighborhood spot run by an owner of 68 Jay Street Bar. The kitchen turns out crostini, salads, and cheese and charcuterie boards; and in addition to wine, the bar offers craft beer and smart takes on all things shaken or stirred. ✉ *54 Jay St., DUMBO* ☎ *718/624–7900* ⊕ *www.olympiawinebar.com* ⊗ *Closed Sun.* Ⓜ *A, C to High St.; F to York St.*

68 Jay Street Bar

Friendly regulars and weekday happy hours (5 to 7 pm) make this casual, unpretentious bar in the former Grand Union Tea Company building a pleasantly low-key affair. As the night goes on and the votive candles come out, patrons take over tables and benches in the spacious side room located behind a terra-cotta archway. ✉ *68 Jay St., DUMBO* ☎ *718/260–8207* ⊕ *www.68jaystreetbar.net* Ⓜ *A, C to High St.; F to York St.*

Superfine

The narrow, bi-level floor plan might seem a little odd, but friendly service and convivial, colorful crowds transform this renovated warehouse into a welcoming, quirky neighborhood spot. The kitchen's organic menu changes seasonally, but the real action is at the bar, where stiff libations are poured near the orange-felt pool table. ⊠ *126 Front St., DUMBO* ☎ *718/243–9005* ⊕ *superfine.nyc* Ⓜ *A, C to High St.; F to York St.*

 Performing Arts

★ St. Ann's Warehouse

The latest iteration of this cutting-edge arts institution (originally launched in the East Village in 1980) occupies a stunningly refurbished tobacco warehouse from 1860 that sits beneath the Brooklyn Bridge in Brooklyn Bridge Park. The 24,000-square-foot space features original brick archways, an elegant outdoor courtyard, an exhibition space, and a theater hosting such performances as an all-female production of *Henry IV* and the American premiere of Irish playwright Edna Walsh's first opera. ⊠ *Tobacco Warehouse, 45 Water St., DUMBO* ☎ *718/254–8779* ⊕ *stannswarehouse.org* Ⓜ *A, C to High St.; F to York St.*

🛏 Hotels

★ 1 Hotel Brooklyn Bridge

$$$ | **Hotel.** An ecofriendly ethos underscores this hip, beautifully designed outpost of the 1 Hotels fleet, including details such as headboards in many guest rooms made from upcycled corrugated steel; a living wall punctuates the tiered, buzzy lobby filled with low-slung leather sofas. **Pros:** beautifully designed and environmentally conscious; near Brooklyn Bridge Park; hip, trendy scene. **Cons:** east-facing rooms overlook busy thoroughfare; hotel guests have priority to rooftop bar on weekdays; uneven service. *Rooms from: $479* ⊠ *60 Furman St., DUMBO* ☎ *877/803–1111* ⊕ *1hotels.com/brooklyn-bridge* ⤳ *194 rooms* ❢❂❢ *No meals.*

Brooklyn Heights and Downtown Brooklyn

DUMBO

BROOKLYN HEIGHTS

DOWNTOWN BROOKLYN

Fort Greene

Red Hook

Cobble Hill

Boerum Hill

Brooklyn Heights is the borough's oldest neighborhood, and this area immediately south of where the Brooklyn Bridge now stands still has an air of historical mystique: it's very much the enclave of shady lanes, cobblestone streets, centuries-old row houses, and landmark buildings that Walt Whitman rhapsodized about. Many brownstones and redbrick row houses are on display, but take note, too, of the wooden-frame beauties that predate them; most of the latter are over near the "Fruit" streets. Along the East River waterfront, and above it from the Brooklyn Heights Promenade, the views of the Manhattan skyline and the Brooklyn Bridge have inspired countless artists and photographers over the years. From the early to mid-20th century, Brooklyn Heights was a bohemian haven, home to such writers as Arthur Miller, Truman Capote, Carson McCullers, Paul Bowles, Marianne Moore, Norman Mailer, and W. E. B. DuBois. Montague Street, the main retail and dining artery, heads east from Brooklyn Heights toward bustling Downtown Brooklyn, which goes about its modern-day business. The eastern corner of Downtown has the 16-acre MetroTech Center, built as part of the area's revitalization in the 1980s and '90s. Its high-rises are now among the many that continue to rise in the borough's main financial, commercial, and civic center.—*Updated by Kelsy Chauvin*

◉ Sights

Brooklyn Borough Hall
Built in 1848 as Brooklyn's city hall, this Greek Revival landmark, adorned with Tuckahoe marble, is one of the borough's handsomest buildings. The statue of Justice atop its cast-iron cupola was part of the original plan but wasn't installed until 1988. Today the building serves as the office of Brooklyn's borough president and the home of the Brooklyn Tourism & Visitors Center. ✉ *209 Joralemon St., Brooklyn Heights* ☎ *718/802–3700* ⊕ *www. explorebk.com* ⊙ *Closed weekends* Ⓜ *2, 3, 4, 5 to Borough Hall; R to Court St.; A, C, F, R to Jay St.–MetroTech.*

★ Brooklyn Bridge Park
This sweeping feat of green urban renewal stretches from the Manhattan Bridge in DUMBO to the Brooklyn Bridge and south all the way to Pier 6, carpeting old industrial sites along the waterfront with scenic esplanades and lush meadows. The park has playgrounds, sports fields, food concessions, the wonderfully restored Jane's Carousel, and lots of grass

for lounging. You can access the park at various points; just head down the hill toward the East River and you can't miss it. ✉ *Brooklyn waterfront, Brooklyn Heights* ☎ *718/222-9939* ⊕ *www.brooklyn-bridgepark.org* Ⓜ *2, 3 to Clark St.; A, C to High St.; F to York St.*

★ **Brooklyn Heights Promenade**
Strolling this mile-long path, famous for its magnificent Manhattan views, you might find it surprising to learn that its origins were purely functional: the promenade was built as a sound barrier to protect nearby brown-stones from highway noise. Find a bench and take in the skyline, the Statue of Liberty, and the Brooklyn Bridge; in the evening, the lights of Manhattan sparkle across the East River. Below are the Brooklyn–Queens Expressway and Brooklyn Bridge Park. ✉ *Between Remsen and Cranberry Sts., Brooklyn Heights* Ⓜ *2, 3 to Clark St.; A, C to High St.; R to Court St.*

★ **Brooklyn Historical Society**
Four centuries' worth of art and artifacts bring Brooklyn's story to life at this marvelous space. Housed in an 1881 Queen Anne–style National Historic Landmark building, the society surveys the borough's changing identity through permanent exhibits that include interactive displays, landscape paintings, photographs, portraits of Brooklynites, and fascinating memorabilia. The gift shop features an eclectic assortment of Brooklyn-themed books and tchotchkes. Stop by the society's DUMBO outpost in

the Empire Stores development at 55 Water Street for special exhibits. ✉ *128 Pierrepont St., Brooklyn Heights* ☎ *718/222-4111* ⊕ *www.brooklynhistory.org* ✎ *$10 suggested donation* ⊘ *Closed Mon. and Tues.* Ⓜ *2, 3, 4, 5 to Borough Hall; R to Court St.; A, C, F to Jay St.–MetroTech.*

"Fruit" Streets
The quiet blocks of Pineapple, Cranberry, and Orange streets contain some of Brooklyn Heights's most picturesque brownstones and brick homes. A few homes made of wood still exist here, too, although new construction of this type has been banned in this area as a fire hazard since the mid-19th century. The wood-frame Federal-style house at 24 Middagh Street dates to the 1820s, its lane commemorating one Lady Middagh, whom we can thank for bestowing such memorable fruit-themed names on this enclave. ✉ *Pineapple, Orange, and Cranberry Sts., Brooklyn Heights* Ⓜ *2, 3 to Clark St.; A, C to High St.*

New York Transit Museum
Step down into an old 1930s subway station to experience this entertaining museum's displays of vintage trains and memorabilia. You can wander through trains and turnstiles and sit behind the wheel of a former city bus (it's not only the kids who do this). Original advertising, signage, and upholstery make this feel like a trip back in time. The gift shop carries subway-line socks, decorative tile reproductions, and other fun stuff. ✉ *Boerum Pl., Brooklyn Heights* ☎ *718/694-1600* ⊕ *www.mta.info/museum* ✎ *$10*

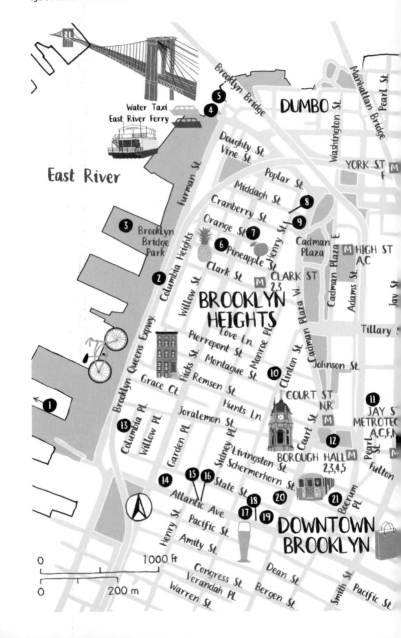

Brooklyn Bridge

Water Taxi
East River Ferry

East River

DUMBO

Manhattan Bridge

Pearl St

Washington St

YORK ST M
F

Doughty St.
Vine St.

Poplar St.

Middagh St.

Cranberry St.

Orange St.

Pineapple St.

Clark St.

3 Brooklyn
Bridge
Park

Columbia Heights

8

9

Henry St.

Cadman
Plaza

HIGH ST
A,C

Furman St.

Willow St.

Cadman Plaza E

Adams St

Jay St

CLARK ST
23

BROOKLYN
HEIGHTS

Cadman Plaza W.

Tillary St

Brooklyn Queens Expwy.

Hicks St.

Pierrepont St.

Montague St.

Remsen St.

Love Ln

Monroe Pl.

Clinton St.

Johnson St.

Grace Ct.

Hunts Ln.

10

COURT ST
N,R

JAY ST
METROTEC
A,C,F,N

Columbia Pl.

Willow Pl.

Joralemon St.

Garden Pl.

Sidney Pl.

Livingston St.

Schermerhorn St.

Court St.

BOROUGH HALL
2,3,4,5

Pearl St.

Fulton

13

14

15 16

State St.

Atlantic Ave

Henry St.

Pacific St.

Amity St.

18

17 19

20

11

12

21

Boerum Pl.

DOWNTOWN
BROOKLYN

0   1000 ft

0   200 m

Congress St.

Verandah Pl.

Warren St.

Dean St.

Bergen St.

Smith St.

Pacific St.

🚫 *Closed Mon.* Ⓜ *2, 3, 4, 5 to Borough Hall; A, C, G to Hoyt–Schermerhorn Sts.; A, C, F, R to Jay St.–MetroTech.*

Plymouth Church

Built in 1849, this barnlike neoclassical Congregational church was a stop on the Underground Railroad. The famous abolitionist Henry Ward Beecher was the first pastor; a sculpture of him stands in the colonnaded courtyard visible from Orange Street. The brick building's open, theaterlike interior inspired many subsequent American Protestant churches. Three Louis C. Tiffany stained-glass windows were added in the 1930s. A fragment of Plymouth Rock is in an adjoining arcade. ✉ *75 Hicks St., Brooklyn Heights* ☎ *718/624–4743* ⊕ *www.plymouthchurch.org* 🕐 *Tours available Mon. and Tues. by appointment only, or Sun. after services* Ⓜ *2, 3 to Clark St.; A, C to High St.*

Shopping

Barnes & Noble. Branch listing at 106 Court St. *See Chapter 8, Park Slope and Prospect Park, for full listing.*

★ Collyer's Mansion

Although this housewares shop is named for New York's infamous hoarder brothers, it's actually a thoughtful selection of beautiful textiles, glassware, lighting, and jewelry designed by a mix of local and international artists. The Japanese bath products—Binchotan charcoal soaps and masks, and Yoshii towels made with raw

cotton—are especially popular. ✉ *179 Atlantic Ave., Brooklyn Heights* ☎ *347/987–3342* ⊕ *www.shopthemansion.com* Ⓜ *2, 3, 4, 5 to Borough Hall; R to Court St.; A, C, F to Jay St.–MetroTech.*

★ Sahadi's

Inhale the aromas of spices and dark-roast coffee beans as you enter this Middle Eastern trading post that's been selling bulk foods in Brooklyn since 1948. Bins, jars, and barrels hold everything from nuts, dried fruit, olives, and pickled vegetables to cheeses, chocolate, candy, those intoxicating coffees, and all manner of spices. There's a large selection of prepared food and groceries as well. ✉ *187 Atlantic Ave., Brooklyn Heights* ☎ *718/624–4550* ⊕ *www.sahadis.com* Ⓜ *2, 3, 4, 5 to Borough Hall; R to Court St.; A, C, F, R to Jay St.–MetroTech.*

Coffee and Quick Bites

Damascus Bread & Pastry Shop $ | **Middle Eastern.** Named for the founder's childhood home in Syria, this family-run bakery and market has been a mainstay of the neighborhood's Middle Eastern community since 1930. Specialties include freshly baked pita, vegetable and meat pies, and baklava. **Known for:** baked goods; Mediterranean prepared food; neighborhood mainstay. *Average main: $5* ⊠ *195 Atlantic Ave., Brooklyn Heights* ☎ *718/625-7070* ⊕ *www.damascusbakery.com* Ⓜ *2, 3, 4, 5 to Borough Hall; R to Court St.; A, C, F to Jay St.–MetroTech.*

Dekalb Market Hall

$$ | Eclectic. Taste-test New York at this underground food hall, home to the first satellite of Manhattan's Katz's Delicatessen and an array of other eateries. With 40 mostly local vendors, you can head here for virtually any cuisine category and specialty dish: barbecue, fried chicken, sushi, pierogies, falafel, pickles, seafood, and dessert. **Known for:** Katz's outpost; quick bites or full meals; local vendors. *Average main: $19* ⊠ *445 Albee Sq. W, Downtown Brooklyn* ☎ *929/359-6555* ⊕ *dekalbmarkethall.com* Ⓜ *B, Q, R to Dekalb Ave.; 2, 3 to Hoyt St.*

Table 87

$$ | Pizza. A hot margherita pizza cooked in a coal-fired oven with a dark, smoky crust is basically *the* taste of Brooklyn. Stop by Table 87, "Home of the Coal Oven Slice," for the quintessential Brooklyn snack (a plain slice costs $4), or get a table in the casual back room for a simple but delicious meal. **Known for:** coal oven pizza; slices; iconic Brooklyn taste. *Average main: $14* ⊠ *87 Atlantic Ave., Brooklyn Heights* ☎ *718/797-9300* ⊕ *www.table-87/coalovenpizza.com* Ⓜ *2, 3, 4, 5 to*

Borough Hall; R to Court St.; A, C, F to Jay St.–MetroTech.

🍴 Dining

Chef's Table at Brooklyn Fare

$$$$ | Eclectic. Should you manage to snag a seat at Brooklyn's only Michelin three-star restaurant, you're in for an exceptional culinary experience. Chef Cesar Ramirez prepares more than a dozen courses of French- and Japanese-influenced raw and cooked seafood small plates. **Known for:** French and Japanese small plates; Michelin three-star rating; extremely high set-price menu. *Average main: $330* ⊠ *200 Schermerhorn St., Downtown Brooklyn* ☎ *718/243-0050* ⊕ *www.brooklynfare.com/pages/chefs-table* ☉ *Closed Sun. and Mon.* Ⓜ *2, 3 to Hoyt St.; 2, 3, 4, 5 to Nevins St.; A, C, G to Hoyt–Schermerhorn Sts.; B, Q, R to DeKalb Ave.*

★ Circa Brewing Company

$$ | American. Tucked into the heart of Downtown Brooklyn is this full-scale brewery and inviting restaurant, serving up to 10 of its brews on draft at any time, plus craft cocktails, and wine from Brooklyn's Rooftop Reds Vineyard. Sophisticated fare pairs with the season's changing drafts, spanning stone-oven pizza, meat and cheese plates, grain salads, and wood-grilled burgers. **Known for:** variety of beer brewed on-site; seasonal menu paired with changing drafts; spacious, modern-industrial style. *Average main: $18* ✉ *141 Lawrence St., Downtown Brooklyn* ☎ *718/858–0055* ⊕ *circabrewing.co* Ⓜ *2, 3 to Hoyt St.; A, C, F, N, R to Jay St.–MetroTech.*

★ Colonie

$$ | Modern American. The key to this perpetually popular restaurant's success lies in its use of ultrafresh ingredients, sourced from local purveyors and presented with style in an upscale-casual space that honors its neighborhood's historical roots. There's always an oyster special, along with a selection of small plates. **Known for:** locally sourced ingredients; daily oyster special; open kitchen. *Average main: $20* ✉ *127 Atlantic Ave., Brooklyn Heights* ☎ *718/855–7500* ⊕ *www.colonienyc. com* ⊗ *No lunch weekdays* Ⓜ *2, 3, 4, 5 to Borough Hall; R to Court St.*

Henry's End

$$$ | American. This neighborhood institution made its reputation serving wonderful food and excellent wines in an unpretentious, high-ceiling, exposed-brick dining room. Meat takes center stage here, with several nightly changing preparations of duck and veal, but there are fish and pasta dishes as well. **Known**

for: seasonal ingredients; meat and game dishes; neighborhood favorite. *Average main: $25* ✉ *44 Henry St., Brooklyn Heights* ☎ *718/834–1776* ⊕ *www.henrysend.com* ⊗ *No lunch* Ⓜ *2, 3 to Clark St.; A, C to High St.*

Iris Café

$$$ | Modern American. Run by two Brooklyn-raised brothers, this bar, restaurant, and café sits on a quiet, cobblestone stretch of Columbia Place in Brooklyn's "Willowtown," a historic neighborhood dating to the 1810s. Sun streaming through large storefront windows illuminates daytime fare that includes baked goods, daily soups, well-made sandwiches, and excellent coffee. **Known for:** casual daytime café; upscale dinner menu; cozy atmosphere. *Average main: $26* ✉ *20 Columbia Pl., Brooklyn Heights* ☎ *718/722–7395* ⊕ *www.iriscafe.nyc* ⊗ *No dinner Mon. and Tues.* Ⓜ *2, 3, 4, 5 to Borough Hall; R to Court St.; A, C, F to Jay St.–MetroTech.*

Junior's

$$ | Diner. Famous for its thick slices of cheesecake, Junior's has been the quintessential Brooklyn diner since 1950. Classic cheeseburgers looming over little cups of coleslaw and thick french fries are first-rate, as are the sweet-potato latkes and pretty much all the breakfast offerings. **Known for:** cheesecake; diner classics; quintessential Brooklyn. *Average main: $15* ✉ *386 Flatbush Ave., Downtown Brooklyn* ☎ *718/852–5257* ⊕ *www. juniorscheesecake.com* Ⓜ *2, 3, 4, 5 to Nevins St.; B, Q, R to DeKalb Ave.; A, C, G to Hoyt–Schermerhorn Sts.*

Noodle Pudding

$$ | Italian. Efficient waiters, consistently outstanding food, and the hum of conversation make a visit to this always bustling Italian restaurant exceedingly pleasant. Squeeze lemon over your calamari, savor gnocchi with sage butter, or dig into lasagna Bolognese: whether you're in the mood for pasta, risotto, meat, chicken, or seafood, you're bound to leave satisfied. Just be sure to hear about the daily specials before making your decision. **Known for:** Italian comfort food; large portions; reasonable prices. *Average main: $20* ⊠ *38 Henry St., Brooklyn Heights* ☎ *718/625-3737* ⊗ *Closed Mon. No lunch* ▭ *No credit cards* Ⓜ *2, 3 to Clark St.; A, C to High St.*

★ Pilot

$$ | American. Few lounges can match a New York Harbor location like the one occupied by *Pilot*, a historic 154-foot-long schooner moored for at least half the year at Pier 6 in Brooklyn Bridge Park. The stunning setting is made complete with a killer oyster bar, plus simple, well-done fare like lobster rolls, crispy fries, and ceviche. **Known for:** stunning harbor location; fresh daily oysters; fine cocktails. *Average main: $19* ⊠ *Pier 6, Brooklyn Heights* ☎ *917/810-8550* ⊕ *pilotbrooklyn. com* ⊗ *Closed approximately early Nov.–late Apr.* Ⓜ *2, 3 to Clark St.; 4, 5 to Borough Hall; R to Court St.*

★ The River Café

$$$$ | Modern American. A deservedly popular special-occasion destination, this waterfront institution complements its exquisite Brooklyn Bridge views with memorable top-shelf cuisine served by an unfailingly attentive staff. Lobster, lamb, duck, and strip steak are among the staples of the prix-fixe menu ($130 for dinner, $47 for Saturday lunch, $60 for Sunday brunch). **Known for:** unforgettable location; top-shelf cuisine; refined atmosphere. *Average main: $130* ⊠ *1 Water St., Brooklyn Heights* ☎ *718/522-5200* ⊕ *www.therivercafe.com* ⊗ *No breakfast weekends, no lunch Sun.–Fri., no brunch Mon.–Sat.* Ⓜ *2, 3 to Clark St.; A, C to High St.; F to York St.*

🍸 Bars and Nightlife

★ Floyd

Comfy sofas, a relaxed scene, and large boccie courts have made this bar a neighborhood staple. And while the beer cheese dip is memorable, locals flock here for the solid selection of drafts and bourbons, plus weekday happy hours and other specials like the ever-popular bucket of assorted beer by the can. The same folks run Union Hall in Park Slope and the Bell House in Gowanus. ⊠ *131 Atlantic Ave., Brooklyn Heights* ☎ *718/858-5810* ⊕ *www.floydny.com* Ⓜ *2, 3, 4, 5 to Borough Hall; R to Court St.; A, C, F to Jay St.–MetroTech.*

Livingston Manor

A pink neon sign reading "Manor" guides you to this downtown hangout where the after-work crowd heads for happy hour (daily between 4 and 7 pm). The bar is inspired by and named for a quaint hamlet in the Catskills, and the pockmarked cement walls, black leather banquettes, and diagonal-striped wood paneling impart a lived-in feel even though the place only opened in 2014. The drink of choice? A pint from the Catskills Brewery, of course. ⊠ *42 Hoyt St., Downtown Brooklyn* ☎ *347/987–3292* ⊕ *www. livingstonmanorbk.com* Ⓜ *2, 3 to Hoyt St.; A, C, G to Hoyt-Schermerhorn Sts.; B, Q, R to DeKalb Ave.*

 **Performing Arts**

Alamo Drafthouse Cinema

On the fourth floor of Downtown Brooklyn's City Point complex is this cinematic destination, where first-run movies, cult classics, and specialty and late-night screenings run daily. Unique to Alamo Drafthouse, however, is roomy seating with table service for a simple, tasty menu that spans beer, wine, cocktails, and (mostly) cinema-friendly snacks and entrées. Yes, popcorn is available—butter, truffle, or herb-Parmesan. ⊠ *445 Albee Sq. W, Downtown Brooklyn* ☎ *718/513–2547* ⊕ *drafthouse.com* Ⓜ *B, Q, R to Dekalb Ave.; 2, 3 to Hoyt St.*

Bargemusic

Founded in 1977, this classical music series on a barge floating on the East River hosts small audiences of about 130 for intimate chamber-music concerts. In this refined, isolated environment the focus is on enjoying the music and making new friends during intermission. ⊠ *2 Old Fulton St., Brooklyn Heights* ☎ *718/624–4924* ⊕ *www.bargemusic.org* Ⓜ *2, 3 to Clark St.; A, C to High St.; F to York St.*

🛏️ Hotels

Aloft New York Brooklyn

$$ | Hotel. A funky boutique chain operation in the heart of Downtown Brooklyn, Aloft is a lively yet comfortable space. **Pros:** easy subway access; reasonable prices; guests have access to the adjacent Sheraton's indoor swimming pool and room service. **Cons:** neighborhood can be noisy. *Rooms from: $359* ⊠ *216 Duffield St., Downtown Brooklyn* ☎ *718/256–3833* ⊕ *www. aloftnewyorkbrooklyn.com* ⤺ *176 rooms* ❍ *No meals* Ⓜ *2, 3 to Hoyt St.; A, C, F, N, R to Jay St.–MetroTech.*

New York Marriott at the Brooklyn Bridge

$$ | Hotel. The rooms at this well-situated hotel are classic Marriott—large and enhanced by high ceilings, massaging showerheads, rolling desks, and other nice touches. **Pros:** near some of Brooklyn's hipper neighborhoods; traditional full-service hotel; good subway access. **Cons:** on a busy downtown street. *Rooms from: $369* ⊠ *333 Adams St., Downtown Brooklyn* ☎ *718/246–7000* ⊕ *www. marriott.com* ⤺ *665 rooms* ❍ *No meals* Ⓜ *2, 3, 4, 5 to Borough Hall; A, C, F, N, R to Jay St.–Metro Tech.*

Boerum Hill and Cobble Hill

GO FOR

Village Feel

Corner Cafés

Youthful Energy

Brooklyn Heights

Downtown

Fort Greene

Red Hook

COBBLE HILL

BOERUM HILL

Carroll Gardens

Park Slope

Gowanus

seeing ★☆☆☆☆ | Shopping ★★★★☆ | Dining ★★★★★ | Nightlife ★★★☆☆

Aside-by-side duo in the heart of Brooklyn, Boerum Hill and Cobble Hill are among the borough's most picturesque areas for strolling past redbrick row houses and brownstone town houses and churches. Greek Revival and Italianate styles predominate among the 19th-century structures, but many other influences can be detected as well. Strong Place and Tompkins Place, two sedate one-block streets, contain a cross-section of Cobble Hill's architectural styles. Cobble Hill, south of Brooklyn Heights, and Boerum Hill, south of Downtown Brooklyn, are classic working-class neighborhoods with hints of their largely Italian-American roots. The area has become more upscale, though, and is now better known for housing many of New York's intelligentsia—and the restaurants and cafés they love. Cobble Hill is named for the piles of cobblestones used as ballast for ships leaving the port in Red Hook, to the southwest, during the 19th century; a family farm back in colonial times provided Boerum Hill its moniker. Smith and Court streets, the two main commercial arteries, run parallel to each other through the neighborhoods and offer excellent dining and shopping. Busy Atlantic Avenue tempts with its antiques stores, home-decor boutiques, and Middle Eastern delis and bakeries.—*Updated by Kelsy Chauvin*

⋯⋯⋯⋯⋯⋯⋯⋯⋯⋯⋯⋯⋯⋯⋯⋯⋯⋯⋯⋯⋯⋯⋯⋯⋯⋯⋯⋯⋯⋯⋯⋯

◎ Sights

Invisible Dog
A 19th-century factory building that for a few recent decades was home to the maker of the famous "invisible dog" leashes is now an interdisciplinary arts center with more than two dozen studios for artists. The gallery exhibits their works and those of their peers from Brooklyn and beyond, and other spaces host musical performances, dance recitals, and other cultural events. ⊠ *51 Bergen St., Boerum Hill* *347/560–3641* ⊕ *www.theinvisi-bledog.org* ⊗ *Closed Mon.; open by appointment only Tues. and Wed.* Ⓜ *F, G to Bergen St.*

Strong Place and Tompkins Place
These pretty redbrick- and brownstone-lined streets are quint-essential parts of the neighborhood and well worth a stroll. Single-block streets, often designated as "places," emerged across the borough to fill in extra space when nearly parallel streets swerved too far apart. The Gothic Revival brownstone church at the corner of Strong and Degraw streets dates to

1849, but many homes on Tompkins Place were erected during the first decade of the 20th century. Two Christian churches (first a Dutch Reformed church, then Trinity German Lutheran Church) previously occupied what's now Kane Street Synagogue at the corner of Tompkins and Kane streets; the structure was built in the mid-1850s. ⊠ *Between Kane and Degraw Sts., Cobble Hill* Ⓜ *F, G to Bergen St. or Carroll St.*

 Shopping

Barneys New York

This location of the legendary Manhattan retail store is a spacious, relaxed place to browse designer collections like A.P.C. or Givenchy without dealing with the hustle and bustle of the Madison Avenue flagship. Shoppers here appreciate the wide selection of men's and women's clothing, shoes, handbags, hats, coats, and other accessories, plus an ever-changing sale section. ⊠ *194 Atlantic Ave., Cobble Hill* ☎ *718/637-2234* ⊕ *www.barneys.com* Ⓜ *2, 3, 4, 5 to Borough Hall*

Books Are Magic. *See Chapter 13, Carroll Gardens, for full listing.*

★ Exit 9 Gift Emporium

The beloved East Village kitsch emporium and card shop—where "childish" is both a selling point and a compliment—expanded to Smith Street. Its wide array of merchandise is often zany yet practical, and includes cool NYC-themed souvenirs and everyday objects like hand sanitizer, bandages, and breath mints turned into gag gifts. The sassy cards, themed gift boxes, and gift wrap come with far more personality than you'll find in any run-of-the-mill drugstore. ⊠ *127 Smith St., Boerum Hill* ☎ *718/422-7720* ⊕ *www.shopexit9.com* Ⓜ *F, G to Bergen St.*

Horseman Antiques

Brooklyn antiques shops have become increasingly precious and expensive of late, but Horseman has resolutely avoided the trend. Its five floors of mid-century-modern furniture, fixtures, and salvaged items—not to mention one of the largest collections of stained glass on the East Coast—remain reasonably priced. ⊠ *351 Atlantic Ave., Boerum Hill* ☎ *718/596-1048* ⊕ *www.horsemanantiques.net* Ⓜ *2, 3, 4, 5 to Borough Hall; A, C, G to Hoyt–Schermerhorn St.; F, G to Bergen St.*

Sterling Place

Painstakingly well stocked, this antiques store and gift shop prides itself on offering one-of-a-kind objects with heirloom potential. Danish-modern furniture is a specialty, but quirky finds such as a pinball-machine coffee table also pop up. Handcrafted inlay jewelry boxes are among the suitcase-friendly items for sale. ⊠ *363 Atlantic Ave., Boerum Hill* ☎ *718/797-5667* ⊕ *www.sterlingplace.com* Ⓜ *A, C, G to Hoyt–Schermerhorn Sts.*

Twisted Lily

All-natural scents from around the world are this fragrance boutique's specialty. This is a good place to

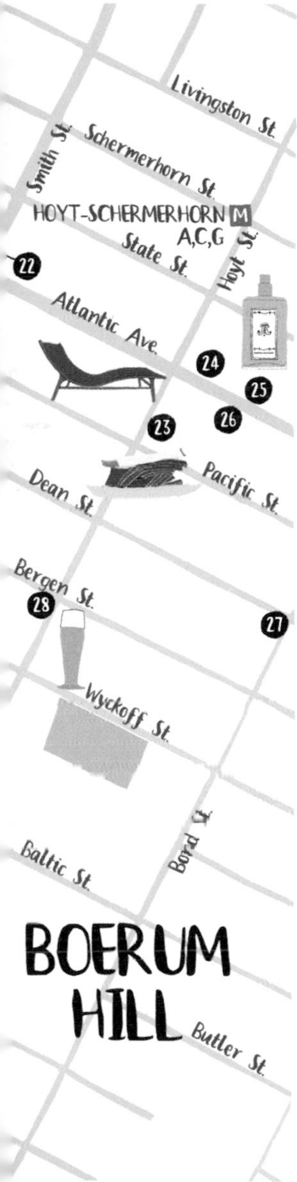

Livingston St
Smith St
Schermerhorn St
HOYT-SCHERMERHORN M
A,C,G
State St
Hoyt St
22
Atlantic Ave
24
25
26
23
Pacific St
Dean St
Bergen St
28
27
Wyckoff St
Bond St
Baltic St
BOERUM HILL
Butler St

SIGHTS

Invisible Dog.............15

Strong Place and Tompkins Place.......12

SHOPPING

Barneys New York.....5

Exit 9 Gift Emporium.................19

Horseman Antiques....................24

Sterling Place..........25

Twisted Lily..............26

COFFEE & QUICK BITES

Bien Cuit...................18

Blue Bottle Coffee...21

Café Pedlar................9

Court Street Pastry Shop.............13

One Girl Cookies......17

Shelsky's of Brooklyn.................6

Van Leeuwen Artisan Ice Cream.................20

DINING

Bar Tabac.................16

Henry Public...............1

Hibino..........................2

La Vara..........................7

Mile End....................23

Rucola.........................27

Sam's Restaurant....10

Watty & Meg.............11

Yemen Café................4

BARS & NIGHTLIFE

Boat...........................29

Brooklyn Inn.............28

Camp.........................30

Congress....................8

Elsa.............................3

61 Local...................14

HOTELS

NU Hotel Brooklyn...22

check out the latest offerings from Penhaligon's of London, Unum of Italy, Maison Francis Kurkdjian of France, and other perfumers. The shop also sells modern skin care, grooming, and beauty products. ⊠ *360 Atlantic Ave., Boerum Hill* ☎ *347/529–4681* ⊕ *www. twistedlily.com* Ⓜ *A, C, G to Hoyt–Schermerhorn Sts.*

GETTING HERE

The Bergen Street stop on the F and G lines exits right onto Smith Street, one of the main drags that cuts through both Boerum Hill and Cobble Hill. You can also get out at Hoyt–Schermerhorn on the A, C, and G lines and walk a few blocks south.

☕ Coffee and Quick Bites

Bien Cuit

$ | Bakery. Locally ground flour, hand-mixed doughs, and European recipes are among this artisanal bakery and café's secrets to success. Some regulars drop by to stock up on classic challah, French *pain de mie* (a sweet bread good for sandwiches or to toast) and baguettes, and Italian Pugliese loaves, but others come for the pastries, sandwiches, or quiches. **Known for:** artisanal pastries; European baked goods; favorite neighborhood stop. *Average main: $5* ⊠ *120 Smith St., Boerum Hill* ☎ *718/852-0200* ⊕ *www.biencuit.com* ⊗ *No dinner* Ⓜ *F, G to Bergen St.*

Blue Bottle Coffee. Branch location at 85 Dean St. *See Chapter 2, Williamsburg, for full listing.*

Café Pedlar

$ | Café. The folks behind Frankie's 457 and Prime Meats in Carroll Gardens operate this bustling café whose limited seating only heightens its cachet. The expert staffers pull espresso drinks and pour-overs made with the latest and greatest roasts from nearby Stumptown. **Known for:** expert baristas; guest roasters; pastries. *Average main: $4* ⊠ *210 Court St., Cobble Hill* ☎ *718/855-7129* ⊕ *cafepedlar.com* Ⓜ *F, G to Bergen St.*

Court Street Pastry Shop

$ | Bakery. A celebrated remnant of Cobble Hill's Italian-American past, this family-owned bakery delivers classics to savor: cannoli, pies, spumoni, custard ices, exquisitely layered Neapolitan-style sfogliatelle,and rainbow cookies by the pound. The vintage sign alone may be reason to visit, but even better is the intoxicatingly delicious interior, where you can discover everything from seasonal pastries to sugar-free cookies. **Known for:** Italian pastries; cookies by the pound; neighborhood classic. *Average main: $3* ⊠ *298 Court St., Cobble Hill* ☎ *718/875-4820* ⊕ *www. courtpastry.com* ⊗ *Closed Sun.* Ⓜ *F, G to Bergen St. or Carroll St.*

★ One Girl Cookies

$ | Bakery. Vintage serving pieces, a hand-painted family tree, and life-size family photos adorn the interior of this aqua-walled bakery and café beloved for its old-world charm and tasty, bite-size cookies. The whoopie pies—chocolate or the very popular pumpkin—and cupcakes are worth checking out, too. **Known for:** tasty cookies; whoopie pies; vintage flair. *Average main: $3* ⊠ *68 Dean St., Boerum Hill* ☎ *212/675–4996* ⊕ *www.onegirl-cookies.com* Ⓜ *F, G to Bergen St.*

Shelsky's of Brooklyn
$ | **Deli.** Owner Peter Shelsky pays homage to the traditional Lower East Side deli by stocking the classics—bagels, *babka* , and the like—but often with a nouveau-Brooklyn twist. Gravlax, Nova, and smoked salmon, for example, share space in the refrigerator with house-cured Jamaican jerk salmon, Mexican achiote salmon, and other deli delectables like pickled herring, whitefish salad, knishes, and prepared salads. **Known for:** Jewish deli classics; smoked and cured fish; sandwiches. *Average main: $12* ⊠ *141 Court St., Cobble Hill* ☎ *718/855–8817* ⊕ *www.shelskys.com* Ⓜ *2, 3, 4, 5 to Borough Hall.*

Van Leeuwen Artisan Ice Cream.
Branch location at 81 Bergen St. *See Chapter 3, Greenpoint, for full listing.*

Dining

Bar Tabac
$$ | **Bistro.** A happening French bistro, with well-worn decor and live jazz several nights a week, Bar Tabac has been a neighborhood mainstay since opening in 2001. The aperitifs are impeccably chilled, the steak *au poivre* sizzles seductively on the grill, and the *moules* have just the right amount of broth for dipping your *frites.* **Known for:** French bistro fare; live jazz; brunch or late-night. *Average main: $19* ⊠ *128 Smith St., Boerum Hill* ☎ *718/923–0918* ⊕ *www.bartabacny.com* Ⓜ *F, G to Bergen St.*

Henry Public
$$ | **American.** On a quiet Cobble Hill street, this dimly lit tavern is charmingly styled like an old-time saloon, and the antique and wood decor and fabulous zinc bar set just the right tone for simple standards cooked well. Best bets include the grass-fed burger, a grilled-cheese sandwich with apple slices, and the signature turkey-leg sandwich. **Known for:** simple, delicious dishes; zinc bar; regional beer and wine. *Average main: $15* ⊠ *329 Henry St., Cobble Hill* ☎ *718/852–8630* ⊕ *www.henrypublic. com* ☾ *No lunch weekdays* Ⓜ *2, 3, 4, 5 to Borough Hall; F, G to Bergen St.*

Hibino
$$ | **Japanese.** There's something almost zenlike about the food at this open, airy restaurant. The traditional and modern sushi rolls, the Kyoto-style *obanzai* (Japanese tapas), and the smooth, creamy homemade tofu served in small glass bottles will leave you feeling relaxed and satisfied. **Known for:** traditional and modern Japanese; daily specials; zenlike atmosphere. *Average main: $17* ⊠ *333 Henry St., Cobble Hill* ☎ *718/260–8052* ⊕ *www. hibino-brooklyn.com* ☾ *No lunch weekends* Ⓜ *2, 3, 4, 5 to Borough Hall.*

★ La Vara

$$ | Spanish. The accent at this diminutive restaurant with exposed-brick walls and ample bar space is on Spanish tapas with Moorish and Jewish influences. Choose among many tasty small plates, including eggplant with cheese, fried artichokes, and a daily selection of savory croquettes. **Known for:** authentic Spanish tapas with flair; intimate atmosphere; garden seating. *Average main: $17* ⊠ *268 Clinton St., Cobble Hill* ☎ *718/422–0065* ⊕ *www.lavarany.com* ⊘ *No lunch weekdays* Ⓜ *F, G to Bergen St.*

Mile End

$$ | Deli. Smoked meat in the form of brisket, turkey, chicken, and duck plays a starring role at this Montréal-style Jewish deli-restaurant that's nearly always full. The brisket finds its way into the signature smoked meat sandwich, the breakfast hash, and even poutine—french fries blanketed with gravy and cheese curds. **Known for:** Montréal-style Jewish-deli menu; smoked meats; modern diner decor. *Average main: $17* ⊠ *97A Hoyt St., Boerum Hill* ☎ *718/852–7510* ⊕ *www.mileenddeli.com* Ⓜ *A, C, G to Hoyt–Schermerhorn Sts.*

★ Rucola

$$ | Italian. Magnificently prepared seasonal vegetables in sides, salads, appetizers, and pastas are the focal point of the menu at this dark-wood Italian restaurant, but don't overlook entrées that range from roast chicken to perfectly prepared branzino or a leg of lamb. Dining at the communal table in the center of the restaurant is fun; opt for bar seating or the few two-tops for a more intimate meal. **Known for:** seasonal ingredients; fine cocktails and desserts; romantic setting. *Average main: $20* ⊠ *190 Dean St., Boerum Hill* ☎ *718/576–3209* ⊕ *www.rucolabrooklyn.com* Ⓜ *A, C, G Hoyt–Schermerhorn St.; F, G to Bergen St.*

Sam's Restaurant

$$ | Italian. If it looks old-school, it's because it is: Sam's has been around since the 1930s, and though the decor is a bit tired, the red leather banquettes and walls hung with faded photos from days gone by have a decidedly charming effect. The Italian fare is classic and comforting, including good thin-crust pizzas. **Known for:** classic red-sauce dishes; thin-crust pizza; old-school Brooklyn-Italian style. *Average main: $15* ⊠ *238 Court St., Cobble Hill* ☎ *718/596–3458* ⊘ *Closed Tues.* ⊟ *No credit cards* Ⓜ *F, G to Bergen St.*

Watty & Meg

$$ | American. A neighborhood favorite for its handsome bar, ample seating, and friendly wait-staff, Watty & Meg dishes up New American fare with flair and a hint of Southern comfort. Dine here for indulgent short ribs, fresh-made pasta, tangy green or grain salads, and fish and other daily specials. **Known for:** eclectic American menu; weekend brunch; friendly, sophisticated atmosphere. *Average main: $20* ⊠ *248 Court St., Cobble Hill* ☎ *718/643–0007* ⊕ *wattyandmeg.com* Ⓜ *F, G to Bergen St.*

Yemen Café

$$ | **Middle Eastern.** Head up the steps to sample some of Brooklyn's finest, authentic Yemeni cuisine, from savory *haneeth* (slow-cooked meat with basmati rice and sauce), to delectable baba ghanoush and hummus, to kebabs, to fish and vegetarian dishes—though the succulent lamb is the real star here. The setting is somewhat nondescript, but portions are large and the flavors are unforgettable. **Known for:** authentic Yemeni fare; memorable lamb dishes; filling portions. *Average main: $19* ⊠ *176 Atlantic Ave., Cobble Hill* ☎ *718/834–9533* ⊕ *www.yemencafe.com* Ⓜ *R to Court St., 4, 5 to Borough Hall.*

Bars and Nightlife

Boat

This popular dive bar, hidden behind a bright-red facade, has many draws, including the casual, borderline grungy ambience, a classic pinball machine, a jukebox, and cheap happy hour specials. ⊠ *175 Smith St., Boerum Hill* ☎ *718/254–0607* Ⓜ *F, G to Bergen St.*

★ Brooklyn Inn

One of Brooklyn's oldest and most unassuming bars, the Brooklyn Inn doesn't rely on gimmicks: it just serves reasonably priced beer and mainstay cocktails. The formula must work, because the place dates back to the 19th century. With high ceilings and large windows in front—there's a pool table in back—this is the quintessential neighborhood spot. ⊠ *148 Hoyt St.,* *Boerum Hill* ☎ *718/522–2525* Ⓜ *F, G to Bergen St.*

Camp

Board games cover the tables, canoes and taxidermied deer heads hang from the walls, and the smell of roasting s'mores fills the air at this homage to country-lodge living. If you appreciate kitsch, you'll dig this place. ⊠ *179 Smith St., Boerum Hill* ☎ *718/852–8086* ⊕ *www.camp-brooklyn.com* Ⓜ *F, G to Bergen St.*

Congress

A cool vibe, great selection of craft beers, and bartenders who know how to mix the perfect cocktail make this a go-to spot in the neighborhood. The perennially popular, meal-in-itself Bloody Mary—one secret ingredient is pickle brine—is garnished with beef jerky, smoked cheddar, celery, an olive, and crostini. There's not much seating in the softly lit space, which encourages people to mix and mingle. ⊠ *208 Court St., Cobble Hill* ⊕ *www.congressbarbk.com* Ⓜ *F, G to Bergen St.*

Elsa

The sleek, modern take on art deco decor is part of Elsa's feminine-leaning style, which successfully draws in women for marvelous cocktails worth their Manhattan-caliber prices. The shallow banquettes make conversation easy, and there's a large back garden for enjoying warm evening breezes. The Singer sewing machine at the bar is no longer for hems but converted as a draft-beer stand. Don't miss Brooklyn's coolest washrooms, with mirror-clad arches and marble finishes. ⊠ *136 Atlantic Ave., Cobble Hill* ☎ *917/882–7395* ⊕ *elsabarnyc.com* Ⓜ *R to Court St.; 4, 5 to Borough Hall.*

61 Local

A pleasant place to linger with a glass of wine or a craft beer, this low-lit bar with exposed-brick walls and a high ceiling has an extensive menu of nibbles, sandwiches, and large plates, most with ingredients sourced from the tristate area and Brooklyn. ⊠ *61 Bergen St., Boerum Hill* ☎ *718/875–1150* ⊕ *www.61local.com* Ⓜ *F, G to Bergen St.*

🛏 Hotels

NU Hotel Brooklyn

$ | **Hotel.** The hip-yet-affordable NU, on one of Brooklyn's main nightlife and shopping streets, is perfect for visitors seeking a perch near the best of the borough. **Pros:** great Brooklyn launching pad; knowledgeable staff; 24-hour fitness center. **Cons:** subway or cab ride to anything in Manhattan; bar area can be a little too quiet; limited in-room amenities. *Rooms from: $299* ⊠ *85 Smith St., Boerum Hill* ☎ *718/852–8585* ⊕ *www.nuhotelbrooklyn.com* ⤵ *93 rooms* ❏ *Breakfast* Ⓜ *F, G to Bergen St.; A, C, G to Hoyt–Schermerhorn Sts.*

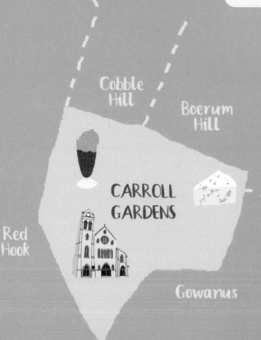

Cobble
Hill

Boerum
Hill

CARROLL
GARDENS

Red
Hook

Gowanus

Carroll Gardens navigates the terrain between trendy and retro with cutting-edge shops, bistros, and cocktail lounges amiably coexisting alongside old-school butcher shops, coffee roasters, and bakeries owned by Italian-American families. Italians began moving into this area in the late 1800s and have lived here for so long that the neighborhood's early-19th-century Irish roots are but a dim memory. One Irish-era legacy current residents appreciate, though, are the spacious front-yard gardens of homes, most notably the "Place" blocks, 1st through 4th, between Henry and Smith streets. These verdant patches lend the neighborhood the "Gardens" half of its name, initiated by real estate agents in the 1960s, when redevelopment commenced. Carroll Gardens is often linked with Boerum Hill and Cobble Hill, sometimes via the ungainly shorthand BoCoCa, and their main retail and dining arteries, Smith and Court streets, perform the same function here. Recent-arrival Manhattanites and French expats have infused the neighborhood with a Parisian–West Village vibe that pairs well with the longtime residents' workaday nonchalance. Many a fine establishment has folded in recent years because of the speculative real estate market in the area. Support the places you love, while they're here.

—*Updated by Christina Knight*

◉ Sights

Court Street

Court Street is the eclectic main artery of Carroll Gardens. It's a quick lesson in gentrification, too, as you'll see shops like D'Amico, the third-generation coffee roaster, and tax offices sharing walls with cool dive bars and yoga studios. But Court Street, and Carroll Gardens in general, is not a story of "us versus them": sit on a bench in leafy Carroll Park and you'll find nannies with strollers and octogenarian Italian men playing bocce coexisting in perfect harmony. ⊠ *Carroll Gardens* Ⓜ *F, G to Bergen St., Carroll St., or Smith–9th Sts.*

St. Mary Star of the Sea

One of the oldest operating Catholic churches in Brooklyn, the neo-Gothic St. Mary Star of the Sea opened in 1855 and once had a clear view to the New York Harbor. Its well-known architect Patrick C. Keely was an Irish immigrant, the stained-glass windows were imported from Munich in 1897, and the altar rail—installed two years later—is made of marble from several Italian quarries. The church may be more interesting to some for the fact that Al Capone was married here back on December 18, 1918. Mass is held daily and open to the public. ⊠ *467 Court St., Carroll Gardens* ☎ *718/625–2270* ⊕ *www. stmarystarbrooklyn.com* Ⓜ *F, G to Carroll St. or Smith–9th Sts.*

Smith Street

While Court Street is home to some of the neighborhood's oldest businesses, Smith is a street of transition—a result of booming real estate prices and the neighborhood's changing tastes. These days, you can find trendy bars and restaurants alongside long dormant storefronts and sleek new constructions awaiting new occupants. On weekends the street can be packed day and night. This is the best drag of all the nearby neighborhoods to hear live music on Sunday evenings. ⊠ *Carroll Gardens* Ⓜ *F, G to Bergen St., Carroll St., or Smith–9th Sts.*

 Shopping

Articlo&

This is the place to go for eclectic, anything-but-basic separates and accessories. Rollas straight-leg jeans, kitschy PepaLoves blouses, and style splurges like a statement kitten heel pump by Intentionally Blank come together in this fabulous shop. Look for on-trend yet affordable brands like Seaworthy, Jeffrey Campbell, and BB Dakota. ⊠ *198 Smith St., Carroll Gardens* ☎ *718/852–3620* ⊕ *www.articleand. com* Ⓜ *F, G to Bergen St.*

Bird

Looking for the chicest women's wear in Brooklyn? You'll find it at this beloved boutique known for its high prices attached to enviable items from Tsumori Chisato, Marni, and Ulla Johnson, to name a few of the indie designers. Everything from knit sweater dresses and cardigans to statement shoes and delicate gold jewelry share the cozy space. There are a few items for men as well. ⊠ *220 Smith St., Carroll Gardens* ☎ *718/797–3774* ⊕ *www.birdbrooklyn. com* Ⓜ *F, G to Bergen St.*

Black Gold Records

If you're skilled, you can sip coffee and simultaneously flip through new and used record albums—all genres of music are the main trade here, other than the quirky examples of taxidermy, vintage posters, some terrariums and antiques, and the Black Gold Blend roasted privately in nearby Red Hook. The coffee-record shop also serves pastries from Goodbatch, Ovenly, and Balthazar. Check the website for occasional $1 sales. ⊠ *461 Court St., Carroll Gardens* ☎ *347/227–8227* ⊕ *http://blackgoldbrooklyn.com/* Ⓜ *F, G to Carroll Gardens or Smith–9th Sts.*

Books Are Magic

A bookstore's conversation starter is the shelving closest to the entrance, and the opening is biography/ memoir, current events, and New York Review of Books. There are no small-talk gift items in sight but the chatter increases in the large children's section that has helpful labels like "New Middle Grade" for the well-read child and "New York,"

BERGEN ST.
F,G

Dean St.

Bergen St.

Wyckoff St.

Hoyt St.

Bond St.

Baltic St.

Douglass St.

Butler St.

Degraw St.

Sackett St.

Gowanus Canal

Bond St.

Union St.

Nevins St.

Carroll St.

1st St.

CARROLL GARDENS

3rd Ave.

0 _____ 1000 ft

0 _____ 200 m

plus a comfy couch. Several author talks are held each week which accounts for the signed paperbacks by writers like Michael Chabon. ✉ *225 Smith St., Carroll Gardens* ☎ *718/246–2665* ⊕ *booksaremagic. net/* Ⓜ *F, G to Carroll St. or Bergen St.*

Caputo's Fine Foods
Counter service can be slow, but a visit to Italian fine food emporium Caputo's for freshly made mozzarella and handcrafted pastas (fresh or frozen) is worth the wait. Italian-made ladyfinger cookies and mascarpone cheese are other favorites, as are imported olive oils and cured meats like prosciutto and various salami. This is the perfect place to pick up a Carroll Gardens food souvenir (although you might end up eating it on the way home). They close at 2:30 pm on Sunday. ✉ *460 Court St., Carroll Gardens* ☎ *718/855–8852* Ⓜ *F, G to Carroll St.*

★ **Court Street Grocers**
Part sandwich shop, part specialty food store, Court Street Grocers is a one-stop shop for Brooklyn's most food-curious visitors. The shop's owners scour the world for products, including regional sodas, chocolate bars, and potato chips. A long list of delicious sandwiches are sold in back: favorites include the Reuben made with house-corned beef brisket, sauerkraut and "comeback" sauce, and the Ultimate Warrior, with slow-roasted pork shoulder, broccoli rabe, provolone, and hot peppers on a Caputo hero. ✉ *485 Court St., Carroll Gardens* ☎ *718/722–7229* ⊕ *www.courtstreet-grocers.com* Ⓜ *F, G to Smith–9th Sts.*

GETTING HERE

The Bergen and Carroll Street stops on the F and G lines are the most convenient for Carroll Gardens: both are on Smith Street, one of the neighborhood's main drags.

Mama Says Comics Rock
This slim shop fills a void in comic book coverage in this area of Brooklyn. Take a seat on the long pew and leaf reverently through your find. New arrivals of Marvel, DC, Image, Vertigo, IDW, and others are posted online on Wednesdays and the young, friendly owners are happy to make recommendations. They'll mail a mystery bag or care package of six to eight comics to your happy (or unhappy) camper in the summer, or friend who needs some new material. ✉ *306 Court St., Carroll Gardens* ☎ *718/797–3464* ⊕ *www.mamasayscomics.com* Ⓜ *F, G to Court St.*

Néda
Women's boutique Néda specializes in edgy (yet not too flashy) party frocks, sundresses, and statement sweaters in bold colors, jumbo florals, and flirty and festive prints and patterns. Designers represented include Plenty By Tracy Reese, Umsteigen, Pepaloves, Atelier Nicole Miller, and Weston Wear. Check out the jewelry selection, which can be more affordable than the clothing. ✉ *302 Court St., Carroll Gardens* ☎ *718/624–6332* ⊕ *www.nedaboutique.com* Ⓜ *F, C to Bergen St. or Carroll St.*

Refinery

Distinctive scarves and jewelry, durable, handmade fabric bags made by the owner, and mid-century furniture and vintage accessories beckon at this small boutique, but the real draw is the selection of traditional clogs, specifically Troentorp and Sven clogs in a variety of colorful and customizable styles. ⊠ *248 Smith St., Carroll Gardens* ☎ *718/643–7861* Ⓜ *F, G to Bergen St. or Carroll St.*

Stinky Brooklyn

If the name doesn't tip you off, Stinky is a mighty fine cheese shop (the case is typically stacked with a couple dozen selections) that also sells sandwiches, coffee, and a selection of charcuterie and specialty fine foods from both far away and around the block. Craft beer is available by the growler, including brews from throughout Kings County. The staff are always willing to give you a taste, sip, or sniff. ⊠ *215 Smith St., Carroll Gardens* ☎ *718/596–2873* ⊕ *www.stinkybklyn.com* Ⓜ *F, G to Bergen St.*

★ Swallow

If you're looking for a gift or a special trinket for that hard-to-shop-for friend or family member who has exquisite taste and an appreciation for the fine designs of nature, head to Swallow. Anatomy- and nature-inspired jewelry, vases, painted gold-leaf mirrors, chimes made of obsidian shards and dried eucalyptus, and other objets d'art and curiosities are just some of the offerings. Browsing here is a bit like traveling down the rabbit

> ### BRIDGE OVER GOWANUS
>
> The Carroll Street Bridge, over the Gowanus Canal, connects Carroll Gardens and Gowanus. It was built in 1889 and is the oldest retractable bridge in the country. The 26-foot-wide, 107-foot-long bridge retracts horizontally to let barge traffic through. It was designated a New York City landmark in 1987.

hole into a grown-up's housewares wonderland. ⊠ *361 Smith St., Carroll Gardens* ☎ *718/222–8201* ⊕ *www. dearswallow.com* Ⓜ *F, G to Carroll St.*

☕ Coffee and Quick Bites

Brooklyn Farmacy

$ | **American.** Half the fun of this 1920s-style soda fountain is the setting, with swirl-top stools and vintage apothecary drawers and penny-tile floors from the long-closed Longos Pharmacy. The other is a dream menu for sweet tooths. **Known for:** classic Brooklyn desserts; huge sundaes; a vintage feel, courtesy of history and a reality TV show transformation. *Average main: $9* ⊠ *513 Henry St., Carroll Gardens* ☎ *718/522–6260* ⊕ *www. brooklynfarmacyandsodafountain.com* Ⓜ *F, G to Carroll St.*

Mazzola Bakery

$ | **Bakery.** This bakery is all about lard bread. "Lard bread," you ask? It's a loaf of slightly sweet, buttery and crusty Italian white bread with a generous amount of cured pork and provolone cheese baked right in—think of it as "prosciutto bread."

They also sell croissants, muffins, and hazelnut coffee cake but it's the lard bread you must try here, ideally still hot. **Known for:** lard bread; old-world, old Brooklyn feel. *Average main: $8* ⊠ *192 Union St., Carroll Gardens* ☎ *718/643–1719* 🚫 *No credit cards* Ⓜ *F, G to Carroll St.*

★ Milkmade Tasting Room

$ | **American.** This small ice-cream tasting room, both cute and hard-core, keeps fans coming back with two seasonal flavors every month. That's in addition to the eight signature ice creams and gelatos made here like Coffee gelato with a dash of Kings County whiskey, Rock Rock Rockaway Road built on marzipan ice cream, and Gotham Basil Chip made with greens grown on local rooftops. **Known for:** unique, seasonal flavors; organic ingredients; partnering with other small businesses, from bakers to brewers. *Average main: $10* ⊠ *204 Sackett St., Brooklyn* ⊕ *www.milk-madeicecream.com/* 🌙 *Closed Mon.* Ⓜ *F, G to Carroll St.*

Smith Canteen

$ | **Café.** Expertly pulled cappuccinos and a roster of baked goods including salted chocolate cookies and the ingenious "everything" croissant make Smith Canteen (from the owners of Wilma Jean and Nightingale 9) an excellent stop. But the tempting menu of breakfast and lunch fare like the quinoa bowl with fresh vegetables and fried eggs may entice you to linger. **Known for:** the "everything" croissant; healthy breakfast and lunch; good coffee. *Average main:*

$4 ⊠ *343 Smith St., Carroll Gardens* ☎ *347/294–0292* ⊕ *www.smithcanteen.com* Ⓜ *F, G to Carroll St.*

🍴 Dining

Avlee Greek Kitchen

$$ | **Greek.** Authentic dishes and the use of top-grade products (olive oil, feta, freshly baked pita) are the reasons locals adore this restaurant. Start with the Prasini salad, a delicious blend of crisp romaine, dill, scallions, and a generous amount of the aforementioned salty cheese. **Known for:** Greek fries with feta cheese; friendly owners and staff; neighborhood favorite. *Average main: $17* ⊠ *349 Smith St., Carroll Gardens* ☎ *718/855–5125* ⊕ *www.avleegreekkitchen.com* Ⓜ *F, G to Carroll St.*

Battersby

$$$ | **Modern American.** The five-course tasting menu is the $75 ticket to a reservation at this small, acclaimed restaurant. Chefs and co-owners Walker Stern and Joe Ogrodnek met while working for Alain Ducasse and are known for highly seasonal cooking that merges French techniques with the products of Brooklyn, the Hudson Valley, and points beyond. **Known for:** five-course tasting menu; consistently excellent dishes; the bar's deft hand with cocktails. *Average main: $33* ⊠ *255 Smith St., Carroll Gardens* ☎ *718/852–8321* ⊕ *www.battersbybrooklyn.com* 🌙 *Closed Mon. and Tues. No lunch* Ⓜ *F, G to Bergen St. or Carroll St.*

Buttermilk Channel

$$ | American. This Southern-accented new American bistro draws epic brunch lines and a legion of neighborhood families (the Clown Sundae is legendary among Carroll Gardens kids). But when day turns to night, Buttermilk Channel transforms into a surprisingly serious restaurant with an excellent, mostly American wine list. **Known for:** fried pork chop or chicken with cheddar waffles; three-course Monday-night prix fixe; unusual ingredient combinations. *Average main: $23 ⊠ 524 Court St., Carroll Gardens ☎ 718/852–8490 ⊕ www.buttermilkchannelnyc. com* Ⓜ *F, G to Smith–9th Sts.*

Cafe Luluc

$$ | French. This French bistro is a longtime, lively neighborhood favorite, especially for weekend brunch, when lines can spill out onto the sidewalk. Francophiles can get classics like croque monsieur, brioche French toast, and moules marinière but the extensive menu spans contemporary cuisine. **Known for:** three-course, weeknight prix-fixe menu before 7 pm; late evening kitchen; brunch pancakes, which also can be ordered on Sunday evening. *Average main: $20 ⊠ 214 Smith St., Carroll Gardens ☎ 718/625–3815* Ⓜ *F, G to Bergen St.*

Cubano Café

$ | Latin American. The quaint, colorful island decor will pull you in like the tide if you happen upon the eatery in warm weather, when a painted banister is the only thing separating tables from the sidewalk. The vibe is pleasant and as long as you're forewarned that dishes are more Latin American than Cuban, you won't bemoan the lack of authentic cuisine. **Known for:** island vibe; Latin cuisine; affordable meals. *Average main: $12 ⊠ 272 Smith St., Carroll Gardens ☎ 929/337–6476 ⊕ www.cubanacafecarrollgardens.com/* ⊟ *No credit cards* Ⓜ *F, G to Carroll St.*

East One Coffee Roasters

$$ | Contemporary. No, it's not just a coffee shop named after a London postal code. It's also a worthy bar with a great happy hour and $1 oysters, and a restaurant with a small and tasty menu of lunch, dinner, and brunch items. **Known for:** happy hour; vegan and vegetarian options; laid-back atmosphere. *Average main: $16 ⊠ 384 Court St., Carroll Gardens ☎ 347/987–4919 ⊕ www.eastonecoffee.com* ⊘ *No dinner Mon. and Tues.* Ⓜ *F, G to Carroll St.*

Frankies Spuntino 457

$$ | Italian. A longtime favorite culinary pioneer in Carroll Gardens, Frank Castronovo and Frank Falcinelli's Italian-American restaurant has atmosphere to spare between the backyard and former blacksmith stable. Choose from the well-conceived menu's shareable salads (many with vegetables roasted or marinated with the Frankies' own Sicilian olive oil), handmade pastas like the cavatelli with hot sausage and browned sage butter, meatballs, and crusty sandwiches that ask to be shared. **Known for:** outdoor dining; menu options for all kinds of eaters; less than warm staff. *Average main: $20* ✉ *457 Court St., Carroll Gardens* ☎ *718/403–0033* ⊕ *www.frankiess-puntino.com* Ⓜ *F, G to Carroll St. or Smith–9th Sts.*

Gersi
$$ | **Italian.** One of the favorite items at this family-friendly restaurant specializing in northern Italian cuisine is the gently priced spaghetti al limone. Dishes are prepared with ingredients from the Carroll Gardens farmers market. **Known for:** fresh ingredients; welcoming staff; family-friendly service. *Average main: $19* ✉ *316 Court St., Carroll Gardens* ☎ *347/889–5077* ⊕ *www.gersirestaurant.com* ⊘ *No lunch weekdays* Ⓜ *F, G to Carroll St.*

La Slowteria
$ | **Mexican.** The beachside airiness here blew in from Tulum, as did the chef-owner and the small menu of southern Mexican favorites. Dishes are artfully presented and part of the owner's slow-food principles. **Known for:** guacamole made tableside; covered back patio; drinks like avocado-milk-honey. *Average main: $10* ✉ *548 Court St., Carroll Gardens* ☎ *718/858–2222* ⊕ *laslowterianyc.com* Ⓜ *F, G to Smith–9th Sts.*

★ Lucali
$$$ | **Pizza.** If you worship at the altar of Neapolitan pizza—thin-crust pies baked quickly in blistering brick ovens—Lucali is a worthy pilgrimage. Ordering is simple: there's one large pie and a choice of toppings from beef pepperoni to vegetables like grilled artichokes;

and calzones in two sizes, which come with a side of marinara sauce. **Known for:** thin, crispy crusts; hours-long waits; cash-only. *Average main: $25* ✉ *575 Henry St., Carroll Gardens* ☎ *718/858–4086* ⊕ *www.lucali.com* ⊘ *Closed Tues. No lunch* ⊟ *No credit cards* Ⓜ *F, G to Carroll St.*

Nightingale 9
$$ | **Asian Fusion.** Though it's named after an old Brooklyn telephone code, Nightingale 9 takes its culinary inspiration from "long distance": Asia. Dishes are reimagined with Chef Rob Newton's Arkansas childhood in mind, resulting in plates like grilled Mississippi catfish served cha ca style or duck salad with collard greens, sweet potato, chili, and basil. **Known for:** $10 pho bowls on Sunday; crispy spring rolls; the bar's cocktails. *Average main: $17* ✉ *329 Smith St., Carroll Gardens* ☎ *347/689–4699* ⊕ *www.nightingale9.com* ⊘ *Closed Mon. No lunch* Ⓜ *F, G to Carroll St.*

Prime Meats
$$$ | **Steakhouse.** Steak, sausages, and serious Prohibition-era cocktails: it's a winning combination for Frank Castronovo and Frank Falcinelli, who opened this Frankies offshoot as a tribute to turn-of-the-20th-century wood-paneled dining rooms. Try a chilled iceberg-lettuce salad with Maytag blue cheese and a Vesper or dry martini to start, followed by a grilled heritage pork chop or perhaps an order of steak frites—though there are

many other options, including three kinds of German-style house-made sausages. **Known for:** meat dishes in large portions; extensive brunch menu. *Average main: $26 ⊠ 465 Court St., Carroll Gardens ☎ 718/254–0327 ⊕ www.frankspm.com Ⓜ F, G to Carroll St. or Smith–9th Sts.*

Ugly Baby
$$ | Thai. Spicy, regional Thai food by chef Sirichai Sreparplarn heats up this end of Smith Street where businesses peter out. Dishes can be shared family-style, from the Laab Ped Udon (spicy duck salad) to Kao Tod Nam Klook (curried rice, pork skin, peanut and ginger sauce) to Tom Som Pla Kra Pong (Central-style red snapper in a complex ginger and tamarind sauce). **Known for:** chili heat (if you want it); authentic regional Thai dishes; scrapping the shrimp/tofu/chicken/beef option. *Average main: $18 ⊠ 407 Smith St., Carroll Gardens ☎ 347/689–3075 ⊕ uglybabynyc.com Ⓜ F, G to Carroll St.*

Wilma Jean's
$ | Southern. The chef/owner of Nightingale 9 sticks closer to his Southern roots in this spot named for his grandmother. Comfort foods on offer include pimento cheese, fried bologna sandwiches, and baskets of perfectly seasoned fried chicken. **Known for:** family-friendly menu and space; Southern takes on Mexican and Asian staples. *Average main: $9 ⊠ 345 Smith St., Brooklyn ☎ 718/422–0444 ⊕ www.wilmajean345.com ☉ Closed Mon. Ⓜ F, G to Carroll St.*

Zaytoons. Located at 283 Smith St., Carroll Gardens. *See Chapter 7, Prospects Heights, for full review.*

🍸 Bars and Nightlife

Bar Great Harry
Though it's named after a small cocktail bar in the Chinatown area of Yokohama, Japan, it feels like a college town hangout and the 24 taps make it the spot for rotating craft beers from all over, including Transmitter Brewing's Bar Great Harry sour ale. There's no pretension here between the friendly bartenders, pinball machines in the back room, and playlist that could be metal or hip-hop. Even kids are welcome (the under-10 kind). ⊠ *280 Smith St., Carroll Gardens ⊕ www.bargreatharry.com Ⓜ F, G to Bergen St. or Carroll St.*

Brooklyn Social
From their black-and-white photos from the 1920s, former members of this erstwhile Sicilian social club watch over the clientele enjoying fancy cocktails at the laid-back bar with period tap, cash box, and clock that now seem enviably luxurious. Pressed sandwiches are on offer, too. A pool table and small but well-manicured backyard have long made this a popular weekend spot. ⊠ *335 Smith St., Carroll Gardens ☎ 718/858–7758 ⊕ www.brooklynsocialbar.com Ⓜ F, G to Carroll St.*

★ Clover Club
Long recognized for excellent drinks—both classic and inspired by the classics—and a cozy vibe,

this is one of the best cocktail bars in Brooklyn. The whole operation is thanks to Julie Reiner, a passionate mixologist and businesswoman who has long been a leader in the industry. Each quarter, she and her bar staff write a seasonal cocktail list, inspired perhaps by a spirit (Chartreuse, for example) or a classic drink style (like the flip). Weekends get busy; we recommend weekdays in the early evening when you can sit at the bar and call bartender's choice. Weekend brunch is very good, too, and not just for the Bloody Mary: the lamb burger is excellent, and there's a nice selection of baked eggs. ⌧ *210 Smith St., Carroll Gardens* ☎ *718/855–7939* ⊕ *www.cloverclubny. com* Ⓜ *F, G to Bergen St.*

Gowanus Yacht Club

Open May through October, this outdoor bar wedged next to a Carroll Street subway entrance is a favorite with fans of both cheap beer (like cans of PBR) and glasses or pitchers of craft brew. Picnic tables line the patio space belonging to the adjacent bagel shop. The menu is driven by the grill, which means hamburgers, hotdogs, kielbasa, and knockwurst. (There's always a vegan option, too.) ⌧ *323 Smith St., Carroll Gardens* ☎ *718/246–1321* Ⓜ *F, G to Carroll St.*

Other Half Brewing Company

Founded in 2014, the Other Half brews its famous IPAs and a few other beers in a former warehouse near the Gowanus Expressway on the edge of Carroll Gardens. Despite the industrial location and small, spartan taproom, fans of hops regularly pack it in here with just enough room to bend an elbow. There are no flights but brews like Cheddar Broccoli, Ain't Nothing Nice, and True Green are poured in four-ounce samples. ⌧ *195 Centre St., Carroll Gardens* ☎ *347/987–3527* ⊕ *www.otherhalfbrewing.com* ⊙ *Closed Sun.–Wed.* Ⓜ *F, G to Smith–9th Sts.*

14

Red Hook and the Columbia Waterfront District

Brooklyn Heights

COLUMBIA WATERFRONT DISTRICT

Cobble Hill

Carroll Gardens

RED HOOK

TACOS TACOS MEXICANOS TACOS

Gowanus

A laid-back area along the western Brooklyn waterfront, Red Hook entices with redbrick Civil War–era warehouses, views of the Statue of Liberty and lower New York Harbor, and destination bars and restaurants. Rural until the mid-19th century, when the area developed into a major shipping and ship-repair hub, Red Hook thrived until after World War II, when the introduction of container ports elsewhere in New York and New Jersey resulted in dockworker layoffs and business closures. The building of the Gowanus Expressway, in 1946, isolated the already remote Red Hook from the rest of Brooklyn, and the neighborhood attracted a growing number of artists and activists as a result of inexpensive rents. Momentum picked up with the arrival of an IKEA store in 2008 and a flourishing number of shops, bars, and restaurants along Van Brunt Street, the main drag. Just north of Red Hook is the mostly residential Columbia Waterfront District, where excellent restaurants are a big draw. Both Red Hook and the Columbia Waterfront District neighborhoods have become more accessible with the expansion of the Citi Bike bikeshare program.

—*Updated by Caroline Trefler*

👁 Sights

Cacao Prieto and Widow Jane

Blending two very worthwhile pursuits, this redbrick building does double duty as both a chocolate factory (Cacao Prieto) and a liquor distillery (Widow Jane). Informative tours of the atmospheric premises (check out the chickens in the courtyard) start in the chocolate factory and then head to the distillery, with tasting samples of both sides of the business. The distressed-wood shop in the front room, with shelves of liquor bottles and gift items, is as lovely as the wrapping on the chocolate bars. ⊠ *218 Conover St., Red Hook* ☎ *347/225–0130* ⊕ *www.*

cacaoprieto.com ✉ *$20 for a 1-hr tour, weekends book in advance* Ⓜ *F, G to Smith–9th Sts.*

★ Louis Valentino, Jr. Park and Pier

This small pier and park, named for a fallen firefighter, has awe-inspiring views of the Statue of Liberty and across the Hudson. You won't need prompting to take pictures. There are a few benches for relaxing. ⊠ *Coffey St. and Ferris St., Red Hook* ⊕ *www.nycgovparks.org* ✉ *Free* Ⓜ *F, G to Smith–9th Sts.*

★ Pioneer Works

Occupying the 19th-century redbrick headquarters of the eponymous machine manufacturer, the Pioneer

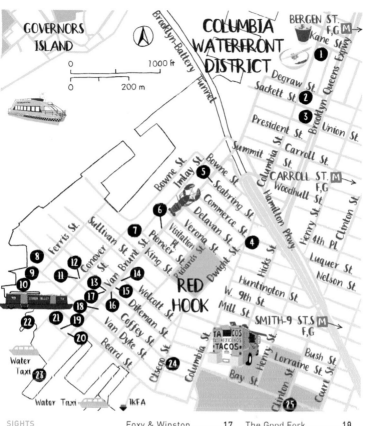

Works Center for Art and Innovation is a soaring three-level space dedicated to the arts. Reclaimed and retooled by Red Hook artist Dustin Yellin, the repurposed building is home to a collection of arts and science residency studios that showcase changing exhibitions and performance art. Lively opening parties, films, and concerts are open to the public as well. The backyard is a miniwonderland of landscaping and artwork. ⊠ *159 Pioneer St., Red Hook* ☎ *718/596–3001* ⊕ *www.pioneerworks.org* ✉ *Free* ⊙ *Closed Mon. and Tues.* Ⓜ *F, G to Smith–9th Sts.*

Raaka Co. Virgin Chocolate

Red Hook has two chocolate factories, not just one, and Raaka stands out from most as they specialize in unroasted or "raw" chocolate. You can learn about their entire bean-to-bar process during in-depth and informative tours that include tastings (book in advance) or, if you really want to explore your inner Willy Wonka, sign up for one of their popular chocolate-making classes. ⊠ *64 Seabring St., Red Hook* ☎ *855/255–3354* ⊕ *www.raakachocolate.com* ✉ *$15 for a 45-min tour* Ⓜ *F, G to Smith–9th Sts.*

★ Red Hook Winery

Based in a warehouse on a riverside pier, the Red Hook Winery bottles an astonishing variety of red, white, and pink wines, all made with New York State grapes. The front rooms of the facility are furnished with a marble-topped bar, several upturned wine barrels, and a few tables and couches,

GETTING HERE

The closest subway stop to Red Hook is Smith–9th Streets on the F and G lines, a brisk 20-minute walk to Van Brunt Street. The B61 and B57 buses also run to the neighborhood as well. The picturesque way to arrive is via the New York Water Taxi. The Columbia Waterfront District is a 10- to 15-minute walk from either the Carroll Street or Bergen Street stations on the F and G. There are also a number of Citi Bike Stations.

where glasses or flights are served. Tours are offered on weekends. ⊠ *Pier 41, 325A, 175–204 Van Dyke St., Red Hook* ☎ *347/689–2432* ⊕ *www.redhookwinery.com/* ✉ *Tastings are $15 for 4 wines* ⊙ *Final tastings start at 5:30 pm* Ⓜ *F, G to Smith–9th Sts.*

Van Brunt Stillhouse

For an up-close look—and taste— into whiskey making, head to the Van Brunt Stillhouse for a tour ($10) of the distillery that includes tastings (rum, whiskey, and grappa are produced here), but if you want to delve deeper, the bar/tasting room serves creative takes on classic cocktails made with the house products. The tasting room is open to the public Thursday and Friday (4–9), Saturday (2–9), and Sunday (2–6). ⊠ *6 Bay St., Red Hook* ☎ *718/887–6012* ⊕ *www.vanbrunt-stillhouse.com* ⊙ *Closed Mon.–Wed.* Ⓜ *F, G to Smith–9th Sts.*

Waterfront Museum and Showboat Barge

Back before the age of giant shipping containers, barges owned by the railroad companies plied the New York Harbor, transporting cargo. The restored all-wooden Lehigh Valley Railroad Barge Number 79 dates back to the beginning of the 20th century and currently operates as a small museum (Saturday 1–5 and Thursday 4–8) dedicated to Brooklyn's maritime heritage. Check out the 1938 *Mary A. Whalen* (weekdays 10–6, and second Sunday of the month May–September; Pier 11, next to the NYC ferry stop) nearby, too. ⊠ *290 Conover St., Red Hook* ☎ *718/624–4719* ⊕ *www.waterfrontmuseum.org* ☉ *Closed mornings; Sun.–Wed, Fri.* Ⓜ *F, G to Smith–9th Sts.*

Shopping

Erie Basin

Heralded for his impeccably modern taste in antique jewelry, Russell Whitmore is the heart, soul, and eye behind Erie Basin. Many an antique wedding ring has been purchased at the classy shop—this is not flea market jumble—but there are also furniture, art, and objects dating from the 18th to the mid-20th century. Prices range from $30 to $30,000. ⊠ *388 Van Brunt St., Red Hook* ☎ *718/554–6147* ⊕ *www.erie-basin.com* Ⓜ *F, G to Smith–9th Sts.*

Foxy & Winston

The selection of quirky items at this small store, ranging from screen-printed textiles, offbeat home ware, elegant soaps, handmade letter-press cards and stationery, as well as children's toys and clothes, will have you racking your brain to think of people to buy presents for. ⊠ *392 Van Brunt St., Red Hook* ☎ *718/928–4855* ⊕ *www.foxyandwinston.com* Ⓜ *F, G to Smith–9th Sts.*

☕ Coffee and Quick Bites

★ Baked

$ | Café. Original creations like the Brookster (chocolate chip cookie dough baked inside a brownie) and delicious interpretations of whoopie pies, blondies, bars, and cookies keep this sleek bakery and café buzzing. There are breakfast items and a few lunchtime savory selections, too. **Known for:** creative brownie recipes; comfy seating, homemade granola (take some home). *Average main: $4* ⊠ *359 Van Brunt St., Red Hook* ☎ *718/222–0345* ⊕ *www.bakednyc.com* Ⓜ *F, G to Smith–9th Sts.*

Nobletree Coffee

$ | Café. If you like to geek out on coffee, the Nobletree headquarters is worth a visit: the facility has been roasting coffee since 2014 (much of it from their own coffee farms in Brazil) and the small café inside functions almost more as a tasting room, serving a variety of blends—brewed to order, of course—as well as specialty drinks that seem almost like coffee and tea cocktails. **Known for:** premiere (and pricey) coffee; super-knowledgeable staff; cozy library lounge. *Average main: $4* ⊠ *499 Brunt St., Red Hook* ☎ *718/643–6080* ⊕ *www.nobletreecoffee.com* Ⓜ *F, G to Smith–9th Sts.*

Red Hook Food Vendors Marketplace

$ | Fast Food. Food trucks selling top-notch, mostly Central American food have been congregating at the Red Hook sports fields on weekends (April–October, 10 am to sundown) for more than 40 years to feed hungry sports enthusiasts and foodies looking for exemplary cheap eats. The nine fields are undergoing a rotating, several-years-long reha-bilitation, and there are fewer food trucks than in years past, but the selection is still tempting. **Known for:** top-notch budget eats; picnic table seating; there's baseball, too. *Average main: $8 ⊠ 160 Bay St., Red Hook ⊕ www.redhookfoodvendors. com* Ⓜ *F, G to Smith–9th Sts.*

Steve's Authentic Key Lime Pies

$ | Bakery. Freshly squeezed key lime juice is just part of what imbues every bite of these pies with a taste of Florida sunshine. Steve Tarpin is a Florida native who's been making pies in Brooklyn for more than 20 years—always, always, always using Florida key lime juice squeezed fresh right before the pies are made. **Known for:** tart-size minipies; picnic table seating; frozen pie dipped in chocolate and served on a stick. *Average main: $6 ⊠ 185 Van Dyke St., Red Hook ☎ 718/858–5333* Ⓜ *F, G to Smith–9th Sts.*

🍴 Dining

Alma

$$ | Mexican. Spread over three levels, Alma is a neighborhood treasure, serving excellent Mexican food. The bottom floor is a busy bar; the second floor is a cozy dining room; and the third is a roof deck, heated in winter, with views of Manhattan. **Known for:** year-round roof deck; excellent margaritas; upscale prices. *Average main: $20 ⊠ 187 Columbia St., Brooklyn ☎ 718/643–5400 ⊕ www.almarestau-rant.com* ☾ *No lunch weekdays* Ⓜ *F, G to Carroll St.*

Brooklyn Crab

$$ | Seafood. Hanging out at this sprawling year-round crab shack can feel like you're a world away from New York City. The food hits all the high points—from peel-and-eat shrimp to seasonal crab specials, crab rolls, po'boys, oysters, and the Crab Royale dinner for two with a selection of crab and a lobster. **Known for:** outdoor spaces; lively atmosphere on weekend nights; laid-back afternoons. *Average main: $23 ⊠ 24 Reed St., Red Hook ☎ 718/643–2722 ⊕ www.brooklyncrab. com* Ⓜ *F, G to Smith–9th Sts.*

Defonte's

$ | Deli. The outrageously good heroes at Defonte's Sandwich Shop, overstuffed with cured meats, mozzarella, chicken parm, or fried eggplant, have made this store-front a Brooklyn institution. And after almost a century in business, they've certainly had time to perfect their recipes. **Known for:** old-school atmosphere; awesome sandwiches; just a few seats. *Average main: $10 ⊠ 379 Columbia St., Red Hook ☎ 718/625–8052* ☾ *No dinner, closed Sun.* ▭ *No credit cards* Ⓜ *F, G to Carroll St.*

Ferdinando's Focacceria

$$ | Italian. Basic decor, a pressed-tin roof, and family photos set the completely unpretentious, old-school mood at this laid-back neighborhood temple of Sicilian comfort food. Everything is delicious, but standouts include the *arancini* (rice balls), the pork-chop *pizzaiola* (cooked with peppers, tomatoes, and capers), and the *panelle* special, in which chickpea fritters meet ricotta in a sandwich with delicious results. **Known for:** great food; reasonable prices; closes at 8 Monday–Thursday. *Average main: $19* ⊠ *151 Union St., Brooklyn* ☎ *718/855-1545* ⊗ *Closed Sun.* Ⓜ *F, G to Carroll St.*

The Good Fork

$$ | Modern American. The husband-and-wife team behind the Good Fork marry Eastern and Western sensibilities at this charming restaurant. He's a native New Yorker and she grew up in South Korea, and the fusion-style menu ranges from homemade dumplings and Korean-style steak 'n' eggs to roasted chicken with fermented black-bean butter sauce. **Known for:** hand-built wooden interior; lovely back garden; creative Korean fusion food. *Average main: $24* ⊠ *391 Van Brunt St., Red Hook* ☎ *718/643-6636* ⊕ *www.goodfork. com* ⊗ *Closed Mon.; no lunch Tues.– Fri.* Ⓜ *F, G to Smith–9th Sts.*

★ Hometown Bar-B-Que

$$ | Barbecue. The smell of barbecue will have your mouth watering even before you get in the door of this cavernous hall, which many say serves the best BBQ around. Head for the counter to order meats by the pound, chicken, sandwiches, tacos, and sides. **Known for:** best BBQ around; lines are long on weekends; live music. *Average main: $20* ⊠ *454 Van Brunt St., Red Hook* ☎ *347/294-4644* ⊕ *www.home-townbarbque.com* ⊗ *Closed Mon.* Ⓜ *F, G to Smith–9th Sts.*

Hope and Anchor

$ | American. There's a full bar and extensive menu at this convivial diner, but breakfast (served all day) is the main event: jerk-chicken or root-vegetable hash, a breakfast burrito that knocks out hangovers, eggs any style, and pancakes deliciously doused with butter and syrup are some of the choices. There are sandwiches and burgers, too, as well as excellent fish tacos. **Known for:** all-day breakfast; chill vibe; weekend karaoke. *Average main: $11* ⊠ *347 Van Brunt St., Red Hook* ☎ *718/237-0276* ⊕ *www. hopeandanchorredhook.com* Ⓜ *F, G to Smith–9th Sts.*

★ Pok Pok Ny

$$ | Thai. The New York outpost of Andy Ricker's famed Portland, Oregon restaurant continues to serve delicious Thai food that goes well beyond the dishes typically found on menus here. Knockouts include the pork belly and pork curry, the boar collar, the wings, and the papaya salad, but it's hard to go wrong—and the servers give excellent guidance. **Known for:** northern Thai food; innovative cocktails; fun atmosphere. *Average main: $17* ⊠ *117 Columbia St., Brooklyn*

☎ 718/923–9322 ⊕ www.pokpokny.com ⊗ No lunch weekdays Ⓜ F, G to Bergen St.

★ **Red Hook Lobster Pound**
$$$ | American. For a taste of Maine in Brooklyn, head to the Red Hook Lobster Pound, where legendary lobster rolls are served with just a touch of mayo. There are variations on the classic, including "Connecticut style" (served warm, with butter) or "Tuscan style " (vinaigrette instead of mayo), as well as lobster dinners, lobster bisque, lobster mac and cheese, and a few noncrustacean options. **Known for:** lobster everything; lobster claw Bloody Mary; casual, fun atmosphere. *Average main: $25* ⊠ *284 Van Brunt St., Red Hook* ☎ *718/858–7650* ⊕ *www.redhooklobster.com* ⊗ *Closed Mon.* Ⓜ *F, G to Smith–9th Sts.*

 Bars and Nightlife

Botanica
Caribbean-style cocktails, many making use of the liquors from the Widow Jane Distillery next door, are the specialty at this pretty bar, where the room is styled after a Venetian hotel lobby. It's especially pleasant when the weather if fine and the front floor-to-ceiling windows are open onto the breezes. ⊠ *220 Conover St., Red Hook* ☎ *347/225–0148* Ⓜ *F, G to Smith–9th Sts.*

Fort Defiance
The food is good at Fort Defiance, but the bar scene and the inventive cocktail list are an even bigger draw. Try the Breukelen Corpse Reviver (made with Breukelen Gin), the Little Italy (a take on the Manhattan), or go for one of the fun tiki drinks. Brunch means specialty drinks, from the excellent Bloody Mary to a breakfast martini with a touch of orange marmalade. ⊠ *365 Van Brunt St., Red Hook* ☎ *347/453–6672* ⊕ *www.fortdefiancebrooklyn.com* Ⓜ *F, G to Smith–9th Sts.*

★ **Sunny's Bar**
This intimate dive bar is a Red Hook landmark, known for its laid-back atmosphere and live bluegrass and jazz. The music is in the back room; up front is the bar and a few banquettes. The small, leafy side patio has eclectic thrift-store furnishings. ⊠ *253 Conover St., Red Hook* ☎ *718/625–8211* ⊕ *www.sunnysredhook.com* ⊗ *Closed Mon.* Ⓜ *F, G to Smith–9th Sts.*

15

Windsor Terrace, Greenwood Heights, and South Slope

GO FOR

Neighborhood Hangouts

Charming Streets

Green Spaces

Gowanus

Park Slope

SOUTH SLOPE

GREENWOOD HEIGHTS

Prospect Park

WINDSOR TERRACE

Sunset Park

Green-Wood Cemetery

Ditmas Park

Kensington

seeing ★★☆☆☆ | Shopping ★☆☆☆☆ | Dining ★★★☆☆ | Nightlife ★★★☆☆

A small-town feel pervades Windsor Terrace, Greenwood Heights, and South Slope, three neighborhoods west and southwest of Prospect Park, where locally owned shops, a quietly flourishing restaurant-and-bar scene, and verdant Green-Wood Cemetery are among the attractions. The cemetery, with its tree-framed, hillside views of Manhattan, and memorials to three centuries of New York City movers and shakers, provides both a respite and a history lesson. This corner of Brooklyn has a mellow pace and easy access to Prospect Park, which has made all three neighborhoods a magnet for young professionals, artists, and families. Windsor Terrace, particularly along Prospect Park Southwest, benefits from the allure of tranquil, tree-lined streets fronted by brick and limestone row houses. The same families have owned many of these homes for multiple generations. Unlike other Brooklyn neighborhoods that have experienced dramatic demographic shifts, Windsor Terrace has retained many of the Irish firefighters, police officers, and working-class residents who have long anchored the community, while welcoming new generations; Greenwood Heights and South Slope have struck a similar balance between new and old. Prospect Park West is the main drag in Windsor Terrace; in Greenwood Heights and South Slope, it's 5th Avenue and 7th Avenue (as in Park Slope to the north).—*Updated by Caroline Trefler*

◉ Sights

★ Green-Wood Cemetery
One of the loveliest places for a stroll in the five boroughs, the 478 acres of Green-Wood Cemetery are also home to more than 560,000 permanent residents. Notables include Jean-Michel Basquiat, Leonard Bernstein, and Horace Greeley, but the elaborate monuments and mausoleums of the non-famous tend to be more awe-inspiring. Equally impressive are the views that stretch to Brooklyn Harbor and Manhattan. Guided walking and trolley tours, as well as special events, are offered. ⊠ *Main Entrance, 500 25th St., Brooklyn* ☏ *718/768–7300* ⊕ *www.green-wood. com* Ⓜ *R to 25th St.; F, G to 15th St.– Prospect Park.*

Kensington Stables
Just around the corner from Prospect Park, the Kensington Stables are the last remaining part of a riding academy founded in 1917, when the horse and carriage was the main mode of transportation around

the area. Experienced staff lead trail rides (from $42 per person) for all skill levels, through wooded and stream-filled Prospect Park. ⊠ *51 Caton Pl., Brooklyn* ☎ *718/972-4588* ⊕ *www.kensingtonstables.com* Ⓜ *F, G to Fort Hamilton Pkwy.*

★ Prospect Park Lake

Every corner of Prospect Park (*see Chapter 8*) is worth exploring, but the part closest to Windsor Terrace includes this lovely man-made lake, home to ducks and swans. Benches and small wooden gazebos dot the waterfront. ⊠ *Prospect Park entrance at Vanderbilt St. and Prospect Park SW, Prospect Park* ⊕ *www.prospectpark. org* Ⓜ *F, G to Fort Hamilton Pkwy.*

Prospect Park Southwest

A stroll along tree-lined Prospect Park Southwest, across from Prospect Park, is one of the highlights of visiting Windsor Terrace. The gracious limestone town houses, many of which were built in the late 19th century and are notable for their beaux arts facades, are an architectural complement to nearby Park Slope's brownstones. ⊠ *Prospect Park SW, Brooklyn* Ⓜ *F, G to 15th St.–Prospect Park or Fort Hamilton Pkwy.*

 Shopping

★ Black Bear

The well-curated selection of secondhand and vintage designer clothing—perhaps a colorful Pucci dress or a child-size coat—sunglasses, hats, and shoes, as well as handmade jewelry and greeting cards, is hard to resist browsing through. The shop is small, but the stock is frequently refreshed. ⊠ *469 16th St., Brooklyn* ☎ *917/715-5889* ⊕ *www.blackbearbrooklyn.com* Ⓜ *F, G to 15th St.–Prospect Park.*

★ Terrace Books

The quintessential neighborhood bookstore, this small shop has extremely friendly staff as well as a small but well-chosen selection of secondhand books and notable new paperbacks and hardcovers. There's a children's nook in back, and the store has events for kids such as story-time readings. ⊠ *242 Prospect Park W, Brooklyn* ☎ *718/788-3475* Ⓜ *F, G to 15th St.–Prospect Park.*

Windsor Place Antiques

This delightful and unmusty antiques shop is stocked with old anatomical charts, vintage maps and globes, posters, and plenty of other intriguing relics and artifacts to get treasure hunters excited. It's the perfect place to find a unique gift. During July and August, the store is closed weekdays. ⊠ *1624 10th Ave., Brooklyn* ☎ *718/986-7615* ⊕ *www.windsorplaceantiques.com* Ⓜ *F, G to 15th St.–Prospect Park.*

🍵 Coffee and Quick Bites

Baked in Brooklyn

$ | Bakery. Follow the smell of fresh bread to this giant bakery with a storefront selling a variety of breads, cupcakes, cookies, danishes, and a select menu of sandwiches. It's especially

GREENWOOD
HEIGHTS

SOUTH
SLOPE

7TH AVE.
F,G M

6th St.
7th St.
8th St.
9th St.
10th St.
11th St.
12th St.

Gowanus Expwy

PROSPECT AVE.
R M

4th Ave.

5th Ave.

6th Ave.

8th Ave.

7th Ave.

14th St.
15th St.
16th St.

17th St.
18th St.
19th St.

11

Prospect Ave.

Prospect Park West

9 10

8

25th ST.
R

24th St.

25th St. M

26th St.

27th St.

21st St.
22nd St.
23rd St.

2

7 6

3

4

5

15TH ST-
PROSPECT PARK
F,G M

Windsor Pl.

Prospect Expwy.

13

14   15   16

12   17   18

Howard Pl.
Fuller Pl.
10th Ave. Sherman

1

WINDSOR
TERRACE

11th Ave.

19

Green-Wood
Cemetery

19th St.
20th St.
E 4th St.
E 3rd St.
E 2nd St.
McDonald Ave.

22

28   27

26

Caton Ave.

0   1000 ft
0   200 m

57th St.

8th Ave.
39th St.
40th St.
41st St.
42nd St.
43rd St.
44th St.

9th Ave.

10th Ave.

38th St.

36th St.

Ft. Hamilton Pkwy.

Chester Ave.

Minna St.
12th Ave.
Tehama St.
Clara St.
Louisa St.

Albemarle Rd.
CHURCH
AVE.
M F,G
Dahill Rd.
Church A

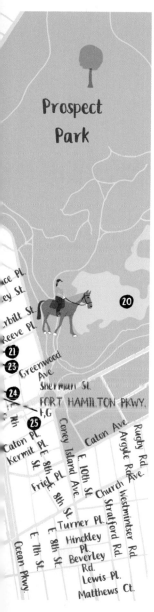

convenient for picnics in Green-Wood Cemetery. **Known for:** fresh pastries; picnic fixings; sandwiches. *Average main: $6 ⊠ 755 5th St., Brooklyn ☎ 718/788–3164 ⊕ www.bakedinbrooklynny.com Ⓜ R to 25th St.*

★ Brancaccio's Food Shop

$ | Deli. In need of picnic supplies, lunch, or a take-home meal? Owner Joe Brancaccio has been feeding the neighborhood with his daily-changing menu of sandwiches, rotisserie chicken, and prepared pastas and vegetables since 2010, and the shop just keeps getting busier. **Known for:** awesome sandwiches; extensive changing menu; renowned rotisserie chicken. *Average main: $8 ⊠ 3011 Fort Hamilton Pkwy., Brooklyn ☎ 718/435 1997 ⊕ www.brancacciosfoodshop.com ☉ Closed Tues. Ⓜ F, G to Fort Hamilton Pkwy.*

East Wind Snack Shop

$ | Asian. The super-flavorful dumplings and pot stickers served at this colorful, casual spot are made fresh daily and cooked to order. There are a few other items on the menu, including chili ribs, a pork-belly bao, and Hong Kong–style waffles for dessert. **Known for:** killer dumplings; cooked-to-order; bright, friendly shop. *Average main: $8 ⊠ 471 16th St., Brooklyn ☎ 718/295–0188 ⊕ www.eastwindsnackshop.com ☉ Closed Sun. Ⓜ F, G to 15th St.–Prospect Park.*

GETTING HERE

The 15th Street–Prospect Park subway stop provides easy access to the heart of Windsor Terrace. The 7th Avenue and Prospect Avenue stops are useful for getting to the South Slope and Greenwood Heights, too. For Green-Wood Cemetery, head to 25th Street.

★ Southside Coffee

$ | Café. This small, unassuming corner café is run by the folks behind the restaurant Lot 2, and they're quietly elevating the neighborhood sandwich scene, one house-made condiment at a time. Breakfast sandwiches like the eponymous Southside (ham, eggs, cheddar, "breakfast mayo," and pickled red onion) are served until 3 pm, but lunch options (including a standout tuna melt with pickles and a grilled cheese with strawberry jam and pickled jalapeños) make it hard to choose. **Known for:** amazing sandwiches; great coffee; limited seating. *Average main: $10 ⊠ 652 6th Ave., Brooklyn ☎ 347/599–2884 ⊕ www.southsidecoffeenyc.com Ⓜ F, G to 15th St.–Prospect Park.*

Steeplechase Coffee

$ | Café. Serving coffee made from Brooklyn Roasting Company beans, and pastries and bagels from the best Brooklyn bakeries, this is the perfect place to start the day or to perk up in the afternoon. Locals love to hang out with their laptops, but ample seating and a computer-free area mean you can almost always find space. **Known for:** laid-back vibe; great coffee and pastries; ample seating. *Average main: $4* ✉ *3013 Fort Hamilton Pkwy., Brooklyn* ☎ *347/799-2640* ⊕ *www.steeple-chasecoffee.com* ⊟ *No credit cards* Ⓜ *F, G to Fort Hamilton Pkwy.*

🍴 Dining

Brooklyn Commune

$ | American. House-baked pastries and breakfast are served every day of the week at this sunshine-filled eatery. Delicious sandwiches and a variety of tasty vegetarian and vegan options make up the rest of the menu offerings. **Known for:** order at the counter; all-day breakfast; vegan sandwich options. *Average main: $10* ✉ *601 Greenwood Ave., Brooklyn* ☎ *718/686-1044* ⊕ *www. brooklyncommune.com* ✆ *No dinner* Ⓜ *F, G to Fort Hamilton Pkwy.*

Della

$$ | Italian. Upmarket, Italian-influenced dinner and brunch are served at this intimate space, run by a well-pedigreed team that owns several spots in the neighborhood. There's a small menu of well executed appetizers, pastas, and entrées, perked up by seasonal specials and a well-chosen wine list (one of the co-owners also runs Juice Box Wine and Spirits down the street). **Known for:** upscale neighborhood spot; house-made pasta; weekend brunch. *Average main: $19* ✉ *1238 Prospect Ave., Brooklyn* ☎ *718/633-0249* ⊕ *www. dellarestaurant.com* Ⓜ *F, G to Fort Hamilton Pkwy.*

The Double Windsor

$$ | American. A place like the Double Windsor is what happens when a few local guys want a casual place in the neighborhood to drink good beer and eat good food, but nothing too fancy. Back in 2009, they couldn't find what they were looking for, so they opened a place themselves and it's become a local institution, for good reason: the beer list is comprehensive, and the comfort food is top quality. **Known for:** beer list; lively atmosphere; family clientele. *Average main: $16* ✉ *210 Prospect Park W, Brooklyn* ☎ *347/725-3479* ⊕ *www. doublewindsorbklyn.com* ✆ *No lunch Mon.–Thurs.* ⊟ *No credit cards* Ⓜ *F, G to 15th St.–Prospect Park.*

Giuseppina's

$$ | Pizza. It's true, there are plenty of excellent, thin-crust pizza spots in Brooklyn, but Giuseppina's stands out with its ample yet cozy dining room, warmed by the fire in the brick oven. It's also notable for what you can't get here, which is anything other than pizza and calzones. **Known for:** thin-crust pizza; cozy atmosphere; no weekday lunch. *Average main: $22 ⊠ 691 6th Ave., Brooklyn* ☎ *718/499–5052* ⊗ *Closed Tues. No lunch* ▭ *No credit cards* Ⓜ *F, G to 15th St.–Prospect Park; R at Prospect Ave.*

Hamilton's

$$ | American. On a relatively quiet stretch of Fort Hamilton Parkway, this gastropub pairs a vibrant atmosphere with classic dishes like mussels in a garlic-and-white-wine broth or decadent macaroni and cheese topped with crunchy bread crumbs and studded with bacon. Weekend brunch options are similarly satisfying: try the Ella Fitzgerald sandwich with grilled chicken, ham, and Gruyère cheese, topped with a fried egg. **Known for:** weekday breakfast; homey atmosphere; interesting dinner options. *Average main: $15 ⊠ 2826 Fort Hamilton Pkwy., Brooklyn* ☎ *718/438–0488* ⊕ *www.hamiltonsbrooklyn.com* Ⓜ *F, G to Fort Hamilton Pkwy.*

Korzo

$$ | Eastern European. The menu at Korzo is Eastern European comfort food with flair, and it's definitely the place to come when you're hungry and you want some very tasty, hearty food. The Hungarian-style burger, served in a fried bread pocket, has a reputation all its own. **Known for:** beet ketchup; hearty food; chill bar scene. *Average main: $17 ⊠ 667 5th Ave., Brooklyn* ☎ *718/499–1199*

⊕ *www.korzorestaurant.com* Ⓜ *R to Prospect Ave. or 25th St.*

★ Krupa Grocery

$$ | American. The eponymous small grocery that used to occupy this space has been completely transformed into an intimate restaurant serving inventive fare for brunch (during the week as well as weekends), lunch, and dinner. The daily-changing menu might include anything from breakfast gnocchi to a shrimp po'boy to steak with chimichurri, and snacks like simply prepared seasonal vegetables, homemade charcuterie, or chicken liver pâté. **Known for:** weekday brunch; market-fresh menu; late-night happy hour. *Average main: $20 ⊠ 231 Prospect Park W, Brooklyn* ☎ *718/709–7098* ⊕ *www.krupagrocery.com* ⊗ *No lunch Tues.* Ⓜ *F, G to 15th St.–Prospect Park.*

Le Paddock

$$ | French. Run by a French and French-Canadian couple, this casual corner restaurant with lots of windows and wood accents serves an outstanding brunch, with egg dishes and breakfast pizzas like the Alsatian-influenced *Flammenkuech,* smothered in leeks, Gruyère, and bacon. At dinner, the Mediterranean menu includes mussels, couscous, and more wonderful pizzas from the wood-burning oven: La Windsor pizza, with prosciutto, fromage blanc, blue cheese, arugula, and fig jam, is a favorite. **Known for:** brunch pizzas; innovative cocktails; rustic atmosphere. *Average main: $20 ⊠ 1235*

Prospect Ave., Brooklyn ☎ *718/435–0921* ⊕ *www.lepaddockbrooklyn.com* Ⓜ *F, G to Fort Hamilton Pkwy.*

★ Lot 2
$$ | American. The changing menu at this romantic, dimly lit restaurant is short but always stellar. The chef has an expert hand, whether exploring unexpected flavor combinations like candied bacon alongside shaved fennel and watermelon or putting together classics like chicken under a brick or the rave-worthy cheeseburger with duck-fat fries. **Known for:** romantic atmosphere; Sunday supper; great burger. *Average main: $23* ⊠ *687 6th Ave., Brooklyn* ☎ *718/499–5623* ⊕ *www.lot2restaurant.com* ⊘ *Closed Mon. and Tues. No lunch* Ⓜ *F, G to 15th St.–Prospect Park; R to Prospect Ave. or 25th St.*

Toby's Public House
$$ | Italian. Loyal patrons of this small spot may have been happy to keep the word from spreading about the top-quality thin-crust pizza, but the secret is undeniably out. There are many delectable options, from classic margherita to fig and Gorgonzola or smoked pancetta and black garlic, and a tempting selection of salads, small plates, and a few pastas. **Known for:** great pizza; neighborhood vibe; friendly bar scene. *Average main: $17* ⊠ *686 6th Ave., Brooklyn* ☎ *718/788–1186* ⊕ *www.tobyspub-lichousebrooklyn.com* ⊘ *No lunch weekdays* ⊟ *No credit cards* Ⓜ *R to Prospect Ave. or 25th St.; F, G to 15th St.–Prospect Park.*

 Bars and Nightlife

The Adirondack
It's just steps from the subway entrance, but the Adirondack feels more like an unpretentious bar somewhere upstate. New York State beer and cider are the specialties, but the friendly bartenders also know how to make good cocktails. The bar snacks are the perfect accompaniment—try the grilled cheese sandwich or a hot pretzel. ⊠ *1241 Prospect Ave., Brooklyn* ☎ *718/871–0100* ⊕ *www.theadirondackbar.com/* Ⓜ *F, G to Fort Hamilton Pkwy.*

Brooklyn Bavarian Biergarten
With several different outdoor areas, including a main bar section and quieter picnic tables along the side arbors, this leafy beer garden (open May–November) can entertain a large number of guests—especially during Octoberfest celebrations. There's a selection of German and New York State beers on tap, as well as wine and cocktails, and a food menu of pretzels, bratwurst, and hearty staples. ⊠ *265 Prospect Ave., Brooklyn* ☎ *718/788–0400* ⊕ *www.brooklynbavarianbiergarten.com* Ⓜ *R to Prospect Ave.; F, G to 4th Ave–9th St.*

★ Freddy's Bar and Backroom
We could tell you this place has history—Freddy's has been in South Slope since 2011, but it occupied its previous home in Prospect Heights for almost a century (relocating when the Barclays Center took over the area)—but what you really want to know is that Freddy's is a good time. There's pretty much

always something going on, whether it's live music, comedy night, or live band karaoke. There's a full menu, too. ✉ *627 5th Ave., Brooklyn* ☎ *718/768-0131* ⊕ *www.freddysbar. com* Ⓜ *R to Prospect Ave.*

Greenwood Park
This former gas station and auto repair shop is now a vast indoor-outdoor beer garden with more than 60 taps dispensing local, domestic, and imported beer, as well as a full bar and a menu of satisfying burgers, salads, and bar snacks. The outside space has picnic tables and several boccie courts. ✉ *555 7th Ave., Brooklyn* ☎ *718/499-7999* ⊕ *www.greenwoodparkbk.com* Ⓜ *F, G to 15th St.–Prospect Park.*

Sea Witch
As the name implies, the Sea Witch is nautically themed—with mermaid murals on the walls and a giant fish tank behind the bar. The back patio, though, with its wooden benches, miniwaterfall, and stone-lined stream, is the real gem. The casual bar fare includes a fillet of fish sandwich and a juicy burger. ✉ *703 5th Ave., Brooklyn* ☎ *347/227-7166* ⊕ *www.seawitchnyc.com* Ⓜ *R to Prospect Ave. or 25th St.*

South
The epitome of a laid-back neighborhood bar, South is known for its friendly bartenders, free popcorn, and extra-long happy hours. Lingering is encouraged and easy to do, especially on a weekend afternoon outside on the patio. There are board games to borrow, too. ✉ *629 5th Ave., Brooklyn* ☎ *718/832-4720* Ⓜ *R to Prospect Ave.*

Ditmas Park and Midwood

GO FOR

Victorian
Architecture

Historic Districts

Eclectic
Restaurants

Prospect Lefferts
Gardens

Prospect
Park

Windsor
Terrace

DITMAS
PARK

Flatbush

Kensington

Midwood

Ditmas Park's majestic Victorian homes with wraparound porches and wide front yards evoke a life more suburban than urban. Yet the neighborhood, which encompasses the Ditmas Park Historic District and the Prospect Park South Historic District, harbors a burgeoning restaurant-and-bar scene that makes it quite cosmopolitan. The area was largely farmland until the early 1900s, when an ambitious developer erected blocks of single-family homes, most in the orderly Colonial Revival style, with a smattering of frothier Queen Annes and neo-Tudors. Also in the present-day mix are Craftsman bungalows and redbrick apartment houses. Starting around the early 2010s, the neighborhood's transformation began on Cortelyou Road, the main commercial artery, where coffee shops, farm-to-table restaurants, bars, and boutiques rub shoulders with longtime Mexican bakeries, pizza parlors, and Caribbean shops and takeout joints. Coney Island Avenue has South Asian eateries and colorful sari shops. Church, Newkirk, and Flatbush avenues follow in Cortelyou's footsteps, with new businesses opening practically every month. The 2015 reopening of the Kings Theatre, a long-shuttered French Renaissance Revival movie palace now glamorously restored as a live performance venue, has already increased foot traffic along Flatbush. Many Orthodox Jews live immediately south of Ditmas Park in Midwood, whose draws include more Victorian houses and famous Di Fara Pizza.—*Updated by Kelsy Chauvin*

◉ Sights

Brooklyn Banya

Head to this small Russian bath-house for a healthful, social experience quite different from the typical modern spa. There are pools and saunas of varying temperatures—moving between them is believed to stimulate the circulation and boost immunity. Bathers (of both genders) can also opt to undergo a variety of treatments, including the traditional *platska* treatment (exfoliation via beating with leafy oak branches). There's a restaurant that serves Russian specialties, and a roof deck. ✉ *602 Coney Island Ave., Brooklyn* ☎ *718/853–1300* ⊕ *www.brooklyn-banya.com* 💲 *$40 for all-day bath access; treatments and massages $30–$90* Ⓜ *Q to Beverley Rd.*

Brooklyn College

The original Georgian-style buildings, elm tree–lined main quad, and lily pond of Brooklyn College were built in the 1930s, and today film and TV crews regularly use the bucolic campus as a location stand-in for Ivy League schools. It's especially beautiful in spring when the cherry blossoms are in bloom. Get a visitor's pass from any security post or sign up for an hour-long guided tour (10 am and 3 pm most weekdays). ⊠ *2900 Bedford Ave., Brooklyn* ☎ *718/951–5000* ⊕ *www.brooklyn.cuny.edu* Ⓜ *2, 5 to Flatbush Ave.–Brooklyn College; Q to Ave. H.*

Flatbush Reformed Church

The last Dutch director-general of New Netherland, Peter Stuyvesant, ordered a church built at this site in 1654, making this one of the oldest places of worship in New York. The current Federal-style stone building, the third at this location, was completed in 1798 and features Tiffany stained-glass windows. The complex, listed on the National Register of Historic Places, also includes the 1853 Greek Revival and Italianate parsonage and the 1924 church house. ⊠ *890 Flatbush Ave., Brooklyn* ☎ *718/284–5140* ⊙ *Check with church office (Tues.–Thurs. until 1 pm) to access church midweek* Ⓜ *B, Q to Church Ave.; 2, 5 to Church Ave.*

Prospect Park South Historic District

Designed in 1899 as a park within the city, the Victorian blocks of this iconic historic district feature stately gateposts that mark the entrances of handsome streets lined with palatial Colonial Revival, Queen Anne, and Tudor Revival homes,

each with striking architectural details. The Ditmas Park Historic District, which also has homes built in the early 1900s, is a few blocks southeast. *(To step inside the houses, see Best Brooklyn Events in Chapter 1 for details about the Victorian Flatbush House Tour.)* ⊠ *From Church Ave. to Beverley Rd., Brooklyn* Ⓜ *B, Q to Church Ave. or Beverley Rd.*

 Shopping

★ Brooklyn ARTery

Jewelry, T-shirts, home decor items, Brooklyn-made artisanal foods like candy from Liddabit Sweets and Mike's Hot Honey, health and beauty products, and much more: this well-stocked gift shop specializes in handmade and reclaimed merchandise made locally and at sustainable cooperatives from around the world. ⊠ *1021 Cortelyou Rd., Brooklyn* ☎ *347/425–7770* ⊕ *www.brooklynartery.com* Ⓜ *Q to Cortelyou Rd.*

Here's a Book Store

On the southern edge of Midwood, this independent bookstore has stood its ground for more than 40 years. Packed with used and new books from the floor to the tin-roof ceiling, it stocks more than 3,000 classic titles, as well as sizable sections for art, children's books, paperback best sellers, and Jewish-interest topics. From Ditmas Park, it's a 10-minute ride from Cortelyou Road on the Coney Island Avenue bus B68 to Avenue P. ⊠ *1964 Coney Island Ave., Brooklyn* ☎ *718/645–6675* ⊙ *Closed Thurs.–Sat.* Ⓜ *B, Q to Kings Hwy.*

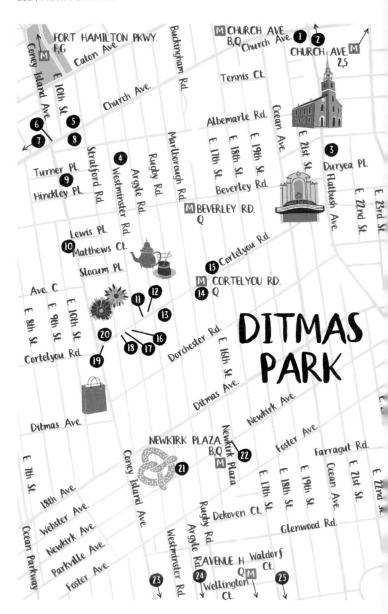

Sherel's

Hats galore, headbands, fascinators (smaller, more decorative hats), purses, and other accessories are family-run Sherel's stock and trade. The shop sells hundreds of styles, textures, and colors of its own label, along with a selection of other brands—from fedoras and berets to straw hats and beanies. You'll be in glamorous company donning your Sherel *chapeau,* since Katy Perry, Betsy Johnson, Blake Lively, and other celebs have sported this label. ⊠ *1314 Ave. J, Brooklyn* ☎ *718/258–5687* ⊕ *www.sherels.com* Ⓜ *Q to Ave. J.*

☕ Coffee and Quick Bites

Café Madeleine

$ | Café. In addition to excellent coffee, tea, and even kombucha (on tap), this bustling café near the Q train serves local farm-fresh and homemade fare from eggs and biscuits to veggie and poke bowls. Sandwiches come piled high with organic ingredients such as fresh avocado, leafy greens, and the "world's best" pastrami. **Known for:** memorable sandwiches; organic ingredients; cozy size. *Average main: $10* ⊠ *1603 Cortelyou Rd., Brooklyn* ☎ *718/941–4020* ⊕ *www.mkt.com/ cafemadeline* Ⓜ *Q to Cortelyou Rd.*

Coffee Mob

$ | Café. Attentive baristas expertly prepare luscious lattes and single-origin cold-brewed coffee in this stylistically minimal corner coffee shop. Owner Buck Berk personally travels to farms around the world

GETTING HERE

The Q line's Cortelyou Road station exits onto the heart of Ditmas Park's main street, Cortelyou Road. To reach Di Fara Pizza, in nearby Midwood, get out at Avenue J.

to find Coffee Mob's beans, which are roasted at Brooklyn's Pulley Collective. **Known for:** single-origin coffee; attentive baristas; natural light in shop. *Average main: $4* ⊠ *1514 Newkirk Ave., Brooklyn* ⊕ *www.coffeemob.com* ═ *No credit cards* Ⓜ *B, Q to Newkirk Plaza.*

Qathra

$ | Middle Eastern. This homey café brews daily-changing coffee roasts (also sold by the bag) and serves a variety of tasty teas, but the real treats are the breakfast pastries and Mediterranean-influenced menu—especially the Egyptian poached eggs with house-made hummus, arugula, and *za'atar* spices. The expansive patio is lovely in summer. **Known for:** Mediterranean flavors; homey café; fine coffee and teas. *Average main: $9* ⊠ *1112 Cortelyou Rd., Brooklyn* ☎ *347/305–3250* ⊕ *www.qathra.nyc* Ⓜ *Q to Cortelyou Rd.*

🍴 Dining

Café Tibet

$ | Tibetan. This brightly painted Tibetan restaurant perched above the subway tracks next to the Cortelyou Road station draws a crowd. The budget- and vegetarian-friendly menu is strong on home-made traditional Himalayan dishes like *momos* (dumplings), curries, *tsam-thuk* (barley soup), *baklap* (patties of minced beef, garlic, and onion), and butter tea, which is salty and usually an acquired taste. **Known for:** homemade Tibetan dishes; vegetarian options; compact, friendly space. *Average main: $12 ⊠ 1510 Cortelyou Rd., Brooklyn ☎ 718/941–2725 ▭ No credit cards Ⓜ Q to Cortelyou Rd.*

★ Di Fara Pizza

$$ | **Pizza.** Brooklyn legend Domenico De Marco has been handcrafting pizzas with top-quality ingredients in this Midwood storefront since 1965, and even the locals wait upward of an hour (and sometimes two) for pizza that's a contender for best in the greater New York area. You can order a slice ($5), but you're better off with a whole pie, because the pizza maker waits until there are enough slice orders to complete a pie. **Known for:** legendary pizza; classic toppings and quality ingredients; long lines. *Average main: $14 ⊠ 1424 Ave. J, Brooklyn ☎ 718/258–1367 ⊕ www.difarany.com ⊗ Closed Mon. ▭ No credit cards Ⓜ Q to Ave. J.*

★ The Farm on Adderley

$$ | **Modern American.** This rustic-chic farm-to-table American restaurant put Ditmas Park on the culinary map when it opened in 2006, and it continues to draw local regulars as well as an in-the-know crowd from Manhattan and beyond. The vegetarian-friendly, locally sourced menu changes seasonally, although the burger, house-made pickles, and award-winning fries with curry mayo are staples. **Known for:** farm-to-table menu; excellent weekend brunch; rustic setting. *Average main: $19 ⊠ 1108 Cortelyou Rd., Brooklyn ☎ 718/287–3101 ⊕ www.thefarmonadderley.com Ⓜ Q to Cortelyou Rd.*

Hunger Pang

$$ | **Asian.** Each dish is an experience in layered flavors at this American Asian eatery, from the Szechuan pepper "Pangry" wings to the "misotto" (an Asian twist on risotto) to the beignets with salted caramel sauce. Chef Medwin Pang, who grew up in the neighborhood, trained at Balthazar and Nobu. **Known for:** layered pan-Asian flavors; vegetable-forward dishes; casual, intimate ambience. *Average main: $17 ⊠ 1021 Church Ave., Brooklyn ☎ 718/552–2869 ⊕ www.hungerpangnyc.com ⊗ Closed Mon. No lunch weekdays Ⓜ B, Q to Church Ave.*

La Loba Cantina

$ | **Mexican.** Lush plants, mixed furniture, and a bright front window enhance the casual-tropical feel of this friendly Mexican restaurant—though its extensive small-batch mezcal menu adds still more authenticity. Specializing in Oaxacan dishes, La Loba serves fresh-made tortillas, tamales, *tlayudas* (similar to tostadas), and other tasty, sometimes-spicy dishes, plus specials, agua frescas, and savory snacks for sharing. **Known for:** Oaxacan-Mexican food; extensive mezcal menu; easygoing ambience. *Average main: $8 ⊠ 709 Church Ave.,*

Brooklyn ☎ 347/295–1111 ⊕ laloba-cantina.com Ⓜ Q to Church Ave.; F, G to Fort Hamilton Pkwy.

Lark Café

$ | **Café.** This sweet little nook along Church Avenue is the area's go-to spot for fresh croissants, bagels, cookies, pies, doughnuts, and oh-so-many other delectable baked goods sourced mostly from nearby Brooklyn bakeries. There's also fine tea, Stumptown coffee, and even beer and wine to sip, plus lunch-time's yummy sandwiches. **Known for:** treats from Brooklyn bakeries; Stumptown coffee; chill café with events and kids' classes. *Average main: $5* ⊠ *1007 Church Ave., Brooklyn* ☎ *718/469–0140* ⊕ *www. larkcafe.com* Ⓜ *Q to Church Ave.*

MangoSeed

$$ | **Caribbean.** Since 2009, MangoSeed has brought the flavors of the Caribbean to central Brooklyn with this breezy eatery at the south-eastern edge of Prospect Park. Jerk chicken, fish tacos, plantains, and other freshly made dishes are as satisfying as the happy hour tropical drinks on the roomy courtyard patio. **Known for:** Caribbean flair; jerk chicken and fish; tropical drinks. *Average main: $17* ⊠ *757 Flatbush Ave., Brooklyn* ☎ *347/529–1080* ⊕ *mangoseedrestaurant.com* ⊘ *Closed Mon. No lunch weekdays* Ⓜ *Q to Parkside Ave.*

Mimi's Hummus

$$ | **Middle Eastern.** This bright, tiny café makes outstanding hummus; the *masabache* version (traditional hummus with lemon garlic dressing) and the mushroom version (which also has onion and cumin) are favorites. Other menu standouts include *shakshuka* (eggs cooked in a tomato sauce) with or without a side of *merguez* sausage, the vegetarian meze sampling plate, the Moroccan tagines, and the weekly specials. **Known for:** Middle Eastern comfort food; flavorful small plates and bowls; friendly local favorite. *Average main: $14* ⊠ *1209 Cortelyou Rd., Brooklyn* ☎ *718/284–4444* ⊕ *www.mimi-shummus.com* Ⓜ *Q to Cortelyou Rd.*

Ox Cart Tavern

$$ | **Modern American.** The exten-sive "burger board" (beef, turkey, fish, or veggie patties with delec-table toppings), brunch, and beer options draw a crowd of regulars to this homey gastropub that often has a sporting event on its TV. The menu, though, runs the gamut from fish-and-chips and roast chicken to pasta dishes and salads—but don't miss the sides, like the soft-baked pretzel with Dijon mustard and cheese sauce, and beer-battered fried pickles. **Known for:** eclectic gastropub menu; array of burger choices; Sunday wings special. *Average main: $15* ⊠ *1301 Newkirk Ave., Brooklyn* ☎ *718/284–0005* ⊕ *www.oxcarttavern.com* ⊘ *No lunch weekdays* Ⓜ *B, Q to Newkirk Plaza.*

Purple Yam

$$ | **Asian Fusion.** The menu at this low-lit, atmospheric pan-Asian restaurant has a heavy Filipino influence, with Korean and other flavors at the forefront. The juicy chicken adobo braised in vinegar, garlic, and soy sauce is the signature dish, but the *bibimbap* (Korean for "mixed rice," with vegetables) is excellent, and adventurous eaters swear by the *sisig*, a succulent Filipino dish of pig cheeks with lime and chilies. **Known for:** flavorful Filipino and Korean dishes; daily dumpling and kimchi specials; homemade ice cream. *Average main: $19 ⊠ 1314 Cortelyou Rd., Brooklyn ☎ 718/940-8188 ⊕ www.purpley-amnyc.com ⊙ No lunch weekdays Ⓜ Q to Cortelyou Rd.*

Werkstatt
$$ | Austrian. Drift a few blocks down Coney Island Avenue to discover real-deal schnitzel, goulash, *palatschinke* (thin pancakes), spaetzle, and other Austrian favorites at this neighborhood spot. Along with a thorough drink menu, you can find beer, cider, and wine on tap at Werkstatt, and enjoy weeknight happy hours and food specials or weekend brunch. **Known for:** Austrian fare; varied draft menu; neighborhood hangout. *Average main: $15 ⊠ 509 Coney Island Ave., Brooklyn ☎ 718/284-5800 ⊕ www.werkstattbrooklyn.com ⊙ No lunch weekdays Ⓜ Q to Beverley Rd.*

★ Wheated
$$ | Pizza. Pizza is the thing at Wheated, and the menu lists nearly 20 Neapolitan-style pies—all named after neighborhoods in Brooklyn, which is fitting for this laid-back, local's-favorite spot. There are several white (no sauce) and vegan options, but meat eaters should try one with Faicco's sweet fennel sausage. **Known for:** Brooklyn-named, sourdough pies; exceptional toppings; major bourbon menu. *Average main: $15 ⊠ 905 Church Ave., Brooklyn ☎ 347/240-2813 ⊕ www.wheatedbrooklyn.com ⊙ Closed Mon. No lunch Ⓜ B, Q to Church Ave.; F to Fort Hamilton Pkwy.*

🍸 Bars and Nightlife

★ Bar Chord
A rotating selection of craft beers and numerous small-batch spirits, nightly live music (never a cover charge), a stellar jukebox, and an expansive year-round backyard (heated in winter) have made Bar Chord a favorite since it opened in 2013. Check out the collection of vintage guitars from the 1950s to the '70s for sale up front. ⊠ *1008 Cortelyou Rd., Brooklyn ☎ 347/240-6033 ⊕ www.barchordnyc.com Ⓜ Q to Cortelyou Rd.*

The Castello Plan
With cozy communal tables and a narrow seasonal patio, this wine bar attracts casually sophisticated neighbors with more than just the eclectic wine list. There are also inventive cocktails and a curated selection of bottled beers and wine, as well as cheese and charcuterie and other small and large plates. ⊠ *1213 Cortelyou Rd., Brooklyn ☎ 718/856-8888 ⊕ www.thecastello-plan.com Ⓜ Q to Cortelyou Rd.*

★ Sycamore Bar & Flowershop
It's a bar, it's a flower shop—and it's the perfect neighborhood hangout. Be lured by the small-batch bourbons, American craft beer,

and locally distilled spirits, as well as fun events like dance parties, live and DJ'ed music, and bingo. A rotating list of food vendors set up on the back patio (tented in winter). There are nightly happy hours and drink specials, like the popular $10 beer-and-bouquet deal; Thursday means $2 off all New York City products. ✉ *1118 Cortelyou Rd., Brooklyn* ☎ *347/240–5850* ⊕ *www.sycamore-brooklyn.com* Ⓜ *Q to Cortelyou Rd.*

 **Performing Arts**

Brooklyn Center for the Performing Arts

Part of the Brooklyn College campus, this community-based arts center offers a variety of performances at affordable prices—their roster of international dance companies is particularly impressive. Most Brooklyn Center events occur at the 2,400-plus-seat Walt Whitman Theatre, but the new Claire Tow Theatre is set to open as a more intimate performance space in early 2018. ✉ *2901 Campus Rd., Brooklyn* ☎ *718/951–4500* ⊕ *www.brooklyncenter.org* Ⓜ *2, 5 to Flatbush Ave.–Brooklyn College.*

★ Kings Theatre

Dormant since 1977, this grand and opulent 1929 movie palace reopened as a 3,000-seat performing-arts venue in 2015, with an exciting schedule of music, theater, dance, and other live performances. One of the Loew's Wonder Theatres from the beginning of Hollywood's Golden Age, the renovated space is quite true to the original. The ornate, French Renaissance–style building's original art deco chandeliers have been restored; the colors on the 70-foot arched ceiling were replicated; and even the original carpeting was re-created. ✉ *1027 Flatbush Ave., Brooklyn* ☎ *718/856–5464 for general info, 800/745–3000 for tickets* ⊕ *www.kingstheatre.com* Ⓜ *2, 5 to Beverley Rd.; Q to Beverley Rd.*

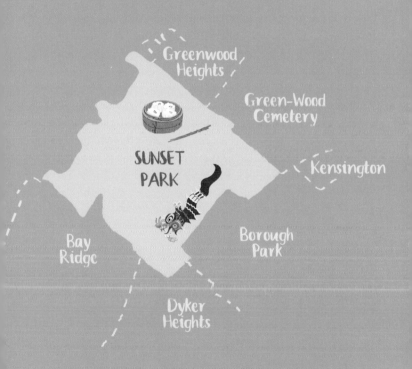

Greenwood Heights

Green-Wood Cemetery

SUNSET PARK

Kensington

Bay Ridge

Borough Park

Dyker Heights

S
tretching along the western Brooklyn waterfront toward the borough's southern end, Sunset Park is best explored when you're hungry—or yearning for spectacular New York Harbor views. Brooklyn's Chinatown (larger than Manhattan's) and its excellent restaurants, bakeries, and sidewalk vendors beckon along 8th Avenue and adjacent side streets, and some of New York City's best Mexican food can be found on or near 5th Avenue. Sunset Park's many Asian and Hispanic residents moved here during the last few decades of the 20th century, replacing some, though not all, of their predecessors, the descendants of the Irish, Polish, and Scandinavian immigrants who arrived during the 19th and early 20th centuries. Many of the earlier settlers came seeking work on the docks or in factories and warehouses, most notably in the sprawling Bush Terminal warehousing and manufacturing complex. As the factories began shuttering after World War II, the neighborhood shifted, developing in fits and starts into the appealing, polyglot middle-class enclave it is today. That Bush Terminal, renamed Industry City, has been reconceived as a multipurpose creative, manufacturing, and retail space with a food hall, artist studios, and neighborhood innovation lab, and that part of the complex is now an 11-acre public park are just a few signs of Sunset Park's 21st-century rejuvenation.
—*Updated by Caroline Trefler*

👁 Sights

Basilica of Our Lady of Perpetual Help
This imposing block-long Romanesque church stands tall on a ridge is unusual because it's actually two churches, one stacked on the other. The lower church opened on Easter Sunday in 1909. The larger, upper one was completed in 1928 in time for Christmas. In recognition of Sunset Park's diversity, masses are said in English, Spanish, Chinese, and Vietnamese. ✉ *526 59th St., Brooklyn* ☎ *718/492–9200* ⊕ *www.olphbkny.org* Ⓜ *N, R to 59th St.*

Bush Terminal Park
The opening of this park in 2014 marked a major milestone in the effort to reclaim Sunset Park's formerly industrial waterfront. Once part of the Bush Terminal port complex, the 11-acre public green space has soccer and baseball fields, as well as a nature preserve containing saltwater tidal pools. The preserve's restored

wetlands are helping to purify the nearby aquatic habitat. Enter the park at 43rd Street and 1st Avenue and walk past several industrial buildings to get to the park gates. The waterfront esplanade has sweeping views of New York Harbor, including the Statue of Liberty and the Manhattan skyline. ⊠ *Marginal St., Brooklyn* ☎ *888/697–2757* ⊕ *www.nycgovparks.org/parks/bush-terminal-park* Ⓜ *R to 45th St.*

Industry City

A makeover and an influx of 21st-century businesses—some in a marvelous food court—have reinvigorated the mammoth former Bush Terminal complex of factories and warehouses. Reincarnated as the 6-million-square-foot Industry City, the space, still evolving, hosts "designers, innovators, start-ups, manufacturers, and artists." Tenants worth checking out at the Food Hall include Colson Patisserie, Blue Marble Ice Cream, and Avocaderia, what may be the world's only avocado-centric restaurant. Events include sample sales, food festivals, and family-friendly dance parties. ⊠ *220 36th St., Brooklyn* ☎ *718/965–6450* ⊕ *www.industrycity.com* Ⓜ *D, N, R to 36th St.*

★ Sunset Park

The neighborhood's namesake park offers fabulous views of New York Harbor and the Lower Manhattan skyline from one of Brooklyn's highest hills. Stretching three blocks between 5th and 7th avenues, the green space has a seasonal public swimming pool, playgrounds, and multiple ball courts. Head to the park at sunset to see why it's worthy of its name. ⊠ *41st to 44th St., Brooklyn* ☎ *718/439–7429* ⊕ *www.nycgovparks.org/parks/sunset-park* Ⓜ *R to 45th St.*

Shopping

Fei Long Market

This massive supermarket is noteworthy for its large selection of Chinese grocery items, fresh produce, and housewares. Come here to stock up on Asian candies and snacks, and check out the food court with its dozen or so options for a quick lunch. ⊠ *6301 8th Ave., Brooklyn* ☎ *718/680–0118* Ⓜ *N to 8th Ave.*

Coffee and Quick Bites

Don Pepe Tortas y Jugos

$ | Café. For fresh juices and smoothies, either straight up or a tonic to cure what ails you, Don Pepe has just the thing. The small shop is plastered with photos and giant menus describing the options. **Known for:** fresh juices and smoothies; stuffed sandwiches; across from the park. *Average main: $8* ⊠ *3908 5th Ave., Brooklyn* ☎ *718/435–3326* Ⓜ *D, N, R to 36th St.*

Dragon Bay Bakery

$ | Bakery. One of several traditional Chinese bakeries along 8th Avenue, this busy café is a good stop for a morning or afternoon pastry and a sweet milk tea. Savory and sweet Chinese classics like the flaky egg tarts, steamed buns, and airy slices of green-tea sponge cake

SUNSET PARK

59th St

32nd St
33rd St
34th St

35th St
36th St
37th St 36TH STREET
D,N,R

41st St
42nd St
43rd St
44th St

40th St

38th St

1st Ave
47th St 2nd Ave
48th St
49th St
50th St
51st St
52nd St
53rd St
54th St
55th St
56th St
57th St
58th St

45th St
46th St
Gowanus Expwy

4th Ave

5th Ave

45TH STREET
R

53RD STREET
R

45th St
46th St
47th St
48th St
49th St
50th St
51st St
52nd St
53rd St
54th St
55th St
56th St
57th St
58th St

6th Ave

59th St
60th St
61st St
62nd St
63rd St

59TH STREET
N,R

4th Ave

5th Ave

59th St
60th St
58th St

Leif Ericson
Park

Senator St

66th St

67th St

68th St   Senator St
Bay Ridge Ave
Ovington Ave

61st St

7th Ave

64th St

8th AVE.
N

8th Ave

9th Ave

65th St

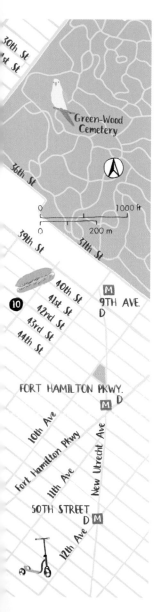

are all between $1 or $2 apiece, so try as many as your appetite allows. **Known for:** fresh egg tarts; Chinese buns; cakes. *Average main: $2* ✉ *5711 8th Ave., Brooklyn* ☎ *718/853–8188* ▭ *No credit cards* Ⓜ *N to 8th Ave.*

★ Kai Feng Fu Dumpling House
$ | **Chinese.** For unbeatable cheap eats, take a slight detour off 8th Avenue to this small and unassuming restaurant. Its sparse dining room doesn't offer much in the way of atmosphere, but the four-for-a-dollar pork-and-leek dumplings are a real deal (and delicious). **Known for:** inexpensive eats; fast service; bustling atmosphere. *Average main: $3* ✉ *4801 8th Ave., Brooklyn* ☎ *718/437–3542* ▭ *No credit cards* Ⓜ *D to 9th Ave.; R to 8th Ave.*

La Gran Via Bakery
$ | **Bakery.** Indulge your sweet tooth with slices of cake at this Latin bakery, open since the 1970s and now run by the children of its founding family. The bakers fashion a silky *tres leches* cake, but also do *quatro leches* and *cinco leches* versions. **Known for:** always open; the quatro leches cake is a neighborhood favorite; so many sweet options. *Average main: $5* ✉ *4516 5th Ave., Brooklyn* ☎ *718/ 853–8021* ⊕ *www.lagranviabakery.com* Ⓜ *R to 45th St.*

Tacos El Bronco
$ | **Mexican.** Head to this 5th Avenue food truck for superb tacos at $2 or less apiece. Options include chicken, veal head, spicy chorizo, and spicy pork. **Known**

GETTING HERE

The 8th Avenue stop is the best place to start an Asian food tour of Sunset Park. For Industry City, get out at 36th Street and walk a block and a half west.

for: inexpensive street food; draws a late-night crowd; neighborhood favorite. *Average main: $2* ✉ *Food truck on west side of 5th Ave., Brooklyn* ☎ *917/568–1592* ⊕ *www. tacoselbronco.com* ▭ *No credit cards* Ⓜ *D, N, R to 36th St.*

🍴 Dining

★ Ba Xuyên
$ | **Vietnamese.** Head to this nondescript spot at the north end of Chinatown for outstanding bánh mì sandwiches that cost just $5. The No. 1, with several kinds of pork, pickled vegetables, and a mound of cilantro on a baguette that's perfectly crusty on the outside and soft on the inside might very well blow your mind. **Known for:** awesome bánh mì; avocado shakes; bare-bones decor but very friendly service. *Average main: $5* ✉ *4222 8th Ave., Brooklyn* ☎ *718/633–6601* ▭ *No credit cards* Ⓜ *D to 9th Ave.*

Bamboo Garden
$$ | **Chinese.** One of the best dim sum halls in the city cranks out excellent classics, like rice rolls, dumplings, shumai, and BBQ pork buns, as well as innovative dishes that are sure to become classics (a

trio of lemon-infused fish cakes on fried-tofu squares and garnished with a slice of conch, a shrimp, and an egg yolk). The entire space has been recently renovated and has a bright blue-and-gold decor, brocade chairs, and an awe-inspiring ceiling dripping with shimmering glass chandeliers **Known for:** innovative takes on dim sum; wonderful ceiling; delicious classics. *Average main: $15* ⊠ *6409 8th Ave., Brooklyn* ☎ *718/238–1122* Ⓜ *N to 8th Ave.*

East Harbor Seafood Palace
$$ | Chinese. For a traditional dim sum brunch experience, this Sunset Park Chinatown institution is a good bet for high quality and variety. Not much English is spoken, so be ready to take a guess and point at whichever plates look good as servers wheel them on carts through the cavernous restaurant. **Known for:** weekend dim sum; friendly and noisy; fresh and tasty dishes. *Average main: $15* ⊠ *714 65th St., Brooklyn* ☎ *718/765–0098* Ⓜ *N to 8th Ave.*

Lucky Eight Restaurant
$$ | Chinese. Dishes are served family style at Sunset Park's go-to spot for Cantonese cuisine so you'll get the most out of a visit if you come here with a large group and share appetizers and entrées. Try the signature dish: the Pride of Lucky Eight, a seafood stir-fry with abalone, squid, and scallops. **Known for:** roast duck is a favorite; popular with local families; bargain lunch specials. *Average main: $16* ⊠ *5204 8th Ave., Brooklyn* ☎ *718/851–8862* Ⓜ *N to 8th Ave., R to 53rd St.*

Maria's Bistro Mexicano
$ | Mexican. Maria's serves classic Mexican breakfast fare like huevos rancheros and *chilaquiles* (a casserole made of tortillas and anything from salsa to mole to eggs to meats, and garnishes such as avocado or *queso fresco*) in a brightly decorated restaurant with a charming backyard space. Every brunch entrée comes with an hour's worth of bottomless mimosas or Margaritas. **Known for:** bottomless brunch; cute outdoor space in summer; happy hour. *Average main: $12* ⊠ *886 5th Ave., Brooklyn* ☎ *718/438–1608* Ⓜ *D, N, R to 36th St.*

Mister Hotpot
$$ | Chinese. Diners at this fun, casual restaurant cook their meals at the table, dunking seafood, meat, and vegetables into hot broth. Hotpot meals are meant for sharing, so it's best to come with a group. **Known for:** great broth; fun group experience; gets very busy on weekends. *Average main: $15* ⊠ *5306 8th Ave., Brooklyn* ☎ *718/633–5197* ⊕ *www.misterhotpotnyc.com* ☺ *No lunch* Ⓜ *N to 8th Ave.; R to 53rd St.*

★ Tacos Matamoros
$ | Mexican. Exceptional tacos large and small are the main attraction at this restaurant with a lengthy menu. Order the small ones, so you can try several different kinds. **Known for:** amazing tacos; potent margaritas; always busy. *Average main: $10* ⊠ *4508 5th Ave., Brooklyn* ☎ *718/871–7627* Ⓜ *R to 45th St.*

Thanh Da

$ | Vietnamese. Authentic *pho* and *bun* noodle soups are this utilitarian spot's specialty. Fans of spicy food should order the Bun Bo Hue, a rice vermicelli soup with three types of beef, including a rich and tender on-the-bone cut. **Known for:** not so much atmosphere but great food; excellent pho; roast pork bánh mì. *Average main: $6 ⊠ 6008 7th Ave., Brooklyn* ☎ *718/492–3253* ⊘ *Closed Tues.* ⊟ *No credit cards* Ⓜ *N to 8th Ave.*

Wong Good Hand Pull Noodle

$ | Chinese. After one bite of Wong Good's springy and tender hand-pulled noodles, you'll understand why area residents depend on this place for a quick and hearty meal. This unadorned shop doesn't offer much in the way of atmosphere or seating, but it's fun to watch as cooks pull noodles to order for the soup dishes. **Known for:** busy all day; good selection of noodles and soups; good for a quick meal. *Average main: $6 ⊠ 5924 8th Ave., No. 3, Brooklyn* ☎ *718/492–7568* ⊟ *No credit cards* Ⓜ *N to 8th Ave.*

🍸 Bars and Nightlife

Irish Haven

A rowdy neighborhood spot, this Irish dive bar is famous for being featured in the scene in *The Departed* in which Leonardo DiCaprio dukes it out over a glass of cranberry juice. Don't expect any real-life bar brawls, but do stop by for the no-frills drinks, down-to-earth bartenders, good jukebox music, and pool table. ⊠ *5721 4th Ave., Brooklyn* ☎ *718/439–9893* Ⓜ *N, R to 59th St.*

Sunset Park

BAY RIDGE

Dyker Heights

tseeing ★★★☆☆ | Shopping ★☆☆☆☆ | Dining ★★★☆☆ | Nightlife ★☆☆☆☆

A large, vibrant, diverse, and residential neighborhood hugging the Narrows waterway in southwest Brooklyn, Bay Ridge is the perfect blend of old and new Brooklyn. It's also a family-oriented area, widely considered one of the best neighborhoods for raising children in Brooklyn. Towering at Bay Ridge's southern end is the photogenic Verrazano-Narrows Bridge, which connects Brooklyn with Staten Island, but it's just a part of what makes Bay Ridge architecturally significant: thanks to its bay views, Bay Ridge was one of Brooklyn's wealthiest areas at the end of the 19th century, evidenced in the mansions dotting the waterfront, as well as the eclectic mix of Victorian, Greek Revival, and neo-Renaissance architecture scattered throughout the neighborhood. Diversity is a key word in Bay Ridge, not just in terms of architecture: since the Dutch West India Company purchased the land from the Nyack Indians in 1652, the area has been home to many waves of immigrant populations, including Scandinavians, Greeks, Italians, Irish, and, more recently, Middle Eastern communities. Third Avenue, considered "restaurant row," is an homage to the neighborhood's diversity with its range of cuisines and mix of casual and upscale dining, while 5th Avenue is home to predominantly Middle Eastern businesses like hookah bars, restaurants, and grocery stores.

—*Updated by Caroline Trefler*

Sights

Bay Ridge Architecture Tour

Bay Ridge has no shortage of eclectic architecture. Wandering the neighborhood, you'll see everything from one of the oldest freestanding Greek Revival homes in Brooklyn (99th Street and Shore Road) to circa-1880 Shingle-style Victorians with conical towers (81st and 82nd streets, between 3rd and Colonial avenues); rows of limestone houses on Bay Ridge Parkway (lit by working gas lamps); and charming cul-de-sacs lined with redbrick, slate-roof homes (68th Street between Ridge Boulevard and 3rd Avenue). The most popular architectural attraction in the neighborhood, though, is the fanciful Arts and Crafts home known to locals as the **Gingerbread House.** Built for shipping magnate Howard E. Jones in 1917, the 6,000-square-foot private home at 8220 Narrows Avenue has a thatched-style shingle roof, rustic stonework, and abundant landscaped greenery that make it look

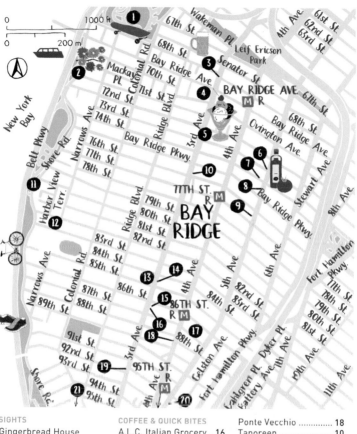

like it came straight out of a Hans Christian Andersen story. ⊠ *8220 Narrows Ave., Brooklyn* Ⓜ *R to 86th St.*

Narrows Botanical Gardens

This 4.5-acre verdant gem of a park between busy Belt Parkway and sleepy Shore Road is modest but worth a visit for a peek at its colorful rose gardens, flower-covered meadow, and waterfront views of the Verrazano-Narrows Bridge. A walk through the volunteer-staffed sanctuary, amid the butterflies, will leave you thinking you've discovered your very own secret garden. Plus, there are chickens wandering around, always a fun sight for urbanites. ⊠ *Shore Rd. between Bay Ridge Ave. and 72nd St., Brooklyn* ☎ *718/748–4810* ⊕ *www.narrowsbg. org* Ⓜ *R to Bay Ridge Ave.*

Owl's Head Park

With gently rolling hills and awe-inspiring views of the Verrazano-Narrows Bridge and Manhattan's skyline, as well as stately old trees, this 24-plus-acre park is a popular retreat for local families, dog walkers, and loungers basking in the view of ships entering and leaving New York Harbor. In addition, there are basketball courts, a playground, a dog run, a skate park, and a spray pool. In winter, kids launch themselves down the park's sledding hill. ⊠ *Colonial Rd. and 68th St., Brooklyn* ⊕ *www.nycgovparks.org* Ⓜ *R to Bay Ridge Ave.*

★ Shore Park and Parkway

This narrow park follows the Bay Ridge waterfront and has spectacular views of the Verrazano-

GETTING HERE

For a close-up view of the Verrazano-Narrows Bridge, exit the subway at 95th Street and walk south to the southernmost point of the Shore Park and Parkway promenade. Most shops and restaurants are convenient to the 77th Street and 86th Street stops. Owl's Head Park is near the Bay Ridge Avenue station. The NYC Ferry stops at the bottom of Bay Ridge Avenue.

Narrows Bridge and the ships in New York Harbor. The promenade is perfect for a long walk or a bike ride. At the north end is the American Veterans Memorial Pier, where the NYC Ferry docks. The pier is also home to Brooklyn's official monument honoring those lost on 9/11. ⊠ *Entrances along Shore Rd., from Bay Ridge Ave. to 4th Ave., Brooklyn* ⊕ *www.nycgovparks.org/ parks/shore-road-park* Ⓜ *R to Bay Ridge Ave., 77th St., 86th St., or Bay Ridge–95th St.*

★ Verrazano-Narrows Bridge

One of the most iconic bridges in New York City, seen worldwide as the starting point of the New York City marathon, this 4,260-foot double-decked bridge connects Brooklyn and Staten Island. It was the longest suspension bridge in the world when it opened in 1964 (it's now 13th) and is named after Giovanni da Verrazzano (his name has two z's, unlike the bridge), an Italian explorer who was the first European to sail into New York Harbor in 1524. There are two times each year when people are allowed to cross the bridge under their own power: for the New York City marathon held every November, and during the Five Boro Bike Tour each May. If you don't want to work that hard for your views (and photos), walk south on 5th Avenue until you hit the bridge or stroll along the **Shore Park and Parkway** promenade. ✉ *Brooklyn* Ⓜ *R to Bay Ridge–95th St.*

Shopping

BookMark Shoppe

The selection of books and knitting materials at this homey neighborhood shop makes it the perfect stop for the craft-loving reader, the book-loving crafter, and every permutation in between. Events range from author readings to book club meetings to learn-to-knit classes. ✉ *8415 3rd Ave., Brooklyn* ☎ *718/833-5115* ⊕ *www.bookmark-shoppe.com* Ⓜ *R to 86th St.*

Century 21

For many New Yorkers, this flagship branch of the behemoth discount designer department store chain anchoring the lively 86th Street shopping strip is *the* reason to visit Bay Ridge—regularly. There are two buildings, one dedicated to home goods, shoes, and children's clothes, and the original building that showcases the latest designer clothing, handbags, accessories, and cosmetics. Note that stock is rotated on Tuesdays if you want to score first dibs. ✉ *472 86th St., Brooklyn* ☎ *718/748-3266* ⊕ *www.c21stores.com* Ⓜ *R to 86th St.*

☕ Coffee and Quick Bites

★ A.L.C. Italian Grocery

$ | Café. Modeled after an old-school salumeria, and run by the grandson of Bensonhurst's beloved Italian food importing and distribution business, D. Coluccio & Sons, this specialty grocery stocks everything from cheese, chocolate, salami, imported pasta, sauces, bread, and pizza dough to prepared foods and salads. **Known for:** Italian sandwiches; many kinds of imported pasta; small but impressive cheese selection. *Average main: $9* ✉ *8613 3rd Ave., Brooklyn* ☎ *718/680-4465* ⊕ *www.alcitalian-grocery.com* Ⓜ *R to 86th St.*

Anopoli Family Restaurant

$ | Café. This Bay Ridge institution has been around for more than a hundred years, and the ice-cream sundaes are the stuff of childhood dreams—the banana split is fantastic. There's a full menu of typical diner fare that's decent, but the sundaes are the real attraction. **Known for:** root beer floats; classic diner vibe; run-of-the-mill diner food. *Average main: $7* ✉ *6920 3rd Ave., Brooklyn* ☎ *718/748-3863* ⊕ *www.anopolifamilyrestaurant.com* ▭ *No credit cards* Ⓜ *R to Bay Ridge Ave.*

Leske's Bakery

$ | Bakery. Alongside traditional Scandinavian treats like limpa bread and flakey chocolate-, fruit-, and custard-filled *kringles*, this 50-plus-year-old bakery offers New York classics like cakey black-and-white cookies, apple turnovers, jelly doughnuts, and cheesecake.

There are many varieties of Italian cookies, including themed ones for occasions like Halloween and Easter. **Known for:** black-and-white cookies; seasonal cookies; too many good things to choose from. *Average main: $3* ⊠ *7612 5th Ave., Brooklyn* ☏ *718/680–2323* Ⓜ *R to 77th St.*

Paneantico
$ | **Italian.** This seemingly always busy corner bakery and café has been serving Bay Ridgers since 2000, with menu offerings that include hearty salads, sandwiches, fresh breads, and prepared foods to go. Its long glass cases are filled with tempting traditional Italian and American desserts; the cannoli are delicious. **Known for:** bustling café vibe; cake, cake, more cake; more than 100 kinds of sandwiches. *Average main: $9* ⊠ *9124 3rd Ave., Brooklyn* ☏ *718/680–2347* ⊕ *www. paneantico.com* Ⓜ *R to 86th St. or Bay Ridge–95th St.*

⑪ Dining

Areo Ristorante
$$ | **Italian.** Bay Ridge families have been coming to this lively, upscale restaurant for old-school Italian food and old-world service for more than 25 years. The waiters are genial and the atmosphere is gregarious, which just goes to show that everyone's having a good time. **Known for:** red sauce joint; lively scene, especially on summer weekends; big portions. *Average main: $20* ⊠ *8424 3rd Ave., Brooklyn* ☏ *718/238–0079* ☾ *Closed Mon.* Ⓜ *R to 86th St.*

Brooklyn Beet Company
$$ | **Eastern European.** Creative interpretations of hearty Eastern European comfort food, with a decidedly beety bent, are what you'll find on the menu at this small, friendly spot. The Korzo burger (named for the sister restaurant, Korzo, in the South Slope), in a lightly fried pocket, is one of the most popular dishes, and it's also available in a vegetarian beet version. **Known for:** beet ketchup; the Korzo burger; brunch. *Average main: $15* ⊠ *7205 3rd Ave., Brooklyn* ☏ *718/492–0020* ⊕ *www.korzorestaurant.com* Ⓜ *R to Bay Ridge Ave.*

Elia Restaurant
$$$ | **Greek.** Something of a Bay Ridge secret, Elia has been serving refined Greek delicacies in the neighborhood since 1998. The menu features grilled meat, fish, and seafood, as well as traditional casseroles and appetizers, all prepared with innovative touches: grilled shrimp, for example, are served with pomegranate couscous and *avgolemono* (egg-lemon sauce), and tender homemade ravioli are filled with braised lamb. **Known for:** whole fish; everything

grilled, especially the octopus; warm Mediterranean vibe. *Average main: $27* ✉ *8611 3rd Ave., Brooklyn* ☎ *718/748–9891* ⊕ *www.eliarestaurant.com* ⊙ *Closed Mon. No lunch* Ⓜ *R to 86th St.*

Gino's

$$ | Italian. Family-owned and -operated since the 1960s, this always crowded restaurant and pizzeria is known for its red-sauce pastas and classic Italian dishes like pasta e fagioli, rigatoni with eggplant and sausage, and spaghetti and meatballs, all served with attentive service in an exposed-brick and white-tablecloth setting. The restaurant is a favorite spot for family gatherings and special-occasion dining. **Known for:** old-school Italian food; casual pizzeria up front; family-friendly. *Average main: $16* ✉ *7414 5th Ave., Brooklyn* ☎ *718/748–1698* ⊕ *www.ginosbayridge.com* ⊙ *Closed Mon.* Ⓜ *R to 77th St.*

Hazar Turkish Kebab

$ | Turkish. In a neighborhood full of excellent Middle Eastern food, this casual restaurant stands out. There's a grill for kebabs, a spit for shawarma, and an oven for delicious made-to-order *pides* (pitas) like the *sucuk* pide (stuffed with mozzarella and Turkish sausage). **Known for:** fresh-baked pides; mixed-grill kebabs; giant sandwiches. *Average main: $8* ✉ *7224 5th Ave., Brooklyn* ☎ *718/238–4040* Ⓜ *R to 77th St.*

Ponte Vecchio

$$ | Italian. Classic Italian fare like veal marsala, linguine alle vongole, and pasta e fagioli isn't hard to find in Bay Ridge, but this lively, upscale Italian eatery has the street cred that comes with being in business since 1978 and having a famous sister restaurant (Angelo's of Mulberry Street, open since 1902) in Manhattan's Little Italy. The namesake Pollo Rollatini Ponte Vecchio—chicken stuffed with prosciutto, mozzarella, and mushrooms, in marsala sauce—is one of the standout entrées. **Known for:** upscale Italian vibe; popular for special occasions; attentive service. *Average main: $24* ✉ *8810 4th Ave., Brooklyn* ☎ *718/238–6449* ⊕ *www.pvristorante.com* Ⓜ *R to 86th St.*

★ Tanoreen

$$ | Middle Eastern. This restaurant put Bay Ridge on the foodie map when it first opened in 1998, and chef-owner Rawia Bishara's refined Palestinian dishes—a tribute to her rich Middle Eastern heritage—continue to draw crowds and accolades. Vaulted ceilings and a glass-enclosed atrium are a stylish backdrop for the inventive interpretations of home-style meals. **Known for:** the freekeh appetizer; pomegranate molasses; save room for dessert. *Average main: $21* ✉ *7523 3rd Ave., Brooklyn* ☎ *718/748–5600* ⊕ *www.tanoreen.com* ⊙ *Closed Mon.* Ⓜ *R to 77th St.*

▼ Bars and Nightlife

The Lock Yard

In an old locksmith shop where owner and local restaurateur (he also owns the Kettle Black bar and Ho'Brah taco joint) Tommy Casatelli

worked as a kid, this neighborhood hot spot summons a young
craft-beer-loving clientele with
its impressive array of American
beers, plus a handful of sustainable
wines and specialty cocktails—and
the 1,300-square-foot heated beer
garden with picnic tables and festive
lights. The menu features artisanal
sausages and hot dogs, knishes,
and fries. ⊠ *9221 5th Ave., Brooklyn*
☎ *718/748–3863* ⊕ *www.lockyard.com*
Ⓜ *R to Bay Ridge–95th St.*

★ The Owl's Head

Located on a quiet block off
busy 5th Avenue, this intimate
wine bar—named for the nearby
waterfront park—was inspired by
a love for wine, food, and design.
Exposed-brick walls, a polished
tin-stamped ceiling, and a chalk-
board wall displaying the day's
carefully selected pours, craft
beers, and small plates (made from
locally sourced ingredients) give
the place a casual vibe. Look for
the mural out front, painted by a
local artist. ⊠ *479 74th St., Brooklyn*
☎ *718/680–2436* ⊕ *www.theowls-
head.com* Ⓜ *R to 77th St.*

Three Jolly Pigeons

This institution has been serving
the neighborhood since the early
1900s, and it's still a laid-back,
welcoming place for a couple of
drinks and perhaps a game of
a pool. The pressed-tin ceiling
and stained-glass details give
the place more atmosphere than
your average dive bar. There's live
music on Saturday nights and lively
karaoke on Fridays. ⊠ *6802 3rd Ave.,
Brooklyn* ☎ *718/745–9350* Ⓜ *R to Bay
Ridge Ave.*

A visit to Brighton Beach and Coney Island, adjacent neighborhoods on the Atlantic Ocean with sandy beaches and colorful boardwalks, is a step back into a different world. Brighton Beach was developed as a seaside resort in the late 1800s, modeled after Brighton, England, and gradually became more residential. Perhaps the most significant factor in Brighton Beach's history, though, was the waves of Soviet citizens immigrating to the United States—leading up to, and after, the collapse of the Soviet Union in 1991—many of whom ended up here, joining the already large population of Jewish-Americans and Holocaust survivors. The neighborhood became known as "Little Odessa," a nickname still used today. Russian, Ukrainian, and Eastern European restaurants and businesses pack the neighborhood, whose main commercial artery is Brighton Beach Avenue, and you're more likely to overhear Russian conversations than ones in English. The avenue extends west to Ocean Parkway and the border with Coney Island, whose main drag is Surf Avenue. More than a century ago Coney ranked among the country's preeminent seaside resorts, but despite a recent economic resurgence, with new restaurants, bars, and a revamped amusement park opening up, an aura of faded carny glory endures. Decades-old concessions line the boardwalk, and plenty of outsize characters keep Coney Island weird, especially at the circus sideshow and the annual Mermaid Parade.—*Updated by Kelsy Chauvin*

◉ Sights

★ Brighton Beach

Just steps from the subway, this stretch of golden sand is the showpiece of Brooklyn's ocean-side playground. Families set up beach blankets, umbrellas, and coolers, and pickup games of beach volleyball and football add to the excitement. Calm surf, a lively boardwalk, and a handful of restaurants for shade and refreshments complete the package. That spit of land in the distance is the Rockaway Peninsula, in Queens. ⊠ *Brighton Beach Ave., Brighton Beach* Ⓜ *B, Q to Brighton Beach; Q to Ocean Pkwy.*

Brighton Beach Avenue

The main thoroughfare of "Little Odessa" can feel more like Kiev than Manhattan. Cyrillic shop signs advertise everything from salted tomatoes and pickled mushrooms to Russian-language DVDs and Armani handbags. When the weather's good, local bakeries sell sweet honey cake, cheese-stuffed *vatrushki* danishes, and chocolatey rugelach from sidewalk tables. ⊠ *Brighton Beach Ave., Brighton Beach* Ⓜ *B, Q to Brighton Beach.*

Brooklyn Cyclones

The minor-league Brooklyn Cyclones are a farm team for the New York Mets, and their waterfront baseball stadium is a great place to see budding talent—they've sent dozens of players to the major leagues since they first started in Coney Island in 2001. The Cyclones play from mid-June through early September at MCU Park, and fireworks after every Friday-night game make it a celebration. ⊠ *1904 Surf Ave., Coney Island* ☎ *718/372-5596* ⊕ *www.brooklyncyclones.com* Ⓜ *D, F, N, Q to Coney Island–Stillwell Ave.*

Coney Island Beach

Just west of Brighton Beach, the Coney Island beach shares many of its neighbor's assets: a gentle surf, golden sand, the famous boardwalk, and plenty of restaurants. The now-defunct Parachute Jump is a great photo op. ⊠ *Coney Island Beach, Coney Island* ⊕ *www.nycgovparks.org, www.coneyislandfunguide.com* Ⓜ *D, F, N, Q to Coney Island–Stillwell Ave.; F, Q to W. 8th St.–NY Aquarium.*

Coney Island Circus Sideshow

The cast of talented freaks and geeks who keep Coney Island's carnival tradition alive include sword swallowers, fire-eaters, knife throwers, contortionists, and Serpentina the snake dancer. Every show is an extravaganza, with 10 different acts to fascinate and impress. ⊠ *Sideshows by the Seashore, 1208 Surf Ave., Coney Island* ☎ *718/372-5159* ⊕ *www.coney-island.com/sideshow.shtml* ⊠ *$10* ⊙ *Closed Oct.–Mar.* Ⓜ *F, Q to W. 8th St.–NY Aquarium; D, F, N, Q to Coney Island–Stillwell Ave.*

★ Coney Island Museum

Founded as a labor of love by Coney Island impresario Dick Zigun, this quirky museum recounts the tumultuous history of the neighborhood and explores the counterculture that still thrives here. Check out the memorabilia from Coney Island's heyday in the early 1900s, as well as video installations, temporary exhibits, and the fabulous collection of funhouse mirrors. ⊠ *1208 Surf Ave., Coney Island* ☎ *718/372-5159* ⊕ *www.coneyisland.com* ⊠ *$5* ⊙ *Labor Day–mid-June closed weekdays; mid-June–Labor Day closed Mon. and Tues.* Ⓜ *D, F, N, Q to Coney Island–Stillwell Ave.; F, Q to W. 8th St.–NY Aquarium.*

The Cyclone

This historic wooden roller coaster first thrilled riders in 1927 and it'll still make you scream. Anticipation builds as the cars slowly clack up to the first unforgettable 85-foot plunge—and the look on your face is captured in photos that you can purchase at the end of the ride. The Cyclone may not have the speed or the twists and turns of more modern rides, but that's all part of its rickety charm. It's one of two New York City landmarks in Coney Island; the other is Deno's Wonder Wheel. ⊠ *Luna Park, 834 Surf Ave.,*

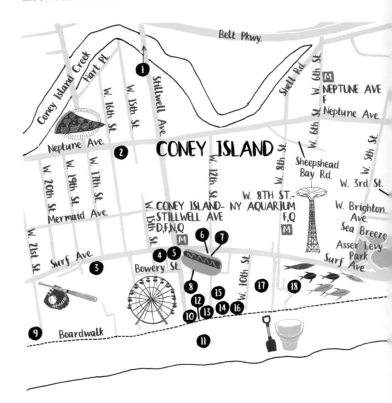

Atlantic Ocean

Coney Island ☎ 718/373–5862 ⊕ www. lunaparknyc.com 🎫 $10 ⊘ Closed hrs vary, but are generally mid-Oct.–early May. Check website for details. Ⓜ F, Q to W. 8th St.–NY Aquarium; D, F, N, Q to Coney Island–Stillwell Ave.

Deno's Wonder Wheel Amusement Park

The star attraction at Deno's is the towering 150-foot-tall Wonder Wheel. The Ferris wheel first opened in 1920, making it the oldest ride in Coney Island, and the spectacular views from the top take in a long stretch of the shoreline. Other rides for tots here include the Dizzy Dragons, the Pony Carts, and a brightly painted carousel. ⊠ 1025 Riegelmann Boardwalk, Coney Island ☎ 718/372–2592 🎫 $8 ⊘ Closed Nov.– early Mar.; hrs vary Ⓜ F, Q to W. 8th St.–NY Aquarium; D, F, N, Q to Coney Island–Stillwell Ave.

Luna Park

The Cyclone and the Wonder Wheel are Coney Island's most famous attractions but they're only the beginning—Luna Park has 19 other rides, including the Slingshot, which will send you soaring and somersaulting more than 90 feet into the air; the Thunderbolt roller coaster with its 90-foot drop; and the Steeplechase, where you'll experience the sensation of riding a horse at top speed around a race track. ⊠ 1000 Surf Ave., Coney Island ☎ 718/373–5862 ⊕ www.lunaparknyc. com ⊘ Closed hrs vary, but are generally mid-Oct.–early May. Check website for details. Ⓜ F, Q to W. 8th St.–NY Aquarium; D, F, N, Q to Coney Island–Stillwell Ave.

GETTING HERE

The beach and boardwalk of Brighton Beach are steps from the Brighton Beach stop on the Q and B lines. For the thick of the Coney Island action, get off at the Coney Island–Stillwell Avenue stop on the D, F, N, and Q lines.

★ New York Aquarium

The oldest continually operating aquarium in the United States is run by the Wildlife Conservation Society; its mission is to save wildlife and wild places worldwide through science, conservation action, and education. The aquarium occupies 14 acres of beachfront property and is home to 266 aquatic species. At the Sea Cliffs, you can watch penguins, sea lions, sea otters, and seals frolic: the best action is at feeding time. The Conservation Hall and Glovers Reef building is home to marine life from Belize, Fiji, and all over the world, including angelfish, eels, rays, and piranhas. The new Ocean Wonders: Sharks! exhibit will bring hundreds more species, including nurse sharks, to the aquarium. The highlight will be a coral-reef tunnel that provides 360-degree views of this underwater universe. ■ TIP→ Purchase tickets online for discounted rates. ⊠ 602 Surf Ave., Coney Island ☎ 718/265–3474 ⊕ www.nyaquarium.com 🎫 $12 Ⓜ F, Q to W. 8th St.–NY Aquarium; D, F, N, Q to Coney Island–Stillwell Ave.

★ Riegelmann Boardwalk

Built in 1923, just one year before legendary Totonno's Pizzeria opened its doors on nearby Neptune Avenue, this famous wood-planked walkway is better known as the Coney Island Boardwalk, and in summer it seems like all of Brooklyn is out strolling along the 2½-mile stretch. The quintessential walk starts at the end of the pier in Coney Island, opposite the Parachute Jump—you can see the shoreline stretched out before you, a beautiful confluence of nature and city. From here to Brighton Beach is a little over a mile and should take about a half hour at a leisurely amble. Those modernistic, rectangular structures perched over the beach are new bathrooms and lifeguard stations. ⊠ *Between W 37th St. and Brighton 15th St., Coney Island* Ⓜ *D, F, N, Q to Coney Island–Stillwell Ave.; F, Q to W. 8th St.–NY Aquarium; B, Q to Brighton Beach; Q to Ocean Pkwy.*

🛍 Shopping

Gastronom Arkadia

The legendary steam tables here are stocked with hot and cold delicacies such as stuffed cabbages and peppers, blintzes, baked fish, pickled watermelon, Russian salads, beef tongue, and *pirozhki* (savory Russian buns with meat or cabbage inside)—fill a plate, or a takeout container. Shop for chocolates and other comestibles that you won't find elsewhere. ⊠ *1079 Brighton Beach Ave., Brighton Beach* ☎ *718/934-7709* Ⓜ *B, Q to Brighton Beach.*

Lola Star Souvenir Boutique

Unique graphics designed by the proprietor herself—who goes by Lola Star—make this the hottest spot for Coney Island– and Brooklyn-branded T-shirts, hats, postcards, and other eye-catching souvenirs and beach gear. The boutique occupies a slim storefront on the boardwalk next to Nathan's oceanfront outpost, and its one-of-a-kind wares make the store an enduring local favorite. ⊠ *1205 Boardwalk, Coney Island* ☎ *646/915-2787* ⊕ *www.lolastar.com* ⊗ *Closed Jan.–late Mar.* Ⓜ *D, F, N, Q to Coney Island–Stillwell Ave.*

Williams Candy

Selling homemade candy apples, marshmallow sticks, popcorn, nuts, and giant lollipops for more than 75 years, this old-school corner candy shop with the yellow awning is a Coney Island mainstay. Owner Peter Agrapides used to visit the store with his mother when he was a kid; he's been the proud owner for 30 years. ⊠ *1318 Surf Ave., Coney Island* ☎ *718/372-0302* Ⓜ *D, F, N, Q to Coney Island–Stillwell Ave.*

☕ Coffee and Quick Bites

Doña Zita

$ | Mexican. Just off the boardwalk, this taco stand has a selection of tasty Mexican standards. The taco *carne asada* (marinated steak) is a favorite; *torta* sandwiches are large enough to share. **Known for:** affordable Mexican food; carne asada tacos; central Coney Island location. *Average main: $5* ⊠ *1221*

Bowery St., Coney Island ☎ *347/492–6160* ⊕ *www.donazita.com* Ⓜ *D, F, N, Q to Coney Island–Stillwell Ave.*

La Brioche

$ | Bakery. Don't be deceived by the French name: this unassuming bakery is Russian-Jewish, right down to its rugelach roots. The wall-to-wall trays are packed with *babka* (a sweet yeast cake filled with swirls of chocolate or cinnamon and sugar), *smetannik* (sour cream layer cake), *vatrushki* (cheese pastries), and honeyed poppy-seed rolls. **Known for:** Russian-Jewish baked goods; cake by the pound; sweet deals. *Average main: $3* ⊠ *1073 Brighton Beach Ave., Brighton Beach* ☎ *718/934–0731* ▭ *No credit cards* Ⓜ *B, Q to Brighton Beach.*

★ Nathan's Famous

$ | Hot Dog. Nathan Handwerker, a Polish immigrant, founded this Coney Island hot dog stand in 1916, and what followed can only be described as a quintessential American success story. With a $300 loan and his wife Ida's secret spice recipe, Nathan set up shop and his success was almost instantaneous—Al Capone, Jimmy Durante, and Cary Grant became regulars early on, President FDR served Nathan's dogs to the king and queen of England, local girl Barbra Streisand had them delivered to London, and Walter Matthau asked that they be served at his funeral. **Known for:** world-famous hot dogs; quintessentially Brooklyn; annual hot-dog-eating contest.

Average main: $5 ⊠ *1310 Surf Ave., Coney Island* ☎ *718/333–2202* ⊕ *www.nathansfamous.com* Ⓜ *D, F, N, Q to Coney Island–Stillwell Ave.*

Paul's Daughter

$ | American. This open-air clam shack right on the boardwalk has been shucking bivalves for more than 50 years. Perch on a stool or just lean against the counter to enjoy a plate of fresh, briny-tasting clams on the half-shell, accompanied by one of the beers on tap, preferably a cold Brooklyn Lager. **Known for:** fresh clams; prime boardwalk location; beach fare and beer. *Average main: $8* ⊠ *1001 Boardwalk, Coney Island* ☎ *718/449–4252* Ⓜ *F, Q to W. 8th St.-NY Aquarium; D, F, N, Q to Coney Island–Stillwell Ave.*

Tom's Coney Island

$ | Diner. Fountain sodas like the cherry-lime rickey or Tom's Famous Egg Cream are favorites at this boardwalk outpost of Tom's in Prospect Heights. As at the original, you can get all-American breakfast items like bacon, ham, or pork sausage omelets, corned beef hash, and silver dollar pancakes. **Known for:** diner classics; rickeys and egg-cream sodas; seasonal outdoor seating. *Average main: $9* ⊠ *1229 Boardwalk, Coney Island* ☎ *718/942–4200* ⊕ *www.toms-brooklyn.com* Ⓜ *D, F, N, Q to Coney Island–Stillwell Ave.*

¶ Dining

Kashkar Cafe

$ | Asian. Uyghur cuisine, from the Chinese region of Xinjiang, is the focus of the menu at this postage-stamp-size café. Standouts include *naryn* (lamb dumplings), *samsa* (empanada-like lamb pies), pickles, vinegary salads, and clay-oven-baked bread. **Known for:** Uyghur and Uzbek cuisine; large portions; colorful restaurant. *Average main: $6* ⊠ *1141 Brighton Beach Ave., Brighton Beach* ☎ *718/743–3822* ⊕ *www.kashkarcafe.com* Ⓜ *B, Q to Brighton Beach.*

Kitchen 21

$$ | American. Occupying an arched Spanish Revival building that is now a city landmark, Kitchen 21 is a massive, airy restaurant, bar, and café with a separate open-air rooftop lounge. The gastropub-style menu features basics like burgers and pizza, along with memorable items like duck wings and lobster nachos. **Known for:** filling gastropub fare; seafood specialties; restored landmark building. *Average main: $20* ⊠ *3062 W. 21st St., Coney Island* ☎ *718/954–9801* ⊕ *www.kitchen-21.com* Ⓜ *D, F, N, Q to Coney Island–Stillwell Ave.*

National Restaurant and Night Club

$$ | Russian. Wear your dancing shoes and dress to impress and you'll fit right in at this lavishly gilded, Brighton Beach institution. The menu has an outstanding selection of Russian specialties, like smoked fish, caviar, kebabs,

and dumplings. **Known for:** Russian specialties; flashy floor shows; no sneakers allowed in the evenings. *Average main: $22* ⊠ *273 Brighton Beach Ave., Brighton Beach* ☎ *718/646–1225* ⊕ *www.nationalrestaurantny.com* ◷ *Closed Mon.–Thurs.* Ⓜ *B, Q to Brighton Beach.*

Skovorodka

$$ | Russian. This family-friendly, Brighton Beach favorite serves home-style Russian classics that could have been prepared by grandma. Dishes like borscht, beef Stroganoff, and stuffed cabbage are all highly recommended. **Known for:** Georgian specialties; classic Russian food; vintage Brighton Beach style. *Average main: $14* ⊠ *615 Brighton Beach Ave., Brighton Beach* ☎ *718/615–3096* ⊕ *www.skovorodkanyc.com* Ⓜ *B, Q to Brighton Beach.*

Tatiana Restaurant and Night Club

$$ | **Russian.** There are two prime times at Tatiana's: day and night. Sitting at a boardwalk table on a summer afternoon, enjoying the breezes and the views of the Atlantic while eating lunch alfresco, is a quintessential Brighton Beach experience. **Known for:** Ukrainian favorites; indoor seating or outdoor along the boardwalk; weekend floor shows. *Average main: $22 ⊠ 3152 Brighton 6th St. (or enter from boardwalk), Brighton Beach ☎ 718/891–5151 ⊕ www.tatianarestaurant.com* Ⓜ *B, Q to Brighton Beach.*

Toné Georgian Bread Bakery & Cuisine

$ | **Eastern European.** The specialty at this off-the-beaten-track Georgian bakery is *khachapuri* (cheese bread) and diners in the know have been coming here and ordering it to go for years. Cozy café seating, though, invites patrons to eat in and try other delicious Georgian cuisines. **Known for:** indulgent bakery finds; Georgian foods; affordable menu. *Average main: $8 ⊠ 265 Neptune Ave., Brighton Beach ☎ 718/332–8082* Ⓜ *B, Q to Brighton Beach.*

Totonno's Pizzeria Napolitana

$$ | **Pizza.** Thin-crust pies judiciously topped with fresh mozzarella and tangy, homemade tomato sauce, then baked in a coal oven—at Totonno's you're not just eating pizza, you're biting into a slice of New York history. Not much has changed since Anthony (Totonno) Pero first opened the pizzeria, in 1924, right after the subways started running to Coney Island—the restaurant is at the same location and run by the same family, who use ingredients and techniques that have been handed down through four generations. **Known for:** legendary New York pizza; family-run; historic location. *Average main: $17 ⊠ 1524 Neptune Ave., Coney Island ☎ 718/372–8606 ⊕ www.totonnosconeyisland.com ⊘ Closed Mon.–Wed. ▭ No credit cards* Ⓜ *D, F, N, Q to Coney Island–Stillwell Ave.*

☕ Bars and Nightlife

★ Ruby's

Patrons from around the world have been drinking at this boardwalk mainstay since much-beloved local boy Ruby Jacobs opened it in 1972. The bar, tables, wainscoting, and ceiling are made from the original 1920s boardwalk wood. Grab a seat and watch the action on the boardwalk, or join the regulars at the 45-foot-long bar and peruse the photographs depicting the neighborhood and the bar's habitués. The jukebox has a great selection of classics. *⊠ 1213 Boardwalk, Coney Island ☎ 718/975–7829 ⊕ www.rubysbar.com* Ⓜ *D, F, N, Q to Coney Island–Stillwell Ave.; F, Q to W. 8th St.–NY Aquarium.*

INDEX

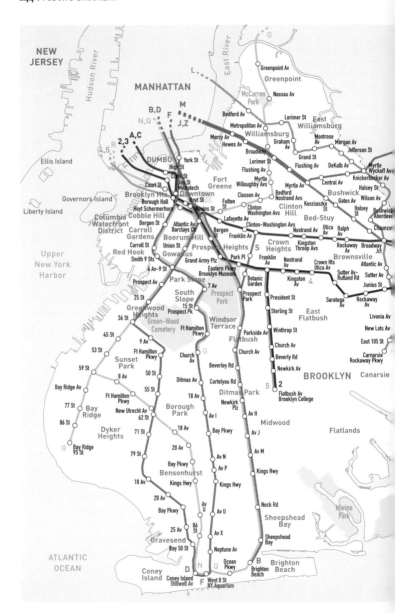

Brooklyn Subway Lines

QUEENS

M

J,Z

Cypress Hills

75th St-Elderts Ln

Crescent St

Av St

St

Norwood Av

Cleveland St

A,C

Van Siclen Av

Alabama Av

Grant Av

Euclid Av

Shepherd Av

Liberty Av

Van Siclen Av

3

New Lots Av

Van Siclen Av

Pennsylvania Av

East New York

Jamaica Bay

Floyd Bennett Field

RESOURCES

New York's extensive **MTA** public transit system (⊕ *www.mta.info*) is the easiest and cheapest way to get to and around Brooklyn. Purchase a reusable MetroCard at any subway stop (single rides cost $3; less with pay-per-ride and unlimited cards). Plan your route with the MTA's online trip planner (⊕ *www.tripplanner. mta.info*), Google Maps (⊕ *www.google. com*), or HopStop (⊕ *www.hopstop.com*), all available as smartphone apps. Our reviews always indicate the nearest stop.

Two ferry lines ply the East River between Manhattan and Brooklyn. The blue-and-white **East River Ferry** (⊕ *www.eastriver-ferry.com*; $4 one-way on weekdays, $6 on weekends) makes the most stops in Brooklyn, connecting Greenpoint, North and South Williamsburg, and DUMBO with each other and Manhattan's 34th Street and Pier 11/Wall Street piers. For Red Hook, board the yellow **New York Water Taxi** (⊕ *www.nywatertaxi.com*) IKEA Express Shuttle from Pier 11/Wall Street in Manhattan (free on weekends; $5 one-way on weekdays); the same company also runs one-way trips to DUMBO ($9) and elsewhere in Manhattan and Brooklyn by all-day pass ($31).

If you want to bike in Brooklyn, look for **Citi Bike** (⊕ *www.citibikenyc.com*) bike share stations in select neighborhoods to rent your own wheels. Parts of the landscaped Brooklyn Greenway (⊕ *www. brooklyngreenway.org*) are open, including Brooklyn Bridge Park.

VISITOR INFORMATION

The **Brooklyn Tourism & Visitor Center** is located at 209 Joralemon Street, inside Brooklyn Borough Hall. You can also visit ⊕ *www.nycgo.com* for more information.

NOTES

NOTES

NOTES

NOTES

NOTES

NOTES

NOTES

NOTES

NOTES

Fodor's BROOKLYN

Editorial: Douglas Stallings, *Editorial Director*; Margaret Kelly, Jacinta O'Halloran, *Senior Editors*; Kayla Becker, Alexis Kelly, Amanda Sadlowski, *Editors*; Teddy Minford, *Content Editor*; Rachael Roth, *Content Manager*

Design: Tina Malaney, *Design and Production Director*; Jessica Gonzalez, *Production Designer*

Photography: Jennifer Arnow, *Senior Photo Editor*

Maps: Rebecca Baer, *Senior Map Editor*

Production: Jennifer DePrima, *Editorial Production Manager*; Carrie Parker, *Senior Production Editor*; Elyse Rozelle, *Production Editor*

Business & Operations: Chuck Hoover, *Chief Marketing Officer*; Joy Lai, *Vice President and General Manager*; Stephen Horowitz, *Director of Business Development and Revenue Operations*; Tara McCrillis, *Director of Publishing Operations*; Eliza D. Aceves, *Content Operations Manager and Strategist*

Public Relations and Marketing: Joe Ewaskiw, *Manager*; Esther Su, *Marketing Manager*

Illustrator: Claudia Pearson

Writers: Kelsy Chauvin, Carly Fisher, Laura Itzkowitz, Christina Knight, Emily Saladino, Caroline Trefler

Editors: Margaret Kelly and Linda Cabasin

Production Editor: Elyse Rozelle

Production Design: Liliana Guia

2nd Edition

ISBN 978-1-64097-030-4

ISSN 2379-8076

All details in this book are based on information supplied to us at press time. Always confirm information when it matters, especially if you're making a detour to visit a specific place. Fodor's expressly disclaims any liability, loss, or risk, personal or otherwise, that is incurred as a consequence of the use of any of the contents of this book.

SPECIAL SALES

This book is available at special discounts for bulk purchases for sales promotions or premiums. For more information, e-mail SpecialMarkets@fodors.com.

PRINTED IN THE UNITED STATES OF AMERICA

10 9 8 7 6 5 4 3 2 1

ABOUT OUR WRITERS & ILLUSTRATOR

Since 2001, **Kelsy Chauvin** has lived among the brownstones of Fort Greene, Brooklyn. She's a writer and photographer who's explored travel, nightlife, food, LGBT culture, and more for *Fodor's*, *Condé Nast Traveler*, *Passport*, *Rand McNally*, and other publications. No matter where she's at, you can always follow her travels on Instagram and Twitter, @kelsycc. This year, Kelsy updated Brooklyn Heights and Downtown Brooklyn, Boerum Hill and Cobble Hill, Ditmas Park and Midwood, and Brighton Beach and Coney Island.

Carly Fisher is a Brooklyn-based editor and writer who lives in Clinton Hill and desperately renews her lease every year to keep it that way. For Brooklyn 2nd Edition, Carly updated Bushwick and East Williamsburg, and the Bedford-Stuyvesant and Crown Heights chapters.

Laura Itzkowitz is a Greenpoint-based freelance writer with a passion for travel, arts & culture, lifestyle, design, food & wine. She co-wrote *New York: Hidden Bars & Restaurants*, the award-winning guide to New York's speakeasy scene published by Jonglez Editions. When not globetrotting, you can probably find her sipping a dirty Martini at one of the city's best bars. Laura updated Williamsburg and Greenpoint.

Christina Knight has lived in Park Slope since 1995 and is a senior digital producer at WNET/Thirteen. She is a former Fodor's editor, launched *In Your Pocket Berlin* and as Zephyr Eurová, penned the *Exberliner's* travel column. Christina took on the Park Slope and Prospect Park, Gowanus, and Carroll Gardens chapters.

Claudia Pearson is a Brooklyn-based artist, Illustrator, and designer. Her work has been published in *New Yorker* and the *New York Times*. Her children's book, *Tribal Alphabet*, was published in 2008. In 2009 Claudia launched a line of prints, tea towels, tote bags, calendars, and note cards based on her world travels and her love of food. She also creates custom designs for West Elm, Crate and Barrel and others.

Emily Saladino is a Brooklyn-based writer, editor, and recipe developer. A former line cook, she is the Executive Editor of VinePair, and has written about the intersection of food, drinks, travel, and culture for *Bloomberg BusinessWeek*, BBC, *Bon Appetit*, *New York Magazine*, *Town & Country*, and many others. Emily updated the Prospect Heights and DUMBO.

Caroline Trefler is a writer and world traveler who still gets excited exploring New York City, where she's lived in for the past 20 years. In that time she's lived in 12 different neighborhoods around Brooklyn and Manhattan. For this edition, Caroline tackled the Experience chapter; Fort Green and Clinton Hill; Red Hook and the Columbia Waterfront; Windsor Terrace, Greenwood Heights, and South Slope; Sunset Park; and Bay Ridge.